# THE FIDDLEHEAD COOKBOOK

# THE FIDDLEHEAD COOKBOOK

## Recipes from Alaska's Most Celebrated Restaurant and Bakery

**Nancy and John DeCherney,
Deborah Marshall,
and Susan Brook**

**Illustrations by Nancy DeCherney**

St. Martin's Griffin
New York

*Design by Diane Stevenson—SNAP•HAUS GRAPHICS*

Library of Congress Cataloging-in-Publication Data

The Fiddlehead cookbook : the best recipes from Alaska's most
   celebrated restaurant and bakery / Susan Brook . . . [et al.].
        p.  cm.
   Includes index.
   **ISBN 0-312-09806-5**
   1. Cookery. 2. Fiddlehead Restaurant and Bakery. I. Brook,
Susan.
TX714.F53  1991
641.5'09798'2—dc20                           91-20932
                                               CIP

10  9  8  7  6  5  4

Dedicated to that spirit of adventure known as hospitality, which draws people together and brings well-being and harmony to the planet.

To Chris Smith, with love and gratitude, for keeping the home fires burning. SB

To my parents, and to my culinary parents: David Glass, who showed me how it should be done; and Vernon and Charlene Rollins, who showed me how it could be done. JD

To my parents, who gave me wings, and to John Novi, who showed me that even the sky is not the limit. ND

To Alice Tucker Biddle, who first taught me the fine art of gracious hospitality, the intricacies of careful meal preparation, and the importance of the freshest and finest ingredients. For you, Granny Biddle. DRM

# ACKNOWLEDGMENTS

Thanks to:

Mary Claire Harris for peanut pasta idea.

Gail Seibert for all her careful testing and kind encouragement.

And all the hundreds of testers: families, friends, and patrons.

The DOT crew for willingly eating lots and lots of variations of many, many dishes, and offering helpful comments and gentle suggestions.

John Hall, for having enough faith in us to more or less force this book to be written.

Chris McQuitty, for aiding and abetting him.

Bruce Steadman, for aiding, abetting, and editing.

Barbara Anderson, for a familiar voice in the wilds of New York, offering constructive guidance and counseling.

Richard Pine, for encouragement and sound advice.

Jim Taggart, for retrieving a manuscript lost inside a computer, on Thanksgiving Day no less.

The Cowpers, for being flexible.

Karen Cantillon, Sharon Gaiptman, Jeanne D'Aurora, Rachel Beck and her dad, who proofread like mad.

Ren and Henry, who patiently stood by while Mom went back into the kitchen.

The entire staff at the Fiddlehead, then and now, without whom this book absolutely would not be.

# C O N T E N T S

# INTRODUCTION

■                              ■                                                    ■

Let's dispel one myth right away. Alaska is not the frigid Far North populated only by intrepid, fur-clad, two- and four-legged animals.

Alaska is a lush, exotic place where the skies are bluer, the mountains taller, the stars closer, and the sun more stunning than any other place on the planet. This is a land of urbane sophisticates, proud tribal leaders, feisty homesteaders, snake-oil peddlers, and authors of The Great American Novel. This is a place where things are possible.

It is the opportunities that keep us here. When fortune or luck or something more divine brought all of us together here in Juneau, we discovered a common sense of spirit and purpose. Modern pioneers, we find in this beautiful and untamed land the chance to shape our future, to contribute to our community and our home.

My first home was Anchorage; my first restaurant was The Bread Factory, where we made soup, we made bread, and we made music all night long. At that point (1974 to 1975) "we" were my sister, Lydia; Scott Miller (a musician from Brooklyn who found himself at "the Top of the World," a long way from Zabar's); and myself. Together we discovered what it takes to make it in the restaurant business: a constantly replenishing stock of creativity, love, energy, innocence, flexibility, vision, more energy, passion, compassion, and the desire to eat as well in Alaska as we had at home.

In 1978, our trio decided to open a restaurant in Juneau, a town in southeast Alaska. Juneau is Alaska's most beautiful and cosmopolitan city—a gentle, gracious town of 30,000, spiced with the excitement and vigor of a state capital and regional center, and blessed with a yearly influx of tourists from all over the world. Nestled along the rugged coastline of America's largest rain forest, the community is strung between the pristine waters of the Inside Passage and the spectacular peaks of the Coast Mountains. Relatively isolated from the rest of the world, Juneau is connected not by roads, but by the Alaska Marine Highway system of ferries to our neighboring towns.

We named our restaurant after one of Alaska's most delicious native foods, the fiddlehead fern. The tiny shoots, which grow in abundance on our mountainsides, are gathered in early spring. Prized as salad ingredients and wonderful sautéed in butter, fiddleheads have a fresh sweet taste that promises melting snows, the return of warming sun, and a lush summer ahead. To us, the fiddlehead symbolizes "Beginner's Mind," the place we must find inside ourselves from which we see problems as opportunities and challenges as adventures.

And challenge and adventure were the themes of those early years as we learned how to run a busy restaurant by doing it—not unlike the way an Alaskan bush pilot learns to land an airplane on a glacier or a beach. The success of the Fiddlehead is due in large part to Scott Miller, who shaped the restaurant's original menu. His natural gift for fine cooking, his good sense, and his unfailing instincts guided this restaurant from the outset. His unbounded and generous creativity attracted like-minded individuals to the

Fiddlehead kitchen, whence amazing, wonderful dishes emerged every day. It was in those early years that first Nancy, then Susan, and then John joined the staff and became part of the development of the restaurant. An eclectic menu has evolved over the years, reflecting our different backgrounds, travels, and tastes. Its flavors include oriental, French, Italian, Mexican, vegetarian, and Alaskan—yet each reflects the Fiddlehead's unique touch: a passion for the freshest ingredients the sea and the land have to offer prepared naturally and healthfully.

The staff of the Fiddlehead has grown to a group of forty individuals, resilient in its diversity, each of whom deserves credit for making the restaurant the success it is today. We pride ourselves on continually trying new ideas, in exploring Alaska's unique resources, and in seeking to put into practice what Alaska's native peoples have known for generations—that one must live with humility and reverence in this wild and pristine country. As we have come to appreciate Alaska's power and beauty, so have we come to understand the fragility of the land we love. We have committed ourselves as individuals and as a business to treat our environment with respect. We use organic ingredients, recycle, and buy our products from socially responsible companies whenever possible.

The 100,000 people who dine with us each year are our friends and our neighbors. They are Alaskans drawn to the capital city by business and to the Fiddlehead by its reputation for fresh, natural, local ingredients prepared creatively by the region's finest cooks. Some of our most treasured guests have been the thousands of visitors from around the world who have enjoyed our meals of fresh Alaska salmon, halibut, sourdough bread, edible greens, and wild berries.

For many years discerning eaters from all over the nation have been requesting our recipes and encouraging us to write a cookbook. We have enjoyed putting together our recipes, our anecdotes, our bits of Alaskana for you. We hope to see you here so that we might share with you the spectacular land we have come to love, and the unique Alaska coastal cuisine we have made our own. But until you can visit us, we hope our book inspires you to prepare your own food and that it will bring you some of the learning, laughter, and love that we have experienced over the years feeding people in the north country.

Remember what Alaska teaches—that it is possible to do what you don't know how to do. If you don't have all the ingredients, substitute. If you lack self-confidence, face the stove and pray. Most important, let your home-cooked meal celebrate your time together and the creativity in your soul. Enjoy your repast.

Deborah R. Marshall

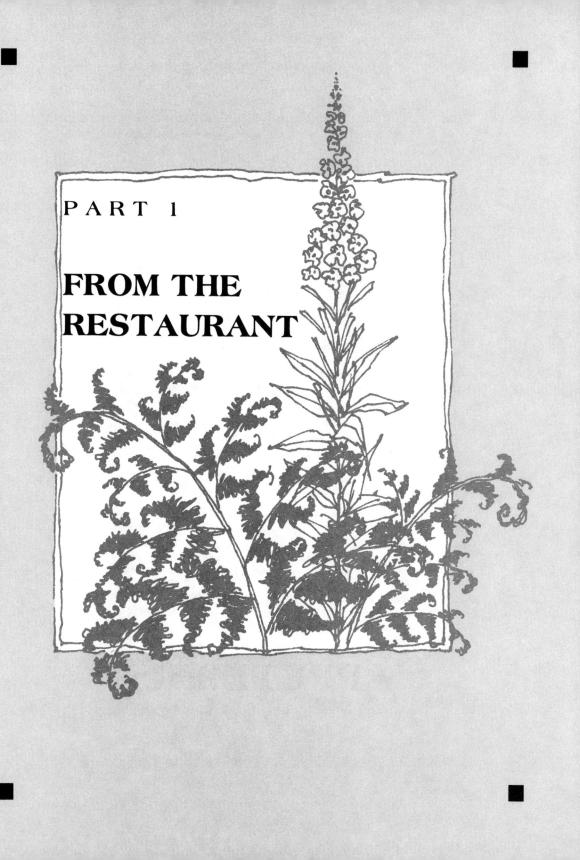

# PART 1

# FROM THE RESTAURANT

Mt. Juneau · Juneau, Alaska

Mount Juneau—Juneau, Alaska's capital, is nestled at the foot of Mount Juneau, a 3,576-foot mountain rising almost straight up from the Gastineau Channel, and Mount Roberts, which rises equally precipitously to a height of 3,819 feet. The steep slopes of the mountains all along the coast have prevented the construction of highways, making Juneau and most southeast communities accessible only by air or sea.

# APPETIZERS

# RED PEPPER PASTA

Robustly flavored and vibrant in appearance, this pasta dish precedes a grilled dinner perfectly.

**Preparation and Cooking Time:** 30 minutes

    12 ounces fettuccine noodles
    6 tablespoons butter
    3 tablespoons extra virgin olive oil
    1½ teaspoons minced fresh garlic (about 2 cloves)
    1½ cups sliced roasted red bell peppers (page 214), or
        substitute roasted bell peppers found in jars in the
        condiment section of the grocery store
    3 tablespoons (about 12) sun-dried tomatoes* (soak in
        ½ cup boiling water until softened, then drain and
        chop) or use sun-dried tomatoes packed in oil,
        chopped
    ¾ cup thinly cut green onions (white and green parts,
        about 4 medium green onions)
    1 tablespoon dried basil
    1 tablespoon dried oregano
    ¼ cup water
    1 teaspoon salt
    ½ teaspoon freshly ground black pepper
    ¾ cup (about 4 ounces) freshly grated Parmesan
        cheese

1. Bring a large pot of water to a boil over high heat. When water is boiling, add pasta and boil until *al dente* (see page 122). Drain pasta in a colander, rinse, and set aside while finishing sauce.

2. Melt butter and olive oil together in a large pot over medium-high heat. Add garlic, red pepper slices, and sun-dried tomatoes. Stir and cook until heated through and you begin to smell garlic (but don't let it brown).

3. Add green onions, basil, oregano, water, salt, pepper, and cooked pasta. Using spaghetti tongs or a large fork, stir to mix ingredients thoroughly. Cook until heated through and sauce begins to thicken or be absorbed by pasta.

4. Mix in Parmesan cheese. Tranfer pasta to a serving dish and serve at once, with additional cheese if you like.

**Yield: 6 appetizers or 4 main courses**

**\*See mail-order sources, page 237.**

# GRILLED SPOT PRAWNS

Inspired by tales of tapas-style shrimp enjoyed by a friend of ours on a visit to the "Outside" (California, in this case), we served these as a special addition to the menu one evening and they've become one of our most requested appetizers. They are quick to prepare, beautiful to look at, and even better to eat.

**Preparation and Cooking Time:** 30 minutes

### ◼ Red Pepper Mayonnaise

> 1 egg yolk (use 1 whole egg if you are using a food processor)
> 2 tablespoons freshly squeezed lemon juice
> 1 cup corn oil or a combination of corn and olive oil
> ¼ cup puréed roasted red peppers (page 214), or substitute roasted bell peppers found in jars in the condiment section of the grocery store
> ½ teaspoon salt
> ¼ teaspoon cayenne

### ◼ Prawns

> 1 tablespoon olive oil
> 1 tablespoon kosher salt*
> 1 to 1½ pounds Alaska spot prawns,* legs removed (or other fresh large shrimp)

### ◼ Garnish

> Fresh red lettuce leaves
> Lemon wedges

1. **To prepare mayonnaise:** (See About Mayonnaise and Other Emulsified Sauces, page 40.) Place egg yolk and lemon juice in a deep bowl. (If you use a food processor with a steel blade or a blender, use the whole egg.) Whisk until foamy. Very slowly, 1 teaspoon at a time, begin to add oil while whisking yolk. After you have added 6 teaspoons oil, begin to add oil by tablespoons, combining thoroughly after each addition. When all oil has been added and mayonnaise is smooth and creamy, fold in pepper purée, salt, and cayenne. Taste and correct seasoning. Pour sauce into a straight-sided serving bowl, cover, and refrigerate until ready to serve the shrimp.

2. Line a serving platter with fresh lettuce leaves. Put red pepper mayonnaise in center of platter and set aside while you cook prawns.

NOTE:
Customarily prawns are deveined, but it is unnecessary: These prawns can be eaten whole, right out of the shell.

3. **To prepare prawns:** Heat olive oil in a large pan over medium-high heat. When oil is hot, sprinkle with kosher salt and add prawns, as many as will fit in a single layer. Cook on both sides until opaque all the way through (cooking time will depend upon size of shrimp). Alaskan spots take about 3 minutes altogether. (Cut one open to check if you are unsure.) Arrange cooked prawns and lemon wedges on serving platter and serve at once.

**Yield: 4 to 6 servings**

**\*See mail-order sources, page 237.**

**NOTE:**
**Prawns are eaten with the fingers, each person shelling his own. Provide bowls for the shells, and because this is a somewhat messy (although finger-licking good) operation, supply small bowls filled with warm water and a slice of lemon, and generous napkins or small towels for your guests.**

---

### It's Uniquely Alaskan

■ ■ ■

*When Alaskans say they are going "Outside," they mean they are headed south, probably to "the Lower Forty-eight," to "the States," to those first forty-eight United States (the contiguous United States).*

*Before satellite communications and air travel, before statehood (in 1959), Alaskans were geographically and politically isolated from the rest of the United States. To early Alaskans, the rest of the world was only peripherally important in their daily lives.*

*Now, even with television, easy access to almost everything under the sun, and full participation as one of the United States, most Alaskans continue to view the rest of the country as a largely indistinguishable region filled with shopping malls, freeways, noise, and a bunch of people rushing around—a nice place to visit, occasionally necessary for business purposes, but otherwise not particularly relevant to Alaskan life.*

*Whatever "Alaskan life" may be! This state crosses four time zones (although for convenience we stick mostly to one time) and climatic conditions ranging from the Arctic to a temperate rain forest. It has modern cities and the most remote, isolated settlements. Given this dramatic diversity, what do Alaskans have in common with each other? Our bond is thin but strong. We all agree that:*

- *Alaska is the most beautiful place in the world and we would and could live nowhere else.*
- *The weather vitally affects your daily life, so you must keep your eye on it.*
- *You have to help your neighbors in times of trouble, no matter how weird they are.*
- *Duct tape fixes anything, so no home should be without it.*
- *Alaska is the land of opportunities.*

*And that begins the debate: Opportunities for what?*

# FIDDLEHEAD PESTO SAUCE

People frequently ask, "Do you serve fiddleheads at the Fiddlehead?" We certainly do. This lemony pesto of fiddleheads was inspired by our good friend and former Fiddlehead manager Susan Kirkness, who creates wonderfully elegant vegetarian dishes.

**Preparation and Cooking Time:**   30 minutes

### ▥ Pesto

¾ cup (3 ounces) washed and cleaned fresh or defrosted frozen fiddleheads* (or substitute 1 cup coarsely chopped fresh asparagus)
¼ cup olive oil
¼ cup grated Parmesan cheese (about 1 ounce)
¼ cup whole almonds
2 tablespoons freshly squeezed lemon or orange juice
1 teaspoon minced fresh garlic (1 large clove)
½ teaspoon lemon zest**
1 teaspoon salt
1 teaspoon freshly ground black pepper

### ▥ Fiddlehead Pesto Pasta

1 pound dried fettuccine noodles
½ cup whipping cream
4 tablespoons butter
1 cup washed and cleaned fiddleheads (or asparagus cut on the diagonal into 1-inch pieces)
½ cup heavy cream

### ▥ Garnish

¼ cup lightly toasted chopped almonds (To toast, bake in a 350°F oven for several minutes until golden brown.

1. **To prepare pesto:**  Place ¾ cup fiddleheads, olive oil, cheese, whole almonds, juice, garlic, zest, salt, and pepper in a blender or food processor and purée until smooth. Using a rubber spatula, scrape pesto into a 2-cup jar. Cover with a thin layer of olive oil and refrigerate until ready to use.

2. **To prepare pasta:**  Bring a large pot of water to a boil over high heat. When water is boiling, drop in fettuccine noodles and boil until they are *al dente* (see page 122). Drain in a colander and set aside until you are ready to add them to sauce.

**NOTE:**
Pesto can be made up to 2 weeks in advance. This recipe doubles easily. Add pesto to steamed vegetables, scrambled eggs, or salad dressings.

3. While noodles are cooking, heat butter in a large pan over medium heat. When foam subsides, add fiddle-heads. Stir with a slotted spoon and cook until lightly crisped but not browned. Remove them from pan and set aside.

4. Add cream and pesto to pan and whisk together.

5. Add fettuccine to pan and, using spaghetti tongs or a large fork, gently toss with sauce until noodles are evenly coated. If pasta seems dry, mix in ¼ cup water. Add cooked fiddleheads and mix together gently.

6. Transfer pasta to a serving dish, sprinkle with toasted almonds, and serve at once.

**Yield: 8 appetizers or light suppers**

**\*Fiddlehead ferns can be gathered early in the spring, or purchased (see mail-order sources, page 237). See the note on Fiddlehead ferns on this page .**

**\*\*Zest is the outside, bright part of the peel, without the white layer.**

---

### Fiddlehead Ferns

■ ■ ■

*For a few weeks in May, we indulge our spring-time food passions and gather fiddlehead ferns from the warming rain forest. The tightly coiled fern shoots have a deli-cate asparagus flavor with the woodsy over-tones of wild mush-rooms.*

*Pick fiddleheads when they're a few inches high, leaving several shoots in each clump to continue growing. Be-fore cooking, rub off the brown chaff that covers the coiled stalks, then rinse thoroughly. Like asparagus, fiddleheads can be steamed, micro-waved, or boiled until tender. Our ultimate springtime indulgence is succulent fiddleheads alongside sourdough English muffins topped with smoked salmon and poached eggs, all bathed in a lemony hol-landaise.*

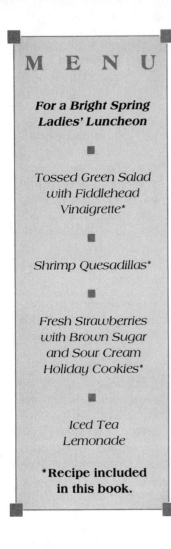

# SHRIMP QUESADILLAS

These are delightfully quick and simple.

**Preparation and Cooking Time:**   15 minutes (longer if you need to make salsa and guacamole)

> 2 8- or 9-inch flour tortillas
> 1 tablespoon salsa (page 220), or use a good-quality brand
> ¾ cup grated Jack or Cheddar cheese (about 3 ounces)
> ½ cup peeled, cooked Petersburg or cocktail shrimp (or flaked poached salmon)
> 1 tablespoon cooking oil

■ **Garnish**

> ½ cup guacamole (page 222)
> ¼ cup sour cream

1. Spread 1 tortilla with salsa and sprinkle half the cheese evenly over it. Distribute shrimp evenly over cheese and top with remaining cheese. Cover with remaining tortilla.

2. Heat oil in a 9-inch fry pan over medium-high heat. When oil is hot, place quesadilla in pan. Cook for 1 to 2 minutes, until the bottom tortilla begins to turn light brown. Carefully flip quesadilla over and fry on other side.

3. When second side is golden brown and cheese is melting, remove quesadilla from pan, cut into 8 wedges, and serve garnished with dollops of guacamole and sour cream.

**Yield: 8 wedges, or 2 to 4 servings**

Mendenhall Glacier · Juneau Alaska

Mendenhall Glacier—The Juneau Icefield, which caps the
Coast Mountains behind Juneau, feeds more than 30 gla-
ciers, including the 12-mile-long Mendenhall Glacier. This
glacier, 1.5 miles wide at its face, is gradually retreating
back into the hills, having receded 2.5 miles since 1750.

# Soups

# HALIBUT BISQUE

This delicate and subtle fish soup is a favorite during halibut season. Its pretty pink color seems to hint that it goes well with any one of the growing number of outstanding Oregon pinot noirs.

**Preparation Time:** 45 minutes

**Cooking Time:** 30 minutes

### ■ Fish and Fish Stock

2 cups water
½ medium onion, trimmed and cut into quarters
1 celery rib, washed, trimmed, and cut into 3-inch pieces
1 carrot, peeled, washed, and sliced into ½-inch-thick disks
½ lemon
¼ teaspoon dried thyme
¼ teaspoon whole black peppercorns
¼ teaspoon salt
¼ cup dry white wine
1 to 1¼ pounds skinned halibut fillet (substitute red snapper or other seafood)

### ■ Bisque

4 tablespoons butter
1⅓ cups medium-diced onions (about 1 large onion)
⅔ cup medium-diced celery (about 2 ribs)
1½ teaspoons minced garlic (2 large cloves)
4 tablespoons all-purpose flour
2 cups reserved fish stock
2 cups milk
1 bay leaf
1 tablespoon minced fresh parsley (or 2 teaspoons dried)
¾ to 1 teaspoon salt
½ teaspoon ground black pepper
½ teaspoon Worcestershire sauce
¼ teaspoon dried thyme
¼ teaspoon celery seed
2 drops Tabasco
2 cups reserved cooked flaked halibut
½ cup canned crushed or diced tomatoes
¼ cup dry sherry or white wine (optional)

NOTE:
If you have cooked halibut on hand, substitute a good-quality clam juice with no MSG and skip making the stock.

1. **To prepare fish and fish stock:** Put water, onion, celery, carrot, lemon, thyme, black peppercorns, salt, and wine in a medium pot and bring to a boil. Reduce heat to a low simmer. Cook on low, uncovered, for 15 minutes, then add halibut. Poach gently for 5 to 10 minutes, just until fish is barely done. (It will be opaque throughout but should not seem dry in the center.)

2. Using a large slotted spoon, carefully remove fish and set aside. Using a wire mesh strainer, strain and reserve stock.

3. **To prepare bisque:** Place butter in a large soup pot over medium-high heat. When it is hot, stir in onion, celery, and garlic. Stir and cook briefly until onion becomes translucent and celery is bright green. (Do not let garlic begin to brown.) Reduce heat to medium, stir in flour, and cook for 3 minutes, stirring frequently.

4. Add reserved fish stock and stir until smooth. Add milk and bay leaf. Increase heat to high and bring soup to a boil, then reduce heat. Stir in parsley, salt, pepper, Worcestershire, thyme, celery seed, and Tabasco. Simmer gently, uncovered, for 15 to 20 minutes.

5. Break cooked halibut into bite-size pieces and add it to soup. Stir in tomatoes and the sherry or white wine. Cook for 5 minutes, until fish is hot. Ladle into bowls and serve immediately.

**Yield: 2 quarts (8 first-course servings)**

*Many of the Fiddle-head's ingredients are grown or processed in Gustavus, a small community of about 200 residents, 50 miles west of Juneau. Accessible only by air or water, it is the gateway community to Glacier Bay National Park and has drawn on its homestead roots to become a tourist destination of its own. From this tiny community come Bobby Lee Daniels's rare and delicious Sitka Hybrid strawberries, Aimée Youman's smoked halibut, Sandy Burd's vegetables, and Jim Mackovjak's fresh seafood.*

*Summer is hectic in Gustavus, bustling with tourists, commercial fishing, and the activities long daylight hours bring. Autumn brings the rain, an incredible array of wild mushrooms, and the potluck season. Rural Alaskans, isolated from the outside world, often with no regular jobs and with no city distractions, relax, enjoy the quiet, and share the finest Alaskan foods.*

# SMOKED HALIBUT CHOWDER

Most New England chowders start with bacon or salt pork to give them their distinctive smokiness. In order to please our "pescatarian" crowd, we have used Alaskan smoked halibut to give our chowder that smoky goodness. This recipe is adapted from one given to us by our friends at the Salmon River Smokehouse in Gustavus.

**Preparation and Cooking Time:**  1½ hours (45 minutes if using prepared stock or clam juice)

6 tablespoons butter
2 tablespoons oil
1 cup small-diced carrots (about 1 large carrot)
1 cup small-diced onion (about 1 onion)
½ cup small-diced celery (about 2 small ribs)
6 tablespoons all-purpose flour
6 cups fish stock (page 228), or use a good-quality clam juice with no MSG
2 cups milk
2 bay leaves
2 teaspoons minced fresh garlic (2 large cloves)
¼ teaspoon dried thyme
⅛ teaspoon white pepper
Pinch of nutmeg
1 cup flaked, skinless smoked halibut* (about 6 ounces), or substitute smoked salmon*

1. In a large pot over medium-high heat, melt butter with oil. When oil is hot, add vegetables. Stir and cook until they are softened and aromatic. Stir in flour, reduce heat to medium, and cook briefly, about 3 minutes. Do not let flour brown.

2. Pour in stock and milk and increase heat to medium high. Stir well and bring soup to a boil, then reduce heat to low. Add seasonings and simmer gently, uncovered, for 15 minutes.

3. Stir in smoked halibut pieces and cook for an additional 10 to 15 minutes, until vegetables are tender but not mushy.

4. Ladle into soup bowls and serve at once.

**Yield: 2 quarts (8 first-course or 4 to 6 main-course servings)**

**\*See mail-order sources, page 237.**

# ITALIAN LENTIL SOUP

This hearty soup, served with crunchy garlic bread and a glass of robust red wine, is easily a meal in itself.

**Soaking Time:** overnight

**Preparation Time:** 15 minutes (if stock is already made)

**Cooking Time:** 2 hours

> "Since we must eat to live, we can be better humans for doing so with grace and love."
> —*M.F.K. Fisher*

1 cup dried lentils
2 tablespoons olive oil
¾ cup medium-diced onion (1 medium onion, about 6 ounces)
¾ cup medium-diced celery (2 large ribs)
1 teaspoon minced fresh garlic (1 large clove)
6 cups vegetable stock (page 227) or instant vegetable soup cubes, or chicken stock (if you are not vegetarian), or water (as a last resort)
1 14-ounce can diced tomatoes or crushed tomatoes in purée
2 teaspoons salt
1 teaspoon Dijon mustard
1 teaspoon dried oregano
1 teaspoon dried basil
½ teaspoon pepper
¼ teaspoon Worcestershire sauce
1 or 2 drops of Tabasco sauce
1 cup cooked chick-peas (optional)

■ **Garnish**

¼ cup freshly grated Parmesan cheese

1. Soak lentils overnight in a large pot with 4 cups cold water.

2. In a large pot over medium-high heat, heat olive oil. When oil is hot, add onion, celery, and garlic. Stir and cook until vegetables are softened and aromatic but not browned.

3. Add stock, tomatoes, and all seasonings. Drain lentils and add to soup. Bring soup to a boil, then cover pot and reduce heat to a simmer. Allow it to cook for 1 to 1½ hours, until lentils are soft. (Cooking time will vary considerably with the age and dryness of the lentils.) Add chick-peas if you like. Taste soup and correct seasoning. Ladle into soup bowls, sprinkle with Parmesan cheese, and serve at once.

**Yield: 2 quarts (6 main-course servings)**

# THAI FISH SOUP

This soup was born out of our growing appreciation for Thai cuisine. (A favorite Fiddlehead sport is to sprint directly out of the Seattle airport to the nearest Thai restaurant.) The light broth with hot-and-sour overtones differs refreshingly from other seafood soups.

**Preparation and Cooking Time:** 1 hour 15 minutes

■ **Fish Stock**

4 cups water
½ cup dry white wine (chardonnay or sauvignon blanc, or choose whatever you prefer to drink)
1 medium onion, trimmed and cut into quarters
2 celery ribs, cut into 3-inch pieces
1 carrot, sliced into ½-inch-thick disks
½ lemon
1 tablespoon dried lemongrass, available in many supermarkets and in oriental groceries* (in a pinch, substitute finely chopped lemon zest; see notes, opposite)
¼ teaspoon dried basil
¼ teaspoon whole black peppercorns
¼ teaspoon salt
1 to 1¼ pounds skinned fillet of lean white fish (halibut, ling cod, or red snapper)

■ **Soup**

1 tablespoon safflower oil
½ cup thinly sliced onion, cut stem to tip (1 small onion)
¼ cup thinly sliced green bell pepper (¼ large pepper)
¼ cup thinly sliced red bell pepper (¼ pepper)
¼ cup thin bias-cut celery (1 small rib)
¼ cup thin bias-cut bok choy (substitute broccoli cut into small florets if necessary)
4 cups reserved fish stock
1 14½-ounce can diced tomatoes
1 to 1¼ pounds reserved cooked fish, broken into pieces
¼ cup chopped fresh cilantro (no flavor substitute; omit if unavailable)
1 tablespoon chopped fresh parsley
¼ teaspoon crushed dried red pepper
2 tablespoons dry sherry
1 tablespoon tamari or soy sauce

**NOTE:**
If you want to use cooked fish, skip making fish stock in step 1 and substitute frozen fish stock or a good-quality clam juice with no MSG.

1 teaspoon oriental sesame oil (available in many supermarkets and in oriental groceries*)
2 drops oriental hot oil (also in oriental groceries*)
1 dash Tabasco sauce
1 dash Worcestershire sauce
Salt to taste

## ■ Garnish

½ cup thinly sliced green onions (tops and bottoms)

1. **To prepare fish stock:** Put water, wine, onion, celery, carrot, lemon, lemongrass, and seasonings in a medium pot and bring to a boil. Reduce heat to a low simmer and cook gently, uncovered, for 15 minutes. Add fish and poach gently for 5 to 10 minutes, until fish is just barely done. (It will flake easily but still appear moist in the center.)

2. Using a large slotted spoon, carefully remove fish and reserve. Strain stock through a wire sieve and reserve.

3. **To prepare soup:** Heat safflower oil in a large soup pot over medium-high heat. Add sliced onion, peppers, celery, and bok choy. Stir to coat evenly with oil and cook briefly, until vegetables are aromatic and barely beginning to soften, about 3 minutes.

4. Add remaining ingredients (except green onions) and cook until just heated through. Taste soup and add salt and pepper to suit your taste.

5. Ladle into soup bowls and serve topped with chopped green onions.

**Yield: 2 quarts (8 first-course servings)**

**\*See mail-order sources, page 237.**

"Sentiment is all very well for a boutonniere, but a well-tied tie is the first serious step in life."
—*Oscar Wilde*

---

### Lemongrass

■ ■ ■

*Lemongrass, a tropical grass commonly used as flavoring in Southeast Asian dishes, adds a unique lemony perfume and flavor to foods. Look for it fresh in the produce section of grocery stores or oriental markets or as dried tea in health food stores.*

*Use the base of the grass, from just above the root to just below the leaves. It is quite fibrous and should be discarded before you serve your dish. Use 2 to 3 tablespoons of dried sliced lemongrass in place of 1 stalk of fresh.*

*Should you be fortunate enough to locate fresh lemongrass, try to root it by sticking it in a glass of water for a week or so. Planted, it makes a tall, graceful houseplant and you will have a supply of lemongrass whenever you need it.*

*If all else fails, substitute 2 strips of fresh lemon zest or 1 teaspoon grated lemon zest for the lemongrass.*

# BEAN SUPREME

One of the most popular combinations at the Fiddlehead is "Pauper's Prerogative": a steaming bowl of homemade soup, a small green salad, and freshly baked bread. This sweet-and-sour three-bean soup has been part of that unbeatable trio for years. Go soak your beans!

**Soaking Time:** overnight

**Preparation Time:** 1 hour, including vegetable stock

**Cooking Time:** 2 hours 15 minutes

1 cup dried black turtle beans
1 cup dried red Mexican beans
1 cup dried navy beans
3 quarts vegetable stock (page 227), or substitute water with 1 tablespoon red miso if necessary, or chicken stock if vegetarian soup is not the point
1 bay leaf
1 tablespoon safflower oil
2½ cups medium-diced onions (about 2 large onions)
2½ cups medium-diced carrots (about ½ pound)
1 teaspoon minced fresh garlic (1 large clove)
4 teaspoons honey
1 tablespoon apple cider vinegar
1 tablespoon Dijon mustard
2¼ cups canned diced tomatoes
2¼ cups tomato purée (or substitute one 28-ounce can crushed tomatoes for both the diced tomatoes and the purée)
2 tablespoons finely chopped fresh parsley
2 teaspoons salt (or to taste)
Pepper to taste

■ **Garnish**

Shredded Cheddar cheese or sour cream

1. Place beans in a large bowl and soak overnight in 8 cups water.

2. Drain beans and place them in a large pot over high heat. Add vegetable stock and bay leaf. Bring to a boil and allow to boil for 10 minutes. Reduce heat to low and simmer, uncovered, until beans are tender, skimming froth from pot as needed. (The time required for beans to cook depends upon their age and dryness. It should take about 1½ hours.)

3. When beans are nearly tender (after about 1 hour), heat safflower oil in a medium-size pan over high heat. When oil is hot, add onions and carrots, reduce heat to medium, and cook until almost tender, stirring frequently. Stir in garlic and honey and cook for 5 minutes.

4. Add cooked vegetables, along with vinegar, mustard, tomatoes, purée, and seasonings, to cooking beans and simmer for 30 minutes, until beans are tender. (Pick one up in a spoon and blow on it gently. If the skin peels back, the beans are done.)

5. Ladle soup into bowls or a tureen and serve at once topped with shredded Cheddar cheese or sour cream.

**Yield: 14 quarts**

NOTE:
**This soup can be made ahead and frozen until needed.**

# CURRIED CREAM OF CARROT SOUP

Smooth and elegantly spicy, this soup is perfect as a first course for a special occasion. It is also refreshing served chilled for lunch on a hot summer day.

**Preparation and Cooking Time:**   2 hours (1 hour if garam masala and chicken stock are already made)

    4 tablespoons butter
    1 cup medium-diced onion (about 1 medium onion)
    1½ teaspoons minced fresh garlic (about 2 large cloves)
    1 tablespoon peeled and minced or finely grated fresh ginger
    2 tablespoons curry powder
    2 teaspoons garam masala (page 208), or combine a bit of powdered cardamom, cumin, freshly ground pepper, ground clove, nutmeg, and cinnamon; toast spices lightly in a pan on low heat before adding to soup
    ½ teaspoon cayenne, or 2 drops of Tabasco sauce
    4 tablespoons all-purpose flour
    2 cups milk
    1 cup heavy cream
    1 cup chicken stock (page 226)
    4 cups carrots, peeled and cut into ½-inch pieces (11 to 12 carrots, about 1¼ pounds)
    1 teaspoon salt

■ **Garnish**

    ¼ cup sour cream
    ¼ cup bias-cut green onions or chives

1. Melt butter in a large soup pot over medium-high heat. When foam has subsided, add onion, garlic, ginger, curry powder, garam masala, and cayenne. Stir and cook briefly, until onion begins to soften but garlic has not started to brown. Add flour and cook for 3 minutes, stirring frequently.

2. Add milk, cream, and chicken stock. Stir until well blended. Add carrots, bring to a boil, reduce heat to low, and cover pot. Cook gently for 20 minutes, or until carrots are tender.

**3.** Carefully purée soup (it's hot) in a food processor fitted with a metal blade, or in a blender or a food mill. Stir in salt. Taste and correct seasonings. Ladle into soup bowls and serve at once garnished with a tablespoon of sour cream and a sprinkling of green onions.

**Yield: 2 quarts (6 as a first course)**

---

### Alaskan-Grown Carrots

■ ■ ■

*You can tell Alaskan carrots by their taste—they are sweet, juicy, and crisp. This perception isn't just regional chauvinism, but is based on horticultural fact: Alaska's cool soils and long hours of daylight during the growing season stimulate sugar production in carrots (and potatoes, too).*

*Knowledgeable Alaskans eagerly pay a few cents more for locally grown carrots because of the superior taste and quality. Those who can, grow their own, looking forward to the crunchy sweet carrots straight from their gardens and the inevitable imitations of Bugs Bunny by their children.*

*Alaskan-grown carrots store particularly well in root cellars, basements, and pantries. For best keeping quality, wash immediately after harvesting and snap off the feathery green tops (but leave the root tails on). Layer the carrots in damp sawdust and store as near to 36°F as you can manage. If the temperature is too high, the carrot tops will send up green shoots. Make sure the sawdust is slightly moist at all times, as drying is the number-one enemy of stored carrots.*

# FRENCH ONION SOUP

East meets West as miso and vegetable stock combine with onions and cheese to create a luxurious meatless variation of the classic onion soup. We developed this soup for our vegetarian friends and it has become a staple on the Fiddlehead menu.

**Preparation Time:**  1 hour (less if stock is already made)

**Cooking Time:**  3 hours

## ▪ Soup

> 2 tablespoons safflower oil
> 2 tablespoons olive oil
> 6 medium onions, cut stem to tip into thin slices (1¾ to 2 pounds)
> 1 cup medium-dry or dry sherry (substitute apple juice)
> 1½ teaspoons minced fresh garlic (about 2 cloves)
> 6 cups vegetable stock (page 227), or substitute chicken stock if you are not vegetarian
> 2 dashes of Tabasco sauce
> 3 tablespoons tomato paste
> 4 tablespoons red or brown miso (often available in the produce section of your grocery store, or in oriental groceries and health food stores*)
> ½ teaspoon salt (or to taste)
> ¼ teaspoon pepper to taste

## ▪ Croutons

> 8 slices day-old sourdough French bread (page 150) or other plain bread

## ▪ Garnish

> 8 slices mozzarella cheese
> 8 slices Swiss cheese
> ½ cup freshly grated Parmesan cheese

**1.** Preheat oven to 325°F.

**2.** Heat safflower and olive oils in a large heavy-bottomed pot over medium heat. Add onions, stir to coat with oil, and cook until they begin to become caramel colored. Add a bit of sherry, stir, and continue to cook slowly. As onions caramelize, add more sherry and stir to evenly distribute the color. Continue cooking slowly until all the sherry is used and onions are a rich honey color. (This process takes almost an hour.)

3. Stir in garlic, stock, Tabasco, and tomato paste. Reduce heat to low and simmer, uncovered, for 2 hours.

4. After soup has simmered for 2 hours, stir in miso and add salt and pepper to taste.

5. **To prepare croutons:** While soup is simmering, re-move crusts from bread and cut into pieces that will fit neatly into ovenproof soup bowls. Lay pieces on a cookie sheet and dry them in oven 5 to 10 minutes, depending on thickness of the pieces. Set aside until ready to serve soup.

6. Preheat broiler.

7. Ladle soup into 4 ovenproof soup bowls. Top each bowl with 2 croutons, then 2 slices of mozzarella and 2 slices of Swiss cheese. Sprinkle 2 tablespoons Par-mesan cheese on each. Place under broiler until cheese has melted and turns slightly brown. Serve im-mediately.

**Yield: 4 main-course or 8 appetizer servings**

**\*See mail-order sources, page 237.**

M E N U

*Fireside Supper*

■

*Tossed Green Salad
with Fiddlehead
House Dressing\**

■

*French Onion Soup\**

■

*Fresh Sourdough
Bread\**

■

*Merlot, or Apple Cider*

■

*Chocolate Amaretto
Cake\**
*Hot Coffee*

**\*Recipe is included
in this book.**

# About Miso

■ ■ ■

Miso, a paste made by fermenting cooked soy beans and various grains, was developed in seventh-century Japan as a way of preserving soy beans. (Tamari sauce is a by-product of rice miso-processing, and so can be wheat-free.) It is loaded with proteins of the same quality as beef or cheese, and packed with vitamins and healthful enzymes. Miso keeps, wrapped and refrigerated, for up to a year.

Like wines or cheeses, miso comes in a staggering variety of colors and textures, each with its own flavor and character. **White miso (shiro)** tends to be slightly sweeter and thinner than the darker varieties. **Light miso (tanshoku)**, any of the yellow or tan varieties, is of medium sweetness and saltiness, while **red miso (aka)**, which can refer to any reddish or dark brown miso, is richer and saltier.

We have found red miso most often fits our needs and tastes. You can experiment with the different types to find the variety that suits you the best, or use several varieties in different situations.

Use miso where you might use salt, soy sauce, Worcestershire sauce, or bouillon cubes to add flavor. One tablespoon of red miso is roughly equivalent to ½ teaspoon of table salt and adds high-quality proteins, vitamins, and other nutrients as well as a good hearty flavor. Add miso at the end of a cooking process: Prolonged cooking destroys the beneficial living organisms it contains.

Store miso tightly wrapped in the refrigerator. Occasionally a thin layer of harmless mold may form on the surface of unpasteurized misos, which contain no preservatives; simply scrape it off or stir it into the miso. White misos may begin to smell of alcohol, but it will be driven off during cooking and does not affect the flavor or healthfulness of the food.

Look for miso in the produce department of your grocery store or in oriental markets or health food stores. Miso-making kits are also available. For mail-order sources, see page 237.

# GERMAN MUSHROOM SOUP

Bruce Massey's passion for soups shines through this one: German mushroom soup is one of our most popular and has warmed many Alaskans on wet, rainy days. The red wine, black pepper, and caraway seasonings bring out the earthy flavors of mushrooms in the satisfyingly rich broth.

**Preparation Time:**   30 minutes if stock is already made

**Cooking Time:**   45 minutes

    2 tablespoons butter
    2 tablespoons safflower oil
    1½ cups thinly sliced onion, cut stem to tip (about 1
        large onion)
    ¼ cup all-purpose flour
    ½ teaspoon ground black pepper
    1 dried bay leaf
    2½ cups vegetable stock (page 227)
    1 14-ounce can diced tomatoes (substitute crushed
        tomatoes, or whole tomatoes that you have
        chopped)
    ½ teaspoon caraway seeds
    1⅓ cups dry red burgundy wine
    4 cups thinly sliced mushrooms (about ¾ pound)
    2 teaspoons soy or tamari sauce
    2 teaspoons Worcestershire sauce
    1 tablespoon red or brown miso (see About Miso,
        opposite page)
    1 teaspoon salt, or to taste

## Garnish

    Sour cream

1. Heat butter and safflower oil in a large soup pot over medium-high heat. Add onion and cook until transparent, stirring frequently. Reduce heat to low.

2. Stir in flour. Cook slowly until golden brown, about 10 minutes, stirring frequently.

3. Add remaining ingredients except miso, salt, and sour cream, increase heat, and bring to a boil. Reduce heat again and simmer, uncovered, for 30 minutes.

4. In a small bowl, dissolve miso with ½ cup hot soup, then add it to soup pot. Season to taste with salt. Ladle into a tureen or soup bowls and serve at once, garnished with a dollop of sour cream.

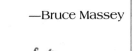

"It was my privilege to work at the Fiddlehead in its infancy. In retrospect, the uniqueness of that time becomes very pronounced. Everyone had a voice in the restaurant's operation, and though this was sometimes frustrating, our debates were nonetheless passionate. You can teach your staff skills but it's very hard to make people care—we had no problem in this area and that's what made this time so special. Soups are my passion. I hope you like the samplings offered here."

—Bruce Massey

**Yield: 2 quarts
(6 to 8 servings)**

# TOMATO-MILLET SOUP

What a difference! Millet adds a little fun to a simply delicious tomato soup.

**Preparation Time:** 30 minutes

**Cooking Time:** 45 minutes

1 tablespoon safflower oil
1 cup small-diced onion (1 medium onion)
1 cup small-diced carrots (2 medium carrots)
1 cup small-diced celery (3 ribs)
2 teaspoons minced fresh garlic (2 large cloves)
1 28-ounce can diced tomatoes with purée
1 20-ounce can tomato purée (or substitute 2 28-ounce cans crushed tomatoes in purée for both the diced tomatoes and tomato purée)
1 bay leaf
1 teaspoon salt
½ teaspoon freshly ground black pepper
½ teaspoon dried rosemary
1 cup water
⅓ cup millet (available in health food stores*)

1. Heat oil in a large pot over medium-high heat. When oil is hot, add onion, carrots, celery, and garlic. Stir and cook until vegetables begin to soften.

2. Add diced tomatoes, tomato purée, bay leaf, salt, pepper, and rosemary. Bring soup to a boil, reduce heat to very low, and cover pot. Simmer gently for 30 minutes, stirring frequently to avoid scorching the bottom of the soup.

3. While soup is cooking, place water and millet in a small pot over high heat. Bring it to a boil, then cover pot and reduce heat to low. Simmer for 30 minutes, until liquid has been absorbed and grain is tender. If necessary add additional water during cooking process. If millet does not absorb all the liquid, take cover off pot and let it simmer gently until dry.

4. When millet is cooked, add it to soup. Taste soup and add salt and pepper to taste. Ladle into soup bowls and serve at once.

**Yield: 2 quarts
(6 to 8 servings)**

*See mail-order sources, page 237.

**NOTE:**
**Millet will thicken the soup, so if you make soup ahead, wait until just before you serve to add millet, or add water as needed to thin the soup.**

carved by Amos Wallace

Harnessing the Atom, Juneau, Alaska

Harnessing the Atom—This totem illustrates the melding of three cultures and world views. The bottom figure, which supports the others, is the raven. According to Tlingit legend, the raven is the creator of everything in the universe. The next two figures, the sun and the man, represent the harnessing of the power of the universe. The Russian Orthodox priest, symbolized by the crossed-arm figure, symbolizes the introduction of Christianity to Alaska, and the eagle, at the top, represents the United States, and symbolizes the transfer of Alaska from Russia to the United States.

# SALADS AND VEGETABLES

# BROWN RICE SALAD

Created by Fiddlehead co-founder Scott Miller, who saw the potential in a simple white rice salad he once tried in Brooklyn, this unusual salad has been a favorite from the minute it was put on the menu. Satisfying and at the same time good for you, it needs nothing more than slices of fresh fruit to be a complete meal. It is a simple dish to prepare for just two.

**Preparation Time:** 25 minutes

**Cooking Time:** 1 hour (15 minutes if you have rice already cooked)

### ▪ Salad

2 tablespoons safflower oil
½ cup medium-diced onion (1 small onion)
½ cup medium-diced green peppers (½ small pepper)
½ cup thinly sliced mushrooms (2 ounces)
2¼ cups cooked brown rice (page 209)
⅔ cup diced firm tofu (4 ounces)
½ cup Fiddlehead vinaigrette (page 218), or other good vinaigrette dressing
2 teaspoons tamari or soy sauce
4 cups cleaned and torn fresh romaine lettuce

### ▪ Garnish

⅔ cup grated Cheddar cheese (about 3 ounces)
4 fresh tomato slices
1 cup alfalfa sprouts (optional)

1. **To prepare salad:** Heat safflower oil in a large deep pan over high heat. When oil is hot, add onion, peppers, and mushrooms and cook, stirring frequently with a wooden spoon, until they are tender but not browned.

2. Add cooked rice, stirring until thoroughly combined and hot.

3. Gently stir in tofu, ¼ cup vinaigrette, and tamari sauce until well combined and warmed.

4. Place lettuce in a very large salad bowl and toss with remaining ¼ cup vinaigrette dressing. Spoon hot rice mixture over dressed lettuce. (Or divide dressed lettuce evenly between 2 plates and top with hot rice.) Sprinkle rice with grated cheese and garnish with slices of tomato and alfalfa sprouts. Serve immediately, with additional salad dressing and soy sauce if you wish.

**Yield: 2 large salads**

# CHARLENE'S SALAD

This wonderful wilted-lettuce salad was inspired by Charlene Rollins, whose style of cooking has influenced us in many ways. Use the leanest smoked bacon and the freshest, creamiest chèvre you can find. It's worth the search.

**Preparation and Cooking Time:** 30 minutes

8 cups torn mixed fresh greens (romaine with a little endive or spinach, or any combination of fresh greens will work: romaine, spinach, leaf lettuce, endive are all good)
2 teaspoons balsamic vinegar (or substitute fresh lemon juice)
Pinch of salt
½ teaspoon freshly ground black pepper
2 ounces chèvre* (substitute feta, if absolutely necessary, and reduce the amount of vinegar or lemon juice)
3 tablespoons extra virgin olive oil
4 slices of bacon cut into ¼-inch pieces
½ cup chopped walnuts (or pecans)
2 teaspoons minced fresh garlic (2 to 3 cloves)

1. Place greens in a very large salad bowl. Sprinkle with balsamic vinegar, salt, and pepper and toss well. Crumble chèvre and sprinkle over greens. Set salad bowl aside.

2. Heat olive oil in a large pan over medium-high heat. Add bacon and cook until translucent but not yet crisp.

3. With a wooden spoon, stir in walnuts and cook just until hot. Add garlic and remove pan from heat. Immediately pour contents of pan over cheese and greens. (It should be so hot it sizzles when it hits the greens.) Using your hands or salad tongs, scoop under greens and toss salad vigorously until there are no large lumps of cheese. (Your hands work best: You won't burn them if you start from under lettuce.)

4. Divide salad onto plates and serve at once.

**Yield: 2 main-course salads or 4 dinner salads**

***Chèvre, a mild-flavored goat cheese, is available in most good cheese shops. See mail-order sources, page 237.**

**M E N U**

*A Simple Supper for Two*

■

*Charlene's Salad\**

■

*Hot Pumpernickel Bread\**
*with Fresh Butter*

■

*Ice Cold Beer*
*(in Frosted Glasses)*

■

*Fresh Pears*

***Recipe included in this book.**

# ELIZABETH'S CHICKEN SALAD

We know a four-year-old who will eat chicken salad only if it has grapes in it: This salad is for her. The delicate fruity dressing makes this a cooling summer salad for eating outside under the trees. Prepare all ingredients ahead and assemble the salad just before you serve it.

**Preparation and Cooking Time:** 1 hour (30 minutes if the chicken is already cooked)

■ **Poached Chicken**

1½ cups water
½ cup dry white wine (optional)
1 onion, quartered
1 carrot, peeled and cut into 2-inch lengths
1 celery rib, cut into 2-inch pieces
½ lemon
3 or 4 parsley sprigs (substitute 1 tablespoon dried)
1 garlic clove, lightly crushed
¼ teaspoon black peppercorns
¼ teaspoon dried thyme
2 large whole chicken breasts, split, 2½ to 3 pounds

■ **Chicken Salad**

3½ to 4 cups cubed (½ inch) cooled poached chicken
4 tablespoons olive oil
4 tablespoons raspberry vinegar *(see note on page 88)
2 tablespoons sour cream or nonfat plain yogurt
2 teaspoons Dijon mustard
1 cup halved seedless grapes (use whatever variety is at its best, or substitute melon balls or diced apple, according to the season)
1 cup chopped walnuts that have been very lightly toasted (Spread the nuts on a cookie sheet and bake in a 350°F oven for 5 minutes, until they become very lightly golden, or spread them in a single layer on a microwave-proof plate and cook, uncovered, in microwave for 2 to 4 minutes.)
1 teaspoon salt
½ teaspoon freshly ground black pepper
3 cups shredded romaine lettuce

1. **To poach chicken:** Place water, wine, onion, carrot, celery, lemon, parsley, garlic, peppercorns, and thyme in a large pot over high heat. Place chicken on top of vegetables. When liquid has come to a boil, reduce heat to low and cover pot. Simmer gently until meat is cooked through, 15 to 20 minutes. (Time will vary depending on thickness of breasts. Take care not to overcook or cook at too high a temperature, which will toughen meat.) With tongs or a large fork, remove chicken from pot and set it aside on a plate to cool. Strain stock through a wire-mesh sieve into a large container and cool in refrigerator. Cover and refrigerate or freeze for use later in soups or sauces. When chicken is cool enough to handle, remove and discard skin and bones and cut meat into ½ -inch cubes. Cover and refrigerate until ready to make salad.

2. **To assemble salad:** Chill 6 salad plates. Place cubed chicken in a large mixing bowl and add olive oil, vinegar, sour cream, mustard, fruit, and nuts. Stir until thoroughly mixed. Taste and add salt and pepper as needed.

**NOTE:**
Chicken can be prepared a day ahead through step 1.

3. Place about ½ cup shredded lettuce on each salad plate and top each with about 1 cup chicken salad.

4. Serve at once.

**Yield: 6 servings**

**\*See mail-order sources, page 237.**

M  E  N  U

*Tea Party for Four or More*

*Elizabeth's Chicken Salad\**

*Miniature Cranberry Muffins with Sweet Butter*

*Apple Juice in Tiny China Cups*

**\*Recipe is included in this book.**

# GRILLED CHICKEN SALAD

This is the next best thing to a trip to Mexico in February. The spirited marinade was inspired by a Caribbean recipe from *The Cooking of the Caribbean Islands*, one of Time-Life's *Foods of the World* books. The zesty chili dressing, borrowed (with kind permission) from *The Frog Commissary Cookbook*, warms with the heat of the tropics. Olé!

**Marinating Time:** 2 to 6 hours

**Preparation and Cooking Time:** 30 minutes

### ▪ Marinade

¼ cup dark rum
¼ cup tamari or soy sauce
¼ cup freshly squeezed lime juice
3 whole chicken breasts, boned and halved (about 3 pounds bone-in or 2 pounds boned)

### ▪ Chili-Cumin Dressing

1 egg
⅓ cup red wine vinegar
1 cup corn oil
2 teaspoons ground cumin
1½ teaspoons chili powder
1 teaspoon salt
1 teaspoon freshly ground pepper
½ teaspoon minced garlic (1 small clove)
¼ teaspoon cayenne

### ▪ Salad

9 to 10 cups torn mixed greens (use any combination of romaine, leaf, or iceberg lettuce, spinach, mizune, rocket, nasturtium leaf, lamb's lettuce— whatever you have available and like best)
1 carrot, peeled and grated
12 tomato wedges (1½ tomatoes)
6 avocado fans: cut avocados into quarters, scoop out of skins using a large spoon, and make thin lengthwise slices three quarters of the length of the avocado; gently fan out (1½ avocados)
½ cup very thinly sliced red onion
6 warmed 8- or 9-inch flour tortillas, folded into quarters

1. **To prepare marinade:** In a small pan, warm rum slightly over low heat. Remove pan from heat and ignite

rum with a match. Let alcohol burn off, gently shaking pan occasionally until flame dies.

2. In a large glass or stainless-steel bowl, combine rum, soy sauce, and lime juice. Using a large spoon, stir in boned chicken breasts, coating each with marinade. Cover and marinate in refrigerator for 1 to 2 hours, or up to 6 hours.

3. **To prepare dressing:** (See note on preparing mayonnaise and other emulsified sauces on page 40.) Put egg in a blender or food processor fitted with a steel blade. Add vinegar and blend briefly on high. While blender is running, add oil slowly, 1 teaspoon at a time at first, then 1 tablespoon at a time. (Do not add oil too fast or the dressing will break down. If it does, start over with an egg yolk and slowly add broken dressing.)

4. When all oil has been added and dressing is smooth, add cumin, chili powder, salt, pepper, garlic, and cayenne. Pour into a 2-cup container, cover, and refrigerate for up to 3 days.

5. **To assemble salad:** Preheat broiler or barbecue. Chill 6 dinner plates.

6. When broiler or barbecue is hot, cook chicken breasts for 3 to 5 minutes on each side. Finish cooking chicken skin side to heat until no longer pink inside (2 to 3 minutes more, depending upon thickness of breasts). If barbecue is quite hot, move chicken to cooler edges of fire and cover barbecue until chicken is done. Remove breasts from heat and slice them thinly on the bias, keeping them neatly together.

7. Divide mixed greens evenly among chilled salad plates and sprinkle with grated carrot. Arrange tomato wedges, avocado fans, and red onion slices on half the greens. Slightly fan out sliced chicken breast on other half of greens. Spoon 2 tablespoons dressing over salad and serve immediately, accompanied by warm tortillas and remaining dressing.

**Yield: 6 large salads**

NOTE:
**Salad can be prepared through step 4 several hours in advance.**

# SMOKED TURKEY AND PASTA SALAD WITH HIGHBUSH CRANBERRY— APPLE BUTTER

Turkey with cranberries is obviously not an original idea, but when our smoked salmon producer tried his hand at smoking turkeys, we gave it a new twist. Highbush cranberries are common in southeast Alaska and the relish, from a recipe published years ago by the University of Alaska's Cooperative Extension Service, is a favorite here.

**Preparation and Cooking Time:**  40 minutes

■ **Salad**

> 12 ounces fettuccine noodles
> 1⅓ cups Fiddlehead vinaigrette (page 218)
> 3 cups seeded and medium-diced fresh tomatoes (to remove seeds, cut tomato in half and squeeze gently)
> 1 cup grated carrots (about 2 medium)
> ⅔ cup bias-cut fresh chives or green onions (6 or 7 medium green onions)
> 1 teaspoon salt
> 9 cups romaine lettuce, washed, dried, and torn into bite-size pieces (1 medium head)
> 1½ pounds smoked turkey, sliced into 2- by ½- by ¼-inch strips

■ **Garnish**

> 6 tablespoons highbush cranberry—apple butter page 207), or substitute other tart preserves or chutney*
> 6 fresh chive flowers (if available)

1. Chill 6 large salad plates.

2. Bring a large pot of water to a boil over high heat. When water is boiling, add fettuccine and boil until cooked through. Pour noodles into a colander, rinse in cold water, and drain thoroughly. Place cooked noodles in a large bowl.

3. Add vinaigrette. Using spaghetti tongs or a large fork, mix well until noodles are well coated with dressing. Mix in diced tomatoes, carrots, chives, and salt.

4. **To assemble salads:** Divide romaine evenly among salad plates. Top each with pasta salad. Arrange strips of smoked turkey over pasta and garnish with a table-spoon of butter and a chive flower. Serve at once.

**Yield: 6 large salads**

*See mail-order sources, page 237.

NOTE:
**Prepare salad through step 3 and hold several hours or overnight, if necessary.**

NOTE:
**Highbush Cranberry–Apple Butter takes 4 hours to prepare. It's best to have it on hand.**

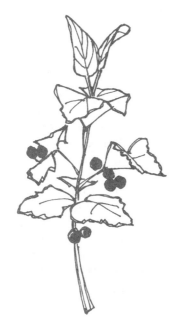

# ALASKAN COASTAL SALAD

An Alaskan's chef salad: Our version of the traditional salad stars a variety of fresh local seafood in place of the usual ham and turkey. Complement the delicately poached seafood with light curried mayonnaise or with Fiddlehead house dressing (page 218).

**Preparation Time:** 30 minutes

■ **Curried Mayonnaise**

1 egg yolk (use a whole egg if you are using a food processor)
3 tablespoons freshly squeezed lemon juice
¾ cup corn or safflower oil
1 teaspoon curry powder
¼ teaspoon garam masala (page 208), or combine pinches of powdered cardamom, cumin, clove, nutmeg, cinnamon, and freshly ground pepper; toast mixture lightly in a pan over low heat before adding to dressing
½ teaspoon salt
½ teaspoon ground black pepper

■ **Salad**

9 to 10 cups torn mixed greens (use any combination of romaine, leaf lettuce, spinach, and greens from your garden)
6 cups chilled cooked seafood broken into bite-size pieces (use any combination you have on hand: Petersburg shrimp, poached salmon, scallops, crab, and squid are all good)
3 tomatoes, each cut into 8 wedges

**NOTE:**
Mayonnaise can be made up to 3 days in advance.

1. **To prepare curried mayonnaise:** (See note on preparing mayonnaise and hollandaise sauces on page 40.) Place egg yolk in a mixing bowl (or whole egg in a food processor). Add lemon juice and whisk or blend briefly. Continue whisking and add oil 1 teaspoon at a time until you have added 6 teaspoons. Then add oil 1 tablespoon at a time, blending thoroughly after each addition until all oil is incorporated and mixture is smooth and thick. Add curry powder, garam masala, salt, and pepper. Whisk just until smooth. Using a rubber spatula, scrape mayonnaise into a 2-cup container, cover tightly, and refrigerate until ready to serve.

2. Chill 6 large salad plates.

3. **To assemble salad:** Divide greens among salad plates. Artfully arrange seafood on greens. Arrange 4 tomato wedges on each salad.

4. Top each salad with 2 tablespoons curried mayonnaise and serve at once, with extra mayonnaise for anyone who wants it.

**NOTE:**
You can assemble salads through step 3, cover with plastic wrap, and refrigerate for 2 to 3 hours, until you are ready to eat.

**Yield: 6 large salads**

---

### Edible Flowers

■ ■ ■

*Flowers add a touch of surprise and elegance to any meal, particularly when they are on the menu as well as the table. Many of the flowers found growing in Alaska are not only edible, but also delicious and nutritious. Here is a list of some of our favorites:*

| | | |
|---|---|---|
| *blueberry blossoms* | *herb flowers* | *sage* |
| *calendula* | *basil* | *sorrel* |
| *chickweed* | *borage* | *honeysuckle* |
| *chrysanthemums* | *chives* | *Johnny-jump-ups* |
| *clover* | *dill* | *lilac* |
| *dandelions* | *lavender* | *nasturtiums* |
| *day lilies* | *marjoram* | *pinks* |
| *fireweed* | *mint* | *roses* |
| *forget-me-nots* | *oregano* | *squash blossoms* |
| *goat's beard* | *rosemary* | *tiger lilies* |
| | | *violets* |

**NOTE:**
**Remember to pick flowers for eating only where you are certain they have not been sprayed with pesticides or otherwise made to be inedible.**

*What to Do With Edible Flowers*
*Dip them in tempura batter and deep-fry them as appetizers*
*Coat a cheese ball with them*
*Add them to scrambled eggs or pancakes*
*Float them in consommé*
*Add them to salads or add them to vinegars or oil used on salads*
*Sprinkle them over pasta*
*Chop them and whip them together with sweet butter to make delicate tea sandwich fillings*
*Fill them with salmon or chicken salad and serve on a bed of lettuce*
*Decorate a whole poached salmon or tuck them around a roast chicken*
*Mix them into herb bread or muffins*
*Add them to ice cream or use them to decorate a wedding cake*
*Drop them into champagne or add them to tea or lemonade*
*Freeze them in ice cubes for punch*
*Make scented jellies*

# SCALLOPS IN LIME SALAD

When weathervane scallops harvested from Kodiak Island became available, we found our customers couldn't get enough of them. This salad, adapted from a recipe found in *The Frog Commissary Cookbook*, blends a piquant and slightly spicy-hot lime dressing with the sweet flavor of gently poached scallops.

**Preparation and Cooking Time:** 45 minutes

■ **Lime Dressing**

> 1 egg
> 1 tablespoon white wine vinegar
> ¼ cup freshly squeezed lime juice (grate zest of 1 lime and squeeze juice, then set aside zest and remaining juice)
> 1¼ cups corn or safflower oil
> 2½ teaspoons red pepper flakes (substitute chili powder to taste if necessary)
> 2 teaspoons grated lime zest (from the lime you squeezed plus 1 more)
> 1½ teaspoons salt
> 1 teaspoon minced fresh garlic (about 1 large clove)

■ **Poached Scallops**

> 2 pounds fresh (or fresh frozen) Kodiak (weathervane) scallops, trimmed of the little white muscle on the side (substitute sea scallops)*
> 1 cup dry white wine (chardonnay or sauvignon blanc)
> 1 cup water
> 2 bay leaves
> 1 tablespoon minced fresh onion
> 3 fresh parsley sprigs (or 1 tablespoon dried)

■ **Salad**

> 6 to 7½ cups washed, dried, and torn lettuce (Boston lettuce is especially nice)
> 1 cup carrot matchsticks (2- by ⅛- by ⅛-inch) or carrot curls (3 carrots)
> 1 cup red pepper strips (⅛ inch wide) (1 pepper)
> 1 cup green pepper strips (⅛ inch wide) (1 pepper)
> 1 cup thinly sliced red onion, cut stem to tip (1 medium onion)

1. **To prepare lime dressing:** (See note on preparing mayonnaise and hollandaise, page 40.) Place egg in a blender or food processor fitted with a steel blade and

add vinegar and lime juice. Blend on high briefly. While motor is running, add oil 1 teaspoon at a time at first. After you have added 6 teaspoons, begin to add by tablespoons, blending thoroughly after each addition. When all oil has been incorporated and dressing is thickened and smooth, add red pepper flakes, lime zest, salt, and garlic. Pour into a 2-cup container, cover, and store in the refrigerator for up to 3 days.

2. **To prepare scallops:** If scallops are large, cut them into ¼-inch disks or 1-inch cubes so they are all uniform in size. Heat wine and water in a large pot over high heat. Add bay leaves, onion, and parsley. When it reaches a boil, turn heat off or to extremely low and add scallops. Cover tightly and steep until scallops are just opaque all the way through (¼-inch-thick scallops will take about 3 minutes; 1-inch cubes 4 to 5 minutes; take care not to overcook). Using a slotted spoon, immediately remove scallops from poaching liquid and place in a mixing bowl. Cover loosely and refrigerate until cold. (Using a wire mesh sieve, strain poaching liquid into a container, cool, cover, and refrigerate or freeze for use later in chowders or sauces.)

**NOTE: Scallops can be poached 1 day ahead.**

3. Chill 4 or 5 salad plates.

4. **To assemble salad:** Place scallops in a fresh mixing bowl and, using a slotted spoon, stir in ½ cup lime dressing. (Add any juices collected in first bowl to reserved poaching liquid.)

5. Divide lettuce among salad plates and top each with scallops. Arrange equal amounts of carrots, peppers, and onion on each salad. Serve immediately, accompanied by remaining dressing.

**NOTE: You can assemble salads several hours in advance, cover with plastic wrap, and refrigerate until ready to serve.**

If you prefer a less structured salad, combine lettuce, scallops, carrots, peppers, and onion in a large bowl. Add ¾ to 1 cup lime salad dressing. Using tongs, toss salad 30 times, until well mixed. Divide among salad plates and serve at once.

**Yield: 4 to 5 main-dish salads**

*See mail-order sources, page 237.

## Smoked Salmon

■ ■ ■

*Visitors from the East Coast comment on how different our smoked salmon looks and tastes. The following descriptions of salmon smokery may help explain the difference:*

*In hot smoking (kippering), fish is first cured briefly in a salt or salt-sugar mix, then smoked and cooked at 250-300°F for a few hours. Hot smoking uses less salt than some of the other methods and produces a fish that is ideal for flaking into soups, salads, quiches, and pasta dishes. Hot smoked salmon is most popular on the Pacific Northwest Coast and is the type we use in our recipes.*

*Cold smoked fish, such as Scotch smoked salmon and Nova lox, is salt-sugar cured until the flesh is firm, then smoked for many hours in an 80-85°F oven. This develops the distinctive flavor, ruddy color, and easily sliced texture. Cold smoked salmon is traditionally served wafer-thin on buttered bread with lemon and pepper.*

*Alaskan natives have perfected hard smoking, where less oily types of fish, such as chum salmon, are briefly salted, then hung whole or in strips in a smokehouse. The drying and smoking process can take up to three weeks, depending on the weather. Salmon comes out jerky-dry and deeply flavored. Hard-smoked fish is excellent for the trail and keeps almost indefinitely.*

*Gravlax and lox are neither smoked nor cooked. For gravlax, salmon fillets are simply sprinkled with a sugar-salt-herb mixture, refrigerated, and allowed to marinate for several days. Gravlax is sliced paper-thin and served garnished with sprigs of fresh dill or capers. Lox is salted salmon that has been freshened in water to remove the excess salt, then cool-dried to firm the fish. Lox is cut into thin slices and enjoyed (do we need to say it?) on toasted bagels slathered with cream cheese.*

# SMOKED SALMON CAESAR SALAD

The world seems to be divided into those who will eat anchovies and those who will not. This variation of the classic Ceasar salad brings them together.

**Preparation Time:** 45 minutes (less if croutons are already made)

- 16 cups torn mixed fresh greens (romaine, leaf lettuce, spinach, rocket, escarole, lamb's lettuce, or other fresh greens)
- ½ pound Alaskan smoked salmon* (not canned), skin and any bones removed
- 4 teaspoons Dijon mustard
- ½ cup Fiddlehead vinaigrette (page 218), or substitute other good vinaigrette
- 2 teaspoons minced fresh garlic (2 large cloves)
- 1 cup salad croutons (page 215), or substitute other garlic-flavored croutons
- ¼ cup freshly grated Parmesan cheese

### ■ Garnish

- 16 marinated artichoke hearts
- 8 tomato slices
- 8 cucumber slices
- 16 black olives

1. Chill 8 salad plates.
2. Place greens in a very large salad bowl.
3. Break smoked salmon into small pieces and sprinkle it over greens.
4. In a small bowl, whisk together mustard, vinaigrette dressing, and garlic.
5. Add croutons, cheese, and dressing mixture to salad bowl. Using your hands or salad tongs, toss salad 30 times, or until thoroughly mixed.
6. Divide salad onto 8 chilled salad plates and garnish each with artichoke hearts, tomato and cucumber slices, and black olives. Serve salad at once.

**Yield: 8 large salads**

*See mail-order sources, page 237.

M E N U

*Lunch for a Bunch*

■

*Italian Lentil Soup* in Mugs*

■

*Smoked Salmon Caesar Salad**

■

*Hot Herb Bread* with Sweet Butter*

■

*Sparkling Cider*

■

*Fresh Fruit Ice**

**\*Recipe is included in this book.**

■ ■ ■

*One impatient day, muttering about gourmet cooking and hectic schedules and life in general, we decided that adding the oil "drop by drop" was unnecessary, time consuming, and completely unrealistic for a modern cook. We simply whisked the lime dressing (for Scallops in Lime Salad, page 36) together and triumphantly concluded that we had overcome the laws of nature and proven old-fashioned methods completely out of date and out of touch with the 90s.*

*Our dressing tasted terrible. It lacked vim and zest. It needed lime juice. It needed flavor.*

*Heads hung low, we slunk back into the kitchen and made the dressing according to the time-honored ritual, adding the oil with care, drop by drop.*

*It came alive! The flavors sang and danced across the salad; the lime stood up and embraced the scallops; the red pepper teased and tickled our taste buds. Drop by drop works. As it has for centuries.*

*Mayonnaise, hollandaise, lime dressing, and custards all rely on egg yolk to hold tiny droplets of oil (or butter) together with tiny droplets of water. The resulting sauce is not only smooth and voluptuous, but the flavor is intense and vibrant. (Is it because there are so many more droplets of flavor to contact our tongue than there are in a simply whisked, unstable emulsion?)*

### What Is Happening
*As the yolks are whisked together with the water (or vinegar or juice or milk), the natural emulsifiers in the egg (mostly lecithin) surround the normally incompatible tiny drops of water and drops of fat from the yolk and create an emulsion. This prevents them from pulling apart into separate pools.*

*Once this initial emulsion is established, a little more fat or oil can be added. But: it must be completely broken into tiny droplets, each surrounded by emulsifier, before any more oil is added. Otherwise, all the oil droplets will break away and separate into a pool of oil.*

*The initial emulsion can assimilate only small amounts of oil at a time. As more and more oil is incorporated, the emulsion becomes more efficient at breaking up the oil into droplets and surrounding them, and can take larger additions at one time. (Roughly speaking, it is safe to add twice the amount of oil with each addition: Add 1 teaspoon first, then 2 teaspoons, then 4.) When all the oil is added, the resulting sauce will be thick, smooth, and full of flavor.*

### Notes
*Emulsions can break down, particularly when overbeaten. For this reason, when making mayonnaise or dressing with a blender or food processor, use the whole egg: The proteins in the egg white stabilize the emulsion.*

*Add only as much oil as a yolk can hold: For 1-yolk mayonnaise: ¾ cup oil.*

*For 1-yolk hollandaise: 3 tablespoons whole butter or ⅔ cup clarified butter.*

*If the sauce does break down, reconstruct it by starting with a new yolk and adding the broken sauce drop by drop.*

*Let the egg come to room temperature before beginning.*

*Make the sauce in a glass or stainless steel bowl: Aluminum discolors these sauces.*

*Use warm emulsified sauces (hollandaise, béarnaise) immediately. (They tend to spoil quickly.) Cold sauces (mayonnaise, salad dressings) can be stored, tightly covered and refrigerated, for up to 3 days.*

*Don't be intimidated: The process is simple.*

*And don't be in such a hurry: A "proper" mayonnaise takes only five to ten minutes, and the flavor is worth every minute.*

**"There is time for everything."**
*—Thomas Edison*

# POACHED SQUID AND RED PEPPER SALAD

Squid is a great favorite at the restaurant (although sometimes we call it calamari so it sounds more enticing), especially in this salad. Roasting the red pepper at home is worthwhile for the smoky sweetness it contributes.

**Preparation Time:** 30 minutes

**Marinating Time:** 4 hours or overnight

**Cooking and Assembly Time:** 15 minutes

■ **Vinaigrette**

>5 tablespoons olive oil
>3 tablespoons red wine vinegar
>2 teaspoons drained capers, coarsely chopped
>1½ teaspoons minced fresh garlic (1½ cloves)
>1 teaspoon Dijon mustard
>½ teaspoon salt
>½ teaspoon freshly ground black pepper
>⅛ teaspoon dried thyme

■ **Poached Squid**

>¾ cup water
>⅓ cup dry white wine
>½ small onion, cut into thin slices
>1 celery rib, cut into 2-inch pieces
>½ lime or lemon
>2 fresh parsley stalks
>4 black peppercorns
>¼ teaspoon dried thyme
>¾ pound cleaned squid (1½ pounds whole squid) or squid steak, cut into 2- by ¼-inch strips. (See Note.)
>1 large red pepper, roasted (page 214)

■ **Salad**

>6 cups torn mixed fresh greens (romaine, red leaf, spinach, or whatever you like best)
>Lemon wedges

**NOTE:**
To clean squid, separate head and tentacles from body. Remove inner cartilage from body. Cut head from tentacles and discard head. Peel outer skin from body. Slice squid into ½-inch rings.

1. **To prepare vinaigrette:** Whisk together olive oil, vinegar, capers, garlic, mustard, salt, pepper, and thyme in a medium bowl. Set aside.

2. **To prepare squid:** Combine water, wine, onion, celery, lime, parsley, peppercorns, and thyme in a medium pot over high heat. Bring to a boil, then reduce heat and

simmer for 15 minutes, until vegetables are cooked through. Remove vegetables and seasonings with a slotted spoon.

3. Add squid to strained court bouillon, cover pot, and turn heat off or to as low as possible. Steep squid just until cooked through, about 3 minutes. It will be opaque white all the way through. Take care not to cook too long or at too high a temperature, as squid will become tough if it is overcooked. Drain and add to vinaigrette. Cover and refrigerate.

4. Cut roasted red pepper in half and remove inner ribs and seeds. Slice into ¼- by 2-inch strips and add to squid and vinaigrette. Toss to combine well and marinate in refrigerator for 4 hours or overnight.

5. **To assemble salad:** Chill 6 to 8 salad plates. Line plates (or a salad bowl) with lettuce leaves. Arrange marinated squid and peppers on lettuce, garnish with lemon wedges, and serve at once.

**Yield: 6 to 8 servings**

"There is an emanation from the heart in genuine hospitality which cannot be described but is immediately felt and puts the stranger at once at his ease."
—*Washington Irving*

# WARM SALMON SALAD

Make this salad on a hot summer day when the salmon are running, the tomatoes are ripe, the barbecue beckons, and it's too hot to eat anything but the essentials.

**Marinating Time:** 4 hours or overnight

**Preparation and Cooking Time:** 30 minutes

### ■ Marinade and Dressing

1 cup olive oil
3 tablespoons fresh lemon juice (1 lemon)
1 tablespoon red wine vinegar
1 generous tablespoon finely chopped fresh parsley
   (substitute 1 teaspoon dried)
1 teaspoon minced fresh garlic (about 1 large clove)
1 teaspoon dried thyme
½ teaspoon salt
½ teaspoon freshly ground black pepper

### ■ Salad

4 fresh salmon fillets or steaks, ½ pound each
12 cups torn mixed fresh greens (use any
   combination of romaine, leaf lettuce, spinach, curly
   endive, or greens you have available)
1 tablespoon extra virgin olive oil
2 cups thinly sliced fresh mushrooms (about ½
   pound)

### ■ Garnish

2 tomatoes, thinly sliced
4 thin slices of red onion
8 thin slices of cucumber
1 cup grated carrots
4 lemon wedges
½ cup cooked fresh beet matchsticks (optional)
½ cup daikon radish matchsticks (optional)

1. **To prepare marinade and dressing:** Whisk together olive oil, lemon juice, red wine vinegar, parsley, garlic, thyme, salt, and pepper in a small bowl. Set aside.

2. Place salmon in a shallow glass or enamel pan and pour half the marinade over it. (Cover and reserve remaining marinade to use as dressing.) Cover and marinate fish in refrigerator for at least 4 hours, or overnight.

3. **To assemble salad:** Preheat broiler or barbecue. Place greens in a large salad bowl.

4. Broil salmon for about 4 minutes on each side, depending on heat of broiler or grill and thickness of salmon.

5. While salmon is cooking, heat olive oil in large pan over medium-high heat. When oil is quite hot, add mushrooms and cook until they are slightly soft. Remove from heat and stir in reserved marinade. Pour mushroom mixture over greens and, using salad tongs, toss salad well. Divide greens among 4 large salad plates and arrange garnishes on each plate.

6. When salmon is cooked through (it will flake easily but not be dry on the inside), use a metal spatula to remove it from broiler or barbecue. Remove and discard skin, and place 1 fillet on each salad. Serve at once.

**Yield: 4 large salads**

■

# SPINACH-CASHEW-RAISIN SALAD

This is a light, refreshing salad with contrasting textures and flavors: chewy and crunchy and sweet and salty.

**Preparation Time:** 30 minutes

>  1 cup raw cashews  (or substitute roasted, salted cashews and skip step 1), coarsely chopped
> 12 cups (about 8 ounces trimmed) washed, dried, and torn fresh spinach
> ½ cup raisins, coarsely chopped
> ½ cup thinly sliced red onion, cut stem to tip
> ½ cup Fiddlehead vinaigrette (page 218)

1. Preheat oven to 350°F. Spread raw cashews on a cookie sheet and roast until golden brown, about 10 minutes (they will burn quickly, so keep an eye on them).

2. Place spinach in a large salad bowl and add ½ cup toasted cashews, raisins, and red onion. Using your hands or salad tongs, toss well.

3. Just before you are ready to serve, add vinaigrette and toss 30 times. Sprinkle salad with remaining ½ cup cashews and serve at once.

**Yield: 6 first-course salads**

■

# CREAMED NEW POTATOES AND PEAS

This is an old-fashioned summer treat well known to everyone who grew up with a potato patch in the backyard.

**Preparation and Cooking Time:** 30 minutes

> 1½ pounds freshly dug new potatoes, well scrubbed and cut into uniform sizes (cold boiled or baked potatoes also work well: skip step 1 if you use cooked potatoes)
> 1½ cups fresh or fresh-frozen peas
> 1½ cups béchamel (page 219)
> Salt and pepper to taste

1. Place potatoes in a large pot, cover with water, and bring to a boil over high heat. Cook until tender when probed with a fork. (Cooking time will depend upon size of potatoes.) Drain them in a colander. (Save potato water to use when making bread.)

2. Add potatoes and peas to the béchamel and cook gently until peas are hot. Taste and add salt and pepper if necessary. Transfer to a serving dish and serve at once.

**Yield: 4 servings**

## M E N U

**Midsummer Supper**

■

*Fresh Salmon
Poached in Court Bouillon\*
Sprinkled with Fresh Chives and Lemon Juice*

■

*Creamed New Potatoes and Peas\**

■

*Slices of Garden-Fresh Tomatoes
With Freshly Ground Pepper*

■

*Pink Lemonade or Sauvignon Blanc*

■

*Strawberries Romanoff\**

**\*Recipe is included in this book.**

# HEALTHY HOME FRIES

We usually serve these at breakfast, but they go well all day long with hamburgers, omelets, steaks, or even late at night all by themselves with a bottle of catsup. What is the secret flavoring that makes these so deliciously different? Nutritious brewer's yeast: It is the perfect complement to the earthy flavor of potatoes.

**Preparation and Cooking Time:** 1 hour (15 minutes if you have cooked potatoes on hand)

■ **Seasoning Mix**

> 2 teaspoons powdered brewer's yeast (available in health food stores*)
> 2 teaspoons garlic powder
> 2 teaspoons salt

■ **Home Fries**

> 1½ pounds red potatoes, scrubbed well but not peeled (substitute any other type of potato)
> 2 tablespoons oil
> 1 tablespoon butter
> ½ teaspoon pepper

1. **To prepare seasoning mix:** Whisk together brewer's yeast, garlic powder, and salt in a small bowl. Transfer to a small jar (an emptied spice jar is perfect) to use as needed.

2. **To prepare home fries:** Place potatoes in a large pot and add water to cover. Place over high heat and bring to a boil. Boil until tender when probed with a fork. Drain and cool potatoes.

3. Cut cooked potatoes into ½-inch cubes.

4. Heat oil and butter in a large heavy-bottomed pan over medium-high heat. When foam subsides and oil is very hot but not browned, add cubed potatoes. Stir to coat evenly and allow to cook for several minutes. When they are crusty-brown on the bottom, stir again and cook until they are crusty on all sides.

5. Sprinkle to taste with seasoning mix and pepper. Transfer to a serving dish to eat at once.

**Yield: 4 to 6 servings (4 cups)**

*****See mail-order sources, page 237.**

NOTE:
Potatoes can be made ahead through step 2 and kept refrigerated for 1 or 2 days, until needed.

# WARM MUSHROOM SALAD

Although this recipe calls for dried mushrooms, it is wonderful with fresh, and with the growing selection of fresh mushrooms available in the market you can enjoy a spectrum of flavors even though you are not necessarily a mycologist. Try fresh shiitake, chanterelles, or oyster mushrooms. If they are available, tiny enoki mushrooms make a charming garnish for this (and many other salads). And when the exotics and dried are unavailable, the basic button mushroom serves very well.

**Soaking Time:**  30 minutes (only if you use dried mushrooms)

**Preparation and Cooking Time:**  15 minutes

> 2 ounces dried shiitake mushrooms (available in many produce stores, oriental groceries, or health food stores*), or about 2 cups thinly sliced fresh mushrooms, 10 to 12 ounces
> 6 to 7 cups washed, dried, and torn romaine lettuce
> 2 tablespoons olive oil
> 3 tablespoons balsamic vinegar* (substitute 2½ tablespoons red wine vinegar)
> ½ teaspoon freshly ground black pepper
> 6 pinches of kosher salt*

1. Soak dried mushrooms in a bowl of lukewarm water for 30 minutes. Drain and lightly pat dry. Cut away stems and slice caps into ¼-inch strips.

2. Place lettuce in a large salad bowl and set aside. Heat olive oil in a large pan over medium-high heat. When oil is hot, add mushrooms and cook quickly, stirring with a wooden spoon, for 3 to 5 minutes.

3. Remove from heat and stir in balsamic vinegar and pepper.

4. Pour mushroom mixture over lettuce. Using your hands or salad tongs, toss together thoroughly. Divide among 6 small salad plates, sprinkle each salad with a pinch of kosher salt, and serve immediately.

**Yield: 6 small salads**

**\*See mail-order sources, page 237.**

**MOREL MUSHROOMS**

■ ■ ■

*We begin to look for morel mushrooms in May, when the leaves on the cottonwood trees are the size of mouse ears. We are continually amazed to find such delicacies growing in the most indelicate environments—under porches, in automobile junk yards, along the edges of dirt roads, or where an old shed has burned.*

*When you hunt for morels, take along a mushroom field guide so as not to confuse the true morel with the dangerous false morel. Once sure of the identification, slice the mushroom off at ground level to preserve the buried strands of mycelium that will produce new mushrooms next year. And most important, remember the spot, because even your best friend won't tell you where the morels are hidden.*

*Always cook morels, as some people are allergic to certain substances in the raw mushroom. Cut the caps into wavy rings and sauté them in hot butter, shaking the pan occasionally to keep them from sticking.*

NOTE:
Leftovers are good in soup, as omelet fillings, or sprinkled with red wine vinegar and added to salads.

# ZUCCHINI PROVENÇAL

We like the colorful tastiness of this side dish.

**Preparation and Cooking Time:** 20 minutes

  2 teaspoons butter
  2 teaspoons olive oil
  1¼ pounds zucchini, quartered lengthwise and cut
    into ¼-inch slices (about 3 cups)
  1 cup seeded and large-diced tomato (cut in half
    around the middle and squeeze gently to remove
    the seeds), about 1 large tomato
  1 teaspoon finely chopped fresh basil (substitute ½
    teaspoon dried)
  1 teaspoon minced fresh garlic (about 1 large clove)
  2 teaspoons freshly squeezed lemon juice
  ½ teaspoon salt
  ¼ teaspoon pepper

1. Heat butter and olive oil in a large pan over medium-high heat. When foam subsides, add zucchini. Stir with a wooden spoon and cook until zucchini begins to soften, about 3 minutes (but avoid browning).

2. Add tomatoes, basil, garlic, and lemon juice; cook 2 to 3 minutes more, until liquid almost completely evaporates. Taste and add salt and pepper as needed.

3. Transfer to a serving dish and serve at once.

**Yield: 4 to 5 side-dish servings**

*"If it comes with the meal, take it."*
*—H. George DeCherney*

St. Nicholas Russian Orthodox Church
Fifth Street, Juneau, Alaska

St. Nicholas Russian Orthodox Church—Constructed in 1894, the St. Nicholas Russian Orthodox Church is the oldest unaltered church in Juneau. Services are held regularly in English, Tlingit (the Native language), and Russian, and the building is open for tours during the summer.

# BREAKFAST

# CRABBY EGGS

Some mornings are like this.

**Preparation and Cooking Time:** 45 minutes

■ **Hollandaise Sauce**

3 egg yolks
2 teaspoons fresh lemon juice
¼ pound butter, melted (use unsalted if you can)
Pinch of cayenne, or 2 drops of Tabasco

■ **Eggs**

1 tablespoon white wine vinegar
12 eggs

■ **Crab**

6 English muffins or croissants
1 tablespoon butter
3 cups (¾ pound) fresh king, dungeness, Tanner, or
   other crabmeat

■ ■ ■

*It's easy to make crabby eggs for a large brunch, especially if you poach the eggs ahead and re-heat them just as you are ready to serve:*

**1.** *Fill a large bowl with very cold water and set it aside.*
**2.** *Poach eggs as you would normally. When they are done, use a slotted spoon to remove eggs from pan and put them into the bowl of cold water. When eggs are cooled, carefully remove them from bowl, trim edges of each egg, and place on a plate lined with absorbent towels. Cover with plastic wrap and refrigerate until you are ready to serve.*
**3.** *When you are ready to serve: Bring a large pot of salted water to a boil and reduce heat to low. Gently place the poached eggs in hot water to heat through (about 2 minutes). Use a slotted spoon to remove eggs from water, drain, and serve according to your recipe.*

1. **To prepare hollandaise sauce:** (See note on preparing mayonnaise and other emulsified sauces on page 40.) Prepare a double boiler with gently simmering water over low heat. Place egg yolks in top of double boiler (or substitute a 1- or 2-quart flat-bottomed stainless steel bowl set directly over extremely low heat). Add lemon juice and whisk gently until egg mixture becomes fluffy and begins to thicken and whisk leaves trails briefly while you are stirring. Remove top of double boiler from heat and set it on a damp towel (to hold it in place while you add butter).

2. Continue to whisk gently, adding melted butter 1 tea-spoon at a time. When you have added 6 teaspoons, begin to add butter by tablespoons, thoroughly incor-porating each addition before adding more.

3. When all butter has been added and sauce is thick and smooth, whisk in cayenne or Tabasco. Taste and cor-rect seasoning. Hold sauce briefly in a warm spot near stove, or transfer to a preheated wide-mouth thermos to hold for up to an hour.

4. **To poach eggs:** Lightly oil the bottom of a medium-size pan and fill it with water to a depth of 1 inch. Add vinegar to pan and bring to a boil over high heat. Re-duce heat to a very low simmer. Crack each egg into a small bowl or saucer and gently slide it into the barely

simmering water. Put as many eggs into pan as will fit comfortably, then cover pan and cook for 4 to 5 minutes (longer if you prefer the yolk hard). The egg whites should be firm to the touch, and the yolk still slightly soft.

5. **While eggs are poaching:** Preheat broiler. Cut English muffins in half and lay them cut side up on a cookie sheet. Toast them lightly under broiler. Turn off broiler, but keep muffins warm.

6. Melt 1 tablespoon butter in a large pan over medium-high heat and toss crab until heated through. Top each half muffin with ¼ cup crab and hold in a warm place.

7. **When eggs are cooked:** Use a slotted spoon or pancake spatula to remove eggs from pan and place on a plate lined with absorbent towels. Trim ragged edges of each egg and place 1 egg on each crab-topped muffin. Hold in a warm spot until all eggs are cooked.

8. Transfer topped muffins to a serving platter, spoon hollandaise over each, and serve at once.

**Yield: 6 servings**

The basic Eggs Benedict can be varied in many delicious ways, of which Crabby Eggs is just one of our favorites. Here are a few more of the many variations we've enjoyed:

### Eggs Benedetto

Whisk 2 teaspoons basil pesto into the hollandaise sauce just before you serve, and substitute thinly sliced prosciutto for the crab.

### Eggs California

Top each muffin with slices of avocado instead of crab. Top with eggs and hollandaise and serve.

### Shrimpy Eggs

Use peeled, cooked cocktail shrimp in place of the crab.

### Alaskan Eggs Benedict

Remove the skin from ¾ pound Alaskan smoked salmon, pick out the bones, and break into small pieces. Use in place of crab.

---

**Extra Egg Whites?**

*Use them in:*

*Beer batter (page 96)*
*Coconut macaroons (page 164)*
*White cake*
*Angel food cake*
*Holiday cookies (page 173)*
*Meringues*

*Or whisk them with a little water and use as a glaze for crusty bread*

# FIDDLEHEAD OMELETS

Simple, fast, and versatile, omelets are welcome any time of day. To do these perfectly, you need a 9-inch nonstick pan or a well-seasoned omelet pan and a flexible-blade metal spatula. This procedure goes fast: Read through the instructions and visualize what you will be doing before you start. It's a snap.

**Preparation and Cooking Time:**  15 minutes

> 1 tablespoon butter
> 3 fresh eggs
> One filling (see suggestions that follow)

1. Preheat broiler and set a plate to warm.

2. Heat butter in a 9-inch nonstick pan or well-seasoned omelet pan over high heat.

3. While butter is melting, beat eggs until they are very frothy.

4. As soon as foam subsides but before butter browns, pour in eggs. (They should sizzle and bubble when they hit the pan.)

5. Working quickly, use a long flexible-blade metal spatula to gently push edges of eggs toward center, letting liquid eggs pour out to the edge. Then, holding the handle of the pan in one hand and the spatula in the other, briskly move pan back and forth while stirring in a circular pattern with the spatula. In about 10 seconds the eggs will be well mixed and will begin to solidify on the bottom, but will still be liquid on the surface. (Eggs should not brown or stick to bottom of pan at all.)

6. Remove pan from heat and put omelet filling, with cheese on top, on the half of the omelet opposite from the handle.

7. Place pan in oven directly under broiler until cheese has melted and eggs have puffed slightly, but are not brown. (When you become skilled, you can start a second omelet on top of the stove while the first is under the broiler.)

8. Remove pan from oven and slip blade of spatula under eggs to loosen them. Fold unfilled part of omelet onto filled part.

9. Tilt pan and gently flip or slide omelet onto your warm plate. Serve at once to the sound of oohs and ahs.

**Yield: 1 large omelet, 1 or 2 servings**

**FILLINGS**

Omelets are delicious wrapped around almost any little tidbit: Use ¼ to ⅓ cup for each omelet. Here are some of our favorite combinations.

■ **Bracken Omelet**

> ¼ cup guacamole (page 222)
> 2 slices Jack cheese

■ **Homesteader's**

This seems like an unusual filling, but it was requested so frequently that we finally put it on the menu. Does it need catsup?

> ¼ cup healthy home fries (page 48)
> 2 tablespoons sour cream

■ **R & H**

> ¼ cup R&H cheese spread (page 214)

■ **Shrimp and Parmesan**

> ¼ cup steamed Petersburg or cocktail shrimp
> 2 tablespoons freshly grated Parmesan cheese

■ **Smoked Salmon and Cream Cheese**

> 2 to 3 tablespoons flaked smoked salmon, all bones
>     and skin removed
> ¼ cup R&H cheese spread (page 214)

■ **Spanish Omelet**

> ¼ cup salsa (page 220)
> 2 slices Cheddar cheese
> Guacamole and sour cream as garnish

# HALIBUT HASH

There is something very comforting about having breakfast for dinner. This quick and easy dish is that perfect comfort food after a long hard day at work. Of course, it's nice for breakfast, too.

**Preparation and Cooking Time:** 45 minutes

4 tablespoons butter
1 pound cubed uncooked boneless halibut (substitute flaked cooked halibut and skip step 1)
1 cup large-diced onion (1 medium onion)
1 cup large-diced green pepper (1 large green pepper)
2 teaspoons minced fresh garlic (2 or 3 large cloves)
2⅔ cups large-diced cooked potatoes (3 small potatoes)
2 to 4 dashes of Tabasco sauce
½ teaspoon dried thyme
¾ teaspoon salt
¼ teaspoon pepper
2 teaspoons white wine
1 tablespoon heavy cream
2 tablespoons butter
8 eggs
⅓ cup cream or milk

■ **Garnish**

½ cup freshly grated Parmesan or Jack cheese
½ cup catsup or salsa

**NOTE:**
**If halibut is unavailable, substitute red snapper, ling cod, or other white fish.**

1. Heat 4 tablespoons butter in a medium fry pan over medium-high heat. When butter is hot, add halibut. Stir with a slotted spoon to coat fish evenly with butter. Cook until cubes are opaque all the way through, about 2 minutes. Remove fish to a large serving dish and set aside.

2. Add onion, peppers, and garlic to pan. Cook over medium heat until they are wilted and lightly browned, stirring occasionally.

**NOTE:**
**Poach or fry the eggs if you prefer.**

3. Add potatoes, Tabasco, thyme, salt, and pepper. Stir in wine and cream. Cook until heated through and lightly golden brown on bottom. Return fish to pan. Reduce heat to very low while you cook eggs.

4. *While potato and fish mixture is simmering*, heat 2 tablespoons butter in a large pan over high heat. Using an electric mixer on high or a wire whisk, beat eggs in a large bowl until foamy, then whisk in cream. As soon

**NOTE:**
**Rumor has it the leftovers are wonderful microwaved the next day.**

as butter is hot and foam subsides, pour in beaten eggs. Stir with a wooden spoon until softly scrambled. Remove from heat.

5. Transfer potato and fish mixture to a serving dish. Sprinkle with cheese and arrange eggs on top. Serve immediately, accompanied by catsup or salsa.

**Yield: 4 servings**

# GRANOLA

Somehow granola became identified with an era, but as the healthful attributes of oats are rediscovered, it seems quite in step with our time. Don't restrict it to breakfast (although, as a deliciously quick morning meal, nothing is better). Try it on ice cream, in crumb pie crusts, sprinkled on pancakes, or as a streusel topping for coffee cakes.

**Preparation Time:** 15 minutes

**Resting Time:** 30 minutes

**Cooking Time:** 30 minutes

> 5 cups old-fashioned rolled oats
> ½ cup sesame seeds
> 1 cup unroasted sunflower seeds
> 1½ teaspoons ground cinnamon
> 2 tablespoons water
> ½ cup honey
> ½ cup safflower oil
> 1 cup dried currants
> ¾ cup chopped almonds

1. In a large mixing bowl, combine oats, seeds, and cinnamon.

2. In a small bowl, whisk together water, honey, and oil. Pour over oats, stir together well, and allow to rest for 30 minutes.

3. Preheat oven to 350°F. Lightly oil a large cookie sheet.

4. Spread oats evenly on cookie sheet and bake for 30 minutes, turning and redistributing oats every 10 minutes, until they are lightly golden brown.

5. Remove from oven and cool on cookie sheet. Stir in currants and almonds. Transfer to an airtight container and store at room temperature for 1 month, or in freezer for longer.

**MENU**

***"Megan's Morning"***
*(The favorite breakfast of one of the Fiddlehead's favorite customers)*

Granola
topped with
unsweetened
yogurt, blueberries,
and brown sugar
Fresh-squeezed
orange juice
Hot chocolate with
whipped cream

**"Kites rise highest against the wind."**
*—Winston Churchill*

**Yield: 2 quarts**

# SOURDOUGH FRENCH TOAST

How can something so simple taste so special? Use a good-quality bread and real maple syrup and cook the toast ever so gently so it is puffy and tender throughout. A friend of ours writes that, as a further indulgence, she likes to sprinkle toasted pecans over the top.

**Preparation and Cooking Time:** 30 minutes

> 8 to 9 eggs
> ½ cup half-and-half or milk
> ¼ teaspoon vanilla extract
> ⅛ teaspoon ground cardamom (substitute cinnamon)
> 8 slices (½ inch thick) day-old sourdough French
>   bread (page 150), or substitute your favorite bread
> 2 teaspoons butter

■ **Garnish**

> Butter
> Warm (real) maple syrup, or fruit syrup*
> Toasted chopped pecans (optional)

**1.** Preheat oven to warm. Set 4 ovenproof plates in oven to warm.

**2.** In a flat-bottomed bowl, whisk together eggs, half-and-half, vanilla, and cardamom until well beaten. Thoroughly soak 2 or 3 slices bread in egg mixture.

**3.** Place 1 teaspoon butter in a large heavy-bottomed skillet set over medium-high heat. When butter has melted and foam subsides, reduce heat to low and add slices of soaked bread. Cook gently until golden brown on bottom, then, using a spatula, flip and cook gently on other side. Toast will puff up very slightly as it cooks through. When it is golden brown on both sides and slightly puffed, top with a dollop of butter and place on a warmed plate in oven while you cook remaining slices. Lightly butter pan, if necessary, before cooking remaining slices of bread.

**4.** Serve with lots of butter and syrup.

**Yield: 4 servings**

**\*See mail-order sources, page 237.**

# TOFU STIR-FRY

The sun rises in the East, as the oriental flavors of this breakfast dish will prove to you. And like an Alaskan morning, it's welcome any time of day.

**Preparation Time:**  1 hour (15 minutes if the rice is already cooked)

**Cooking Time:**  15 minutes

    6 tablespoons corn or safflower oil
    3 tablespoons oriental sesame oil (found in oriental
      groceries or health food stores*)
    ¾ cup thinly sliced mushrooms
    ¾ cup medium-diced red pepper (1 small)
    ¾ cup medium-diced green pepper (1 small)
    ¾ cup medium-diced red onion (1 medium)
    ¾ cup medium-diced yellow onion (1 medium)
    12 ounces firm tofu, cut into ½-inch cubes (about 2
      cups)
    3 tablespoons minced fresh ginger (substitute ½
      teaspoon powdered)
    6 tablespoons tamari or soy sauce
    3 tablespoons butter
    6 eggs
    9 cups cooked brown rice (page 209), warmed

1. Heat oils in a large pan over medium heat. When oil is hot, add vegetables. Stir with a wooden spoon to coat vegetables evenly with oil and cook until tender.

2. Mix tofu into vegetables and add ginger and tamari. Reduce heat to low while you prepare eggs.

3. Heat butter in a small pan over medium-high heat. Using a wire whisk or egg beater, beat eggs until foamy. When butter is melted, pour in eggs. Using a wooden spoon, stir and cook them until softly scrambled. Remove from heat.

4. Line a serving dish with rice and top with vegetable-tofu mixture. Spoon scrambled eggs over vegetables and serve at once, accompanied by extra tamari or soy sauce. (NOTE: Some people prefer to mix the rice, vegetables, and eggs all together before serving. It's delicious either way.)

**Yield: 6 servings**

*See mail-order sources, page 237.

# SOURDOUGH STRAWBERRY WAFFLES

Light as a feather, divine topped with wild strawberries and whipped cream (or creamed salmon), this breakfast treat is based on Marion Cunningham's (*The Breakfast Book*) recipe for raised waffles, which she found in an old edition of *The Fannie Farmer Cookbook*. Set the starter the night before you plan to cook the waffles.

**Preparation Time:** 10 minutes

**Starter (rising) Time:** overnight

**Cooking Time:** 15 minutes

■ **Waffle Starter**

1 cup sourdough starter (page 230)
1½ cups milk, warmed
1 cup white flour
½ cup graham flour* (substitute whole wheat flour, if necessary, but waffles will not have the same nutty, crunchy flavor)
¼ pound butter, melted
1 teaspoon salt
1 teaspoon sugar

■ **To Replenish the Starter Pot**

½ cup sourdough starter (page 230)
1 cup water
1 cup white flour

■ **To Complete Waffles**

2 eggs, beaten
¼ teaspoon baking soda

■ **Garnish**

2 quarts fresh strawberries, washed, patted dry, hulled, and sliced (5 to 6 cups)
2 teaspoons sugar
1 cup heavy cream
1 teaspoon sugar
1 teaspoon vanilla extract

1. **To set waffle starter:** Combine 1 cup starter, milk, 1 cup white flour, graham flour, butter, salt, and sugar in a large crockery or glass bowl. (The mixture will double in size during the night.) Using a wooden spoon, beat until smooth.

2. **To replenish the starter pot:** In your starter pot, stir together ½ cup starter, 1 cup water and 1 cup flour. Mix well.

3. Cover both waffle starter and starter pot and allow to sit overnight at room temperature. In the morning, refrigerate starter pot until the next time you make waffles.

4. **To complete waffles:** Preheat oven to warm. Warm your plates while you are cooking waffles. Preheat waffle iron according to manufacturer's instructions.

5. Put sliced strawberries in a small bowl and sprinkle with 2 teaspoons sugar. Whip cream until stiff and whisk in 1 teaspoon sugar and vanilla. Refrigerate strawberries and cream until waffles are ready.

6. With a wooden spoon, beat eggs and baking soda into waffle starter.

7. Lightly oil waffle iron and spoon or pour batter to within 1 inch of edges of iron. (The amount to use will vary with size of the waffle iron.) Cook until crisp and golden brown.

8. Transfer each waffle to a warm plate and top generously with strawberries and whipped cream. Serve at once.

**Yield: 10 7-inch waffles**

*See mail-order sources, page 237.

**NOTE:**
Waffle batter will keep covered in refrigerator for 1 to 2 days. Any extra waffles (without strawberries and whipped cream) freeze well wrapped in plastic, to be toasted later.

**VARIATION:**
To make Sourdough Pancakes, reduce amount of butter to 4 tablespoons, or substitute ¼ cup corn oil. Follow same mixing procedure, dropping batter by tablespoonfuls onto a hot, lightly oiled griddle. (Sprinkle pancakes with wild blueberries at this point if you like.) Turn pancake when bubbles begin to show through the batter and pancake is lightly browned on the bottom. Cook briefly on other side, remove from pan, and serve with butter and maple syrup.

Gone Fishing

Gone Fishing—Juneauites spend many summer hours out on the water. With about one boat for every fourteen people, most of the community can be found afloat on a sunny summer afternoon.

# SANDWICHES AND QUICHE

# GRILLED SALMON SANDWICH

The Earl of Sandwich would consider this a prince.

**Preparation and Cooking Time:** 30 minutes (15 if the tartar sauce is on hand)

■ **Tartar Sauce**

½ cup mayonnaise
2 teaspoons finely chopped dill pickle or pickle relish
1 teaspoon freshly squeezed lemon juice
1 teaspoon Dijon mustard
1 teaspoon finely chopped fresh parsley
1 teaspoon drained, chopped capers
¼ teaspoon dried tarragon

■ **Sandwich**

1 pound boneless, skinless salmon fillets, cut into 4 portions
4 onion buns (page 144) or other hamburger buns
4 lettuce leaves, washed and dried
4 tomato slices

1. **To prepare tartar sauce:** In a small bowl, stir together mayonnaise, pickle, lemon juice, mustard, parsley, capers, and tarragon. Cover and refrigerate until ready to use.

2. **To prepare sandwiches:** Preheat broiler.

3. Lightly season each piece, of salmon with salt and pepper, then broil 5 minutes on each side (depending on thickness of fish: 10 minutes for each inch of thickness).

4. Just before fish is done, cut buns in half and lightly toast them under broiler.

5. Spread toasted buns with tartar sauce, top with grilled salmon, lettuce, and tomato. Cut each sandwich in half, transfer to a serving platter, and serve at once.

**Yield: 4 sandwiches**

NOTE:
Tartar sauce can be made up to 1 week in advance.

## Kelp Pickles

■ ■ ■

*An old-timey Alaskan treat that's still relished today is sweet pickled kelp. A common sea-weed, bull kelp can best be described as a long, dull-green whip with a pompom. Kelp is easily collected from a boat— but take along a knife. Hauling in a plant that's anchored to the bottom in 100 feet of water isn't easy! Sans skiff, a walk on the beach after a storm may also yield fresh bull kelp. Summer is the best time of year to collect the plant, as kelp collected in the fall must have its dark outer layer peeled away.*

*To make kelp pickles: Cut the hollow kelp stems into rings and soak for a few hours to remove excess salt. Then pack them in a bread-and-butter, dill, or sweet-mustard brine. Use kelp pickles in the same way you would use cucumber pickles— as a meat accompani-ment, mixed with cot-tage cheese, or on a relish tray.*

# FIDDLEHEAD HAMBURGERS

More than quite a few served.

**Preparation and Cooking Time:** 15 minutes

■ **The Basic Burger**

¼ pound lean ground beef
1 tablespoon ice water
Salt and pepper
1 onion bun (page 144), sliced in half and lightly
   brushed with butter
1 lettuce leaf
1 tomato slice
1 red onion slice

■ **Garnish**

1 dill pickle spear
Mustard, mayonnaise, catsup

1. Preheat barbecue or broiler, or set a lightly oiled pan on medium-high heat.

2. Combine ground beef with ice water and pat into a 4-inch patty. Lightly season with salt and pepper. Place it on barbecue, under broiler, or in pan and cook for 3 to 5 minutes on each side, depending on how well done you like your meat. Avoid pressing on burger while it is cooking; this squeezes all the flavor out.

3. **While burger is cooking:** Lightly toast bun, buttered sides to the heat, under broiler or in a small pan over medium heat. When it is golden brown, remove to a plate, arrange lettuce leaf, tomato, and onion on top half; keep warm while finishing burger.

4. Just before burger is done, cover it with topping of your choice. Melt cheese under broiler, or by covering pan. Place burger on bottom half of bun and serve at once, accompanied by the usual condiments.

**Yield: 1 hamburger**

**THE TOPPINGS**

■ **McDunnah Burger**

Named for Grandpa Gene, this is our most popular com-bination.

2 tablespoons guacamole (page 222)
1 ounce Jack cheese (1 or 2 slices)

Top grilled burger with guacamole, then cheese. Place under broiler until cheese has melted.

### ■ Popeye Burger

An inspiration from the New Boonville Hotel in Boonville, California.

> ½ teaspoon olive oil
> ½ teaspoon butter
> ½ teaspoon minced garlic (1 small clove)
> 1 cup washed, trimmed, and chopped fresh spinach
> Salt and pepper to taste
> 1 slice mozzarella cheese

1. Heat olive oil and butter with garlic in a small pan over medium-high heat. Add spinach, stir to combine well, and cover. Sweat spinach for 30 seconds, or until wilted.

2. Place spinach on top of grilled burger and top with cheese. Place under broiler to melt cheese, and serve at once.

### ■ Washington-Wisconsin Burger

> 2 slices (¼ inch thick) good Washington apples that have been cored
> 1 slice (1 ounce) Wisconsin Cheddar cheese

Place apple slices on grilled burger and top with cheese. Melt under broiler. Serve at once.

### ■ DaVinci Burger

> ¼ cup marinara sauce (page 224)
> 1 slice mozzarella cheese

Top grilled burger with marinara sauce, cover with cheese, and melt cheese under broiler. Serve at once with a knife and fork (it can be messy).

### ■ Blue Burger

As unlikely as it sounds, the bank refused to lend McDunnah's Limited the money to purchase Ishi's Restaurant and start the Fiddlehead unless hamburgers were on the menu—specifically, Ishi's blue cheese burger. We have learned this is a combination you can bank on.

> ¼ cup crumbled blue cheese
> 1 to 2 tablespoons mayonnaise

Mix cheese and mayonnaise together and spread on top of burger. Melt under broiler.

"If you aren't satisfied with a good hamburger, you just aren't hungry enough."
—*The Chef*

## MENU

### Brunch for the New Mother

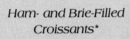

Tossed Green Salad
with
Fiddlehead
Vinaigrette*

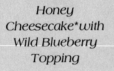

Ham- and Brie-Filled
Croissants*

■

Fresh Fruit Salad
with Yogurt Dressing

■

Sparkling Apple Cider
Champagne

■

Honey
Cheesecake*with
Wild Blueberry
Topping

**\*Recipe included
in this book**

# HAM- AND BRIE-FILLED CROISSANTS

Make this extravagant ham sandwich to spoil yourself or someone who needs a special treat.

**Preparation and Cooking Time:**  15 minutes

■ **Honey Mustard**

> 4 tablespoons honey
> 4 tablespoons Dijon mustard

■ **Sandwiches**

> 4 croissants
> 12 ounces thinly sliced good-quality smoked ham
> 1 apple, halved, cored, and sliced ⅛ inch thick
> 8 ounces Brie, cut into 4 equal portions

1. **To prepare honey mustard:** Whisk together honey and mustard in a small bowl and set aside.

2. **To prepare sandwiches:** Preheat broiler.

3. Using a serrated knife, cut croissants in half horizontally. Spread both halves generously with honey mustard. Set the bottoms of the croissants on a cookie sheet or broiler pan; set tops aside.

4. Neatly arrange ham on croissant bottoms. Top ham with apple slices, then with Brie. Broil sandwiches until Brie melts.

5. Place tops on each sandwich, transfer to a serving platter, and serve at once.

**Yield: 4 sandwiches**

# THE FACTORY WORKER

Deborah Marshall started her career as a restaurateur at the Bread Factory in Anchorage, where this was one of her favorite sandwiches. The Fiddlehead now offers it to workers of all kinds.

**Preparation and Cooking Time:** 30 minutes, including preparing the guacamole

    12 slices sunflower-millet bread (page 152)
    3 cups guacamole (page 222)
    12 tomato slices (2 large tomatoes)
    6 slices (6 ounces) Cheddar cheese
    6 slices (6 ounces) Jack cheese
    6 tablespoons roasted sunflower seeds
    6 tablespoons alfalfa sprouts

1. Preheat broiler.

2. Spread each slice of bread with ¼ cup guacamole and place on a cookie sheet.

3. Lay 1 slice of cheddar on 6 slices of bread, 1 slice of Jack on remaining slices, and place under broiler.

4. When cheese has melted, remove from heat, top each piece of bread with a slice of tomato, and put seeds on the 6 slices with Cheddar cheese, sprouts on the 6 with Jack.

5. Transfer to a serving platter and serve open-face, giving each person a slice with Cheddar and one with Jack cheese.

**Yield: 6 sandwiches**

**"A good workman never blames his tools."**
   *—Harold Hopper*

# BEAN BURGERS

These days everything is available in sandwich form, even beans and rice. Susan Kirkness and Susan Haymes, two gifted Fiddlehead cooks, developed this sandwich, which goes well with all the same toppings you would use on a hamburger.

**Soaking Time:**  overnight

**Preparation Time:**  30 minutes

**Cooking Time:**  2 to 2½ hours

### ▨ Bean Burger Mix

1 cup dried red beans
1 cup dried navy beans
1 cup dried lentils
6 to 7 cups water
⅓ cup brown rice
1 tablespoon oil
1 cup small-diced onion (1 small onion)
2 tablespoons minced fresh garlic (6 to 7 cloves)
1½ teaspoons dried basil
1½ teaspoons salt
¾ teaspoon freshly ground black pepper
½ cup all-purpose flour
2 tablespoons tamari or soy sauce

### ▨ Bean Burger

½ cup bean burger mix
1 teaspoon untoasted sesame seeds.
1 tablespoon oil
1 onion bun, split horizontally (page 144)
Mayonnaise or butter
Lettuce
1 tomato slice
1 red onion slice

1. **To prepare bean burger mix:** Soak beans and lentils overnight in a large bowl with enough water to cover them completely.

2. The next day, drain beans, place in a large pot over high heat, and add 6 to 7 cups water. Bring to a boil, cook for 10 minutes, then cover and reduce heat to low. Simmer about 1 hour and 15 minutes.

3. Add rice to beans, cover, and continue to simmer until beans and rice are soft and tender, 45 minutes to 1 hour. Drain off any excess liquid and set beans aside.

4. Heat oil in a large pan over medium-high heat. When oil is hot, add onion and cook until it begins to soften. Stir in garlic, basil, salt, and pepper. Cook, stirring, for 1 to 2 minutes, until garlic is aromatic and softened, but not beginning to brown.

5. In a large bowl, combine cooked beans, onion mixture, all-purpose flour, and tamari. Using an electric mixer fitted with a paddle, mix together until somewhat puréed, about the consistency of lumpy mashed potatoes. Cover bowl and let mix sit for 10 minutes to cook flour. Refrigerate until cool enough to handle.

**Yield: Enough mix to make 12 bean patties**

6. **To cook basic bean burger:** Preheat broiler.

7. Form ½ cup bean burger mix into a 3-inch patty. Sprinkle it lightly with sesame seeds on both sides. Heat 1 tablespoon oil in a large pan over medium-high heat. When oil is hot, cook patty until golden brown on both sides.

8. Lightly toast onion bun under broiler and spread with mayonnaise or butter. Arrange lettuce, tomato, and onion on top half of bun. Set cooked patty on bottom half. (Garnish as you might a hamburger.) Set on a plate and serve at once, accompanied by all the usual condiments.

**Yield: 1 bean burger**

**NOTE:**
Prepare through step 5 and store, tightly covered, in refrigerator for up to 1 week, or shape into patties and freeze, individually wrapped, for future use.

# ROAST BEEF PIZZAIOLA

Created by an expatriate Philadelphian, this is a cross between a Philly cheese steak and a sloppy Joe. It's a good
reason to keep a little extra marinara sauce around at all
times.

**Preparation and Cooking Time:** 1 hour 15 minutes (15
minutes if you have marinara on hand)

> 8 croissants
> 1½ pounds rare roast beef, thinly sliced
> 2 cups marinara sauce, warmed (page 224)
> 1 pound mozzarella cheese, grated or sliced

1. Preheat broiler. Using a serrated knife, carefully slice
   each croissant in half and set bottom halves on a cookie
   sheet and set tops aside. Cover each croissant bottom
   with 3 ounces roast beef, ¼ cup warm marinara sauce,
   and 2 ounces cheese.

2. Place under broiler until cheese has melted and begins
   to bubble. Place top of each croissant over bottom,
   transfer to a serving platter, and serve at once.

**Yield: 8 sandwiches**

# KT GRILL

Katie Malone, our lunch cook for many years, added a little
extra spark to her grilled cheese sandwiches. This recipe
bears her name and remains one of the best-loved choices
of our customers.

**Preparation and Cooking Time:** 25 minutes

■ **Vegetable Mix**

> 1 teaspoon corn or safflower oil
> ½ cup large-diced onion (about 1 small onion)
> ½ cup large-diced green pepper (½ green pepper)

■ **Sandwiches**

> 8 slices herb bread (page 140)
> 6 slices (about 4 ounces) Cheddar cheese
> 6 slices (about 4 ounces) Jack cheese
> Softened butter

1. **To prepare vegetable mix:** Heat oil in a small pan over medium-high heat. When oil is hot, add onion and peppers. Stir and cook quickly, until vegetables begin to soften. Remove from heat.

2. **For each sandwich:** Cover 1 slice of bread with 1½ slices Cheddar cheese. Top cheese with ¼ cup vegetables and 1½ slices Jack cheese. Cover with 1 slice of bread.

3. Lightly butter outsides of sandwiches and place in a large pan over medium-low heat. Cover pan and cook for 3 for 4 minutes, until bread is golden brown and bottom layer of cheese begins to melt. Turn sandwiches over, cover pan, and cook briefly, until cheese has all melted and bread is golden brown. Transfer to a serving plate, cut in half, and serve at once.

**Yield: 4 sandwiches**

M E N U

*The All-American Lunch*

■

*Tomato-Millet Soup\**

■

*KT Grill Sandwiches\**

■

*Ice-Cold Milk*

■

*Old-Fashioned Chocolate Chip Cookies\**

**\*Recipe is included in this book.**

# GULIANO SANDWICH

This is not just a collection of everything trendy between two slices of bread (note there is no cilantro), but is, in fact, a great combination.

**Marinating Time:** 30 minutes

**Preparation and Cooking Time:** 45 minutes

1 pound eggplant (1 small)
Salt
½ cup all-purpose flour, seasoned with ½ teaspoon each salt and pepper
1 egg, lightly beaten with 1 tablespoon water
1 to 1½ cups dry bread crumbs, seasoned with ¼ teaspoon each dried basil and oregano
2 to 3 tablespoons olive oil
8 slices sourdough French bread (page 150)
¼ cup basil pesto (available in produce department of many grocery stores)
½ cup roasted red pepper (page 214), or substitute roasted red peppers found in jars in the condiment section of the grocery store
8 ounces mozzarella, grated

1. Cut eggplant into ⅛-inch slices (do not peel it) and lay slices in a single layer on absorbent towels on a cookie sheet. Generously sprinkle slices with salt and let them sit at room temperature for 30 minutes.

2. Rinse eggplant and pat dry. Dip each slice first in flour, then egg, then crumbs, and set aside.

3. Heat 2 tablespoons oil in a large pan over medium-high heat. When oil is hot, add breaded eggplant and brown lightly on both sides. Remove from pan and place on absorbent towels. Add additional oil to pan as needed and cook remaining eggplant.

4. Preheat broiler.

5. Spread each slice of bread with pesto and place on a cookie sheet or broiler pan. Top 4 slices of bread with breaded eggplant, 2 tablespoons roasted red peppers, and cheese. Toast under broiler until cheese is melted.

6. Put sandwich halves together, cut in half on the diagonal, transfer to a serving platter, and serve at once.

**Yield: 4 sandwiches**

# SAN FRANCISCO SANDWICH

We haven't the foggiest idea where this name came from, although the sourdough bread should provide a clue.

**Marinating Time:** 1 hour to overnight

**Preparation and Cooking Time:** 30 minutes

### Vegetable Mixture

1⅓ cups Fiddlehead vinaigrette (page 218)
1 cup zucchini, cut into quarters lengthwise, then
    sliced ⅛ inch thick (1 6-ounce zucchini)
1 cup large-diced onion (1 small onion)
1 cup large-diced green pepper (1 small pepper)
1 cup carrot cut into quarters lengthwise, then sliced
    ⅛ inch thick (1 medium)

### Sandwiches

8 slices sourdough French bread (page 150)
8 ounces mozzarella cheese, grated
2 tablespoons freshly grated Parmesan cheese

1. **To prepare vegetables:** Heat 2 tablespoons vinaigrette in a large pan over medium-high heat. When vinaigrette begins to sizzle, add vegetables. Stir and cook for 1 to 2 minutes. Remove from heat, transfer to a nonreactive (nonaluminum) bowl, and add remaining vinaigrette. Cover, refrigerate, and allow to marinate for at least 1 hour, or up to overnight.

2. **To prepare sandwiches:** Preheat broiler. Lay bread on a cookie sheet.

3. Using a slotted spoon, remove vegetables from vinaigrette and divide among 4 slices of bread. (Reserve marinade to use on salads.) Sprinkle vegetables evenly with grated mozzarella cheese.

4. Sprinkle remaining 4 slices of bread with Parmesan cheese.

5. Place cookie sheet under broiler to melt cheeses, then top each vegetable slice with a Parmesan slice. Cut sandwiches in half, transfer to a serving platter, and serve immediately.

**Yield: 4 sandwiches**

**NOTE:**
If you prefer, these can be prepared like grilled cheese sandwiches rather than broiled.

# SALMON-MUSHROOM QUICHE

Quiche gently transforms just a little bit of this and a little bit of that into something special. Welcome at brunch, lovely for lunch, and perfect at supper, quiche simply sat-isfies. (Even here in the Fur-North, where men are men, they like their quiche.)

**Preparation Time:** 45 minutes (less if pie crust is already made)

**Cooking Time:** 40 minutes

1 10-inch unbaked pie crust* (page 212)

■ **Filling**

1 tablespoon butter
1 cup thinly sliced mushrooms (about ¼ pound)
½ cup thinly sliced onion (about ½ medium onion)
1 tablespoon all-purpose flour
2 cups cooked salmon, flaked (remove all bones)
½ cup cream cheese
2 tablespoons finely chopped chives or finely sliced
   green onions

■ **Custard**

2 cups half-and-half
4 large eggs
½ teaspoon salt
Pinch of cayenne
½ cup freshly grated Parmesan cheese

1. Preheat oven to 325°F and set a rack in center.

2. **To prepare filling:** Heat 1 tablespoon butter in a small pan over medium-high heat. When foam subsides, add mushrooms and onion slices. Stir and cook until wilted. Stir in flour and combine well. Remove from heat.

3. Distribute salmon evenly in unbaked pie shell. Dot with lumps of cream cheese and add cooked mushrooms and onions. Sprinkle with chives.

4. **To prepare custard:** In a large bowl (with a spout if you have one), whisk together half-and-half and eggs. Add salt and cayenne and pour over filling. Sprinkle pie with Parmesan cheese.

**5.** Bake for 40 minutes, until quiche is golden brown on top and slightly puffed in center. Remove from oven, cool for 15 minutes, then slice and serve warm.

If you have only a 9-inch pie pan, make custard with 3 eggs and 1½ cups half-and-half.

**Yield: 1 10-inch quiche, or 6 large servings**

**Variations**

### ■ Shrimp and Parmesan Quiche

Substitute 1 cup Petersburg shrimp and 1 cup Parmesan cheese for salmon-mushroom filling.

### ■ Mushroom and Onion Quiche

Brown ½ pound (2 cups) sliced mushrooms and 1 large onion, sliced, in 3 tablespoons butter. Add 4 tablespoons dry sherry, then stir in 3 tablespoons flour. Distribute mixture evenly on pie shell. Top with 1 cup grated Jack cheese, fill with custard, and sprinkle whole pie with ¼ cup Parmesan.

### ■ Broccoli-Cheddar Quiche

Steam 2 cups broccoli florets (1-pound head) until almost tender. Drain well and place in pie shell. Sprinkle with 1 to 1½ cups grated Cheddar cheese, add custard, and sprinkle filled pie with ½ cup sliced almonds.

**NOTE:**
Quiche can be kept refrigerated overnight, or frozen, but is best the same day.

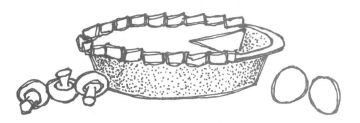

# TONY'S TERRIFIC TOASTED TOFU SANDWICH

Our good friend Tony Tengs described a sandwich he enjoyed on a junket to the "Outside" (Bellingham, Washington, to be exact). It sounded terrific so that's what we call it.

**Preparation and Cooking Time:** 15 minutes

> 1 teaspoon butter
> ¼ cup sliced mushrooms
> 2 slices whole wheat bread
> 4 slices Cheddar cheese (about 1 ounce, enough to cover both slices of bread)
> 2 pieces steamed tofu, 4 to 5 ounces total (available in health food or oriental stores, or in the produce department of the grocery store*)
> 2 thin tomato slices
> 1 tablespoon finely sliced green onions or chives
> 2 tablespoons butter, softened

1. In small pan over medium-high heat, heat 1 teaspoon butter. When foam subsides, add mushrooms and cook until they begin to wilt. Set them aside while you assemble sandwich.

2. Cover 1 slice of bread with 2 slices of cheese. Place tofu on top of that, then tomatoes, mushrooms, and green onions. Place remaining cheese on top and cover with other piece of bread.

3. Lightly butter outsides of sandwich and place in a small pan over medium-low heat. Cover pan and cook for 3 or 4 minutes, until bread is golden brown and bottom layer of cheese is beginning to melt. Turn sandwich over, cover pan, and cook briefly, until cheese has all melted and bread is golden brown. Cut sandwich in half, transfer to a plate, and serve at once.

**Yield: 1 sandwich**

**\*See mail-order sources, page 237.**

Fishing in inside waters
Southeast Alaska

Fishing in Inside Waters—Commercial fishing is Juneau's third largest industry, and the principal industry in many southeast Alaskan communities.

# ENTRÉES

## Chicken Liver Pâté

■ ■ ■

**1.** *While they are still hot, put livers and sauce into a food processor or blender.*

**2.** *Add ¼ cup butter, ¼ cup apple juice, 2 teaspoons minced fresh garlic, and salt to taste. Purée on high until smooth. Pour into a small crock, cover loosely, and refrigerate.*

**3.** *When cold, serve with crackers, apple slices, or toast. Store refrigerated, tightly wrapped, for up to a week.*

**Yield: 2½ cups pâté**

NOTE:
This recipe can be doubled nicely, but you may need to make it in two pots unless you have a very large one (1½-gallon size).

*See mail-order sources, page 237.

# CHICKEN DAVID

This was an improvisation made for a member of the staff who wanted his chicken, pasta, and vegetables all in one bowl. The combination was so good we put it on the menu and named the dish for him.

**Preparation and Cooking Time:** 1 hour (reduce time by using already boned and skinned chicken)

    12 ounces fettuccine noodles
    4 tablespoons butter
    1½ pounds boneless or 3 pounds whole chicken
        breasts, skinned, boned, and cut into ½- by 1½-inch
        strips (3 cups)
    ½ cup all-purpose flour, seasoned with 1 teaspoon
        each salt and pepper
    2 medium zucchini, cut lengthwise into 4 thin layers,
        then diagonally into ¼-inch slices
    ¾ teaspoon dried tarragon
    1 cup dry white wine (chardonnay or sauvignon
        blanc)
    1 cup heavy cream
    1¼ teaspoon salt
    ½ teaspoon ground black pepper
    ½ teaspoon oriental sesame oil (available in the
        oriental section of the supermarket*)
    ¼ cup freshly grated Parmesan cheese (about 1
        ounce)

**1.** Bring a large pot of water to a boil over high heat. Add fettuccine and boil until it is *al dente* (see page 122). Drain pasta in a colander, rinse, and set aside.

**2.** Heat butter in a large deep pot over medium-high heat. When foam subsides, lightly dredge chicken strips in seasoned flour and add to pot. Stir to coat evenly with butter. Cook briefly until chicken is lightly cooked on all sides, but not cooked through.

**3.** Add zucchini, stir, and add tarragon and white wine. Bring to a boil and reduce heat to low. Add pasta and heavy cream.

**4.** Using spaghetti tongs or a large fork, mix and cook until sauce thickens. Add salt and pepper and mix in sesame oil.

**5.** Transfer to a large serving bowl, sprinkle with Parmesan cheese, and serve at once.

**Yield: 4 servings**

# CHICKEN LIVERS
# QUEEN ANNE

Fiddlehead founder Scott Miller created this as a romantic gift when he lived on Queen Anne Hill and worked at Le Tastevin in Seattle. Even those who don't like liver have been won over.

**Preparation and Cooking Time:** 45 minutes

1 pound fresh chicken livers
¼ cup flour, seasoned with ½ teaspoon each salt and pepper
2 tablespoons butter
1 teaspoon minced fresh garlic (about 1 large clove)
½ cup large-diced onion (½ large onion)
½ cup large-diced green pepper (½ pepper)
⅓ cup medium-dry sherry
¼ cup chicken stock
Salt and pepper as needed

■ Accompaniment

Hot cooked rice, toast points, or croissants

1. Dredge livers in seasoned flour.

2. Heat butter in a large pan over medium-high heat. When foam subsides, add livers and brown lightly on all sides.

3. Stir in garlic, onion, and peppers. Reduce heat to medium and cook until vegetables begin to soften.

4. Add sherry and stock. Raise heat slightly until sauce begins to boil, then reduce heat to a simmer and cook until sauce has reduced by one third and has thickened. Taste sauce and add salt and pepper as needed.

5. Arrange hot rice, toast, or split croissants on a serving platter. Spoon livers over top and serve at once.

**Yield: 4 servings**

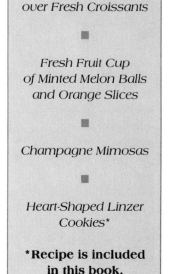

**M E N U**

*Valentine's Day Brunch for Two*

■

*Chicken Livers Queen Anne\* over Fresh Croissants*

■

*Fresh Fruit Cup of Minted Melon Balls and Orange Slices*

■

*Champagne Mimosas*

■

*Heart-Shaped Linzer Cookies\**

**\*Recipe is included in this book.**

NOTE:
This makes a delicious pâté as well. See opposite page.

# CHICKEN MARSALA

Scott Miller, founding father of the Fiddlehead menu, created this variation of the classic Italian dish, veal marsala, and it was the Wednesday night special for years. It is very quick and simple to make, yet so delectably different that it's right for a special occasion.

**Preparation and Cooking Time:**   45 minutes

> 8 boneless, skinless chicken breast halves, 6 to 7 ounces each
> 6 to 8 tablespoons butter
> ½ cup all-purpose flour, seasoned with 1 teaspoon salt and ½ teaspoon pepper
> 6 cups thinly sliced mushrooms (about 1½ pounds)
> ½ teaspoon freshly grated orange peel (substitute 1 teaspoon dried, but flavor will be slightly different)
> 1 cup dry marsala

■ **Garnish**

> Fresh chives (include chive blossoms if you can) or chopped fresh parsley

■ **Accompaniment**

> Hot rice

1. Place each half breast between two pieces of waxed paper and flatten slightly, using a mallet, the bottom of a small pan, or the palm of your hand. Set aside.

2. Melt 3 tablespoons of the butter in a large, lidded, heavy-bottomed pan over medium-high heat.

3. When foam subsides, lightly dredge 4 half breasts in flour and fry them quickly on both sides just until golden brown. Remove from pan and keep warm while you cook remaining pieces of floured chicken (add a little additional butter if necessary). Remove from pan.

4. To same pan, add 3 tablespoons butter. When it has melted, add mushrooms. Stir to coat evenly with butter and cook 2 minutes.

**NOTE:**
Preheat oven to 325°F if you would like to cook the dish in the oven rather than on top of the stove. Do whichever is more convenient.

5. Return chicken to pan. Add orange peel and marsala. Bring to a boil, then immediately lower heat to a simmer. Cover and cook gently on top of stove or in oven until chicken is cooked through. (This takes from 10 to 15 minutes, depending on size of breasts and how far you cooked them initially.)

**6.** Uncover pan, remove chicken, and keep warm. Raise heat and reduce liquid until it thickens to consistency of syrup. (A spoon will leave a trail when drawn across bottom of pan.) Taste sauce and correct seasoning. Return chicken to sauce and coat each breast. Arrange on a serving platter, tucking a few fresh chives along edge or sprinkling with chopped parsley for color. Serve at once, with hot rice.

**Yield: 8 servings**

# CHICKEN TERIYAKI

If all the plates of chicken teriyaki prepared and eaten at the Fiddlehead were laid end to end, they would probably reach from Juneau to Tokyo and back. Somehow we never tire of it. The lightly marinated stir-fried chicken and fresh vegetables over brown rice are satisfyingly *good*!

**Marinating Time:** 2 hours to overnight

**Preparation Time:** 30 minutes

**Cooking Time:** 15 minutes

> 2½ pounds boneless, skinless chicken breast, cut into 1-inch cubes
> 2 cups teriyaki marinade (page 210)

### ▪ Vegetable Mix

> 1 cup carrots, thinly sliced on the diagonal (3 medium)
> 1 cup thinly sliced onion, cut stem to tip (1 medium onion)
> 1 cup zucchini, cut in half lengthwise, then on the diagonal into ¼-inch slices (1 medium)
> 1 cup medium-sliced green pepper (1 medium pepper)
> 1 cup medium broccoli florets, with stems peeled, and cut on the diagonal about ¼ inch thick (½ small head)
> 1 cup medium cauliflower florets (¼ medium head)
> 6 mushrooms, quartered
> 4 tablespoons cooking oil

### ▪ Garnish

> ¼ cup thinly sliced green onions, tops and bottoms
> ¼ cup crushed cocktail peanuts

### ▪ Accompaniment

> Hot brown rice (page 209)

**NOTE:**
Use eggplant, celery, snow peas, parsnips, bok choy, or any other vegetables you like: For 6 servings you need 6 to 7 cups vegetables altogether.

1. Add chicken to marinade and refrigerate for at least 2 hours, or overnight.

2. **To prepare vegetable mix:** Combine all cut vegetables in a large container. Use immediately, or wrap tightly and refrigerate overnight.

3. **To cook teriyaki:** Heat 2 tablespoons oil in a large wok or very large pan over high heat. When oil is quite hot, add vegetables, stirring to coat evenly with oil. Cover pan and cook for 3 minutes. Stir and continue to cook

uncovered for 3 minutes. Vegetables should still be crisp, but beginning to soften. Using a slotted spoon, remove from wok and keep warm.

4. If necessary, add additional oil to wok. When oil is very hot, using a slotted spoon, remove one third chicken from marinade and add to wok. Stir and cook just until no longer pink inside, about 5 minutes. Remove chicken from wok with a slotted spoon and add to cooked vegetables to keep warm. Repeat with remaining chicken.

5. Return cooked chicken and vegetables to wok and stir to combine flavors. Cover and cook 1 to 2 minutes to allow juices to thicken.

6. Line bottom of a serving dish with hot rice and pour chicken and vegetables over top. Sprinkle with green onions and chopped peanuts and serve at once.

**Yield: 6 servings**

### ■ Variations

*For a barbecue:* Cut onions and peppers into thin squares rather than strips. Skewer bits of marinated chicken between onions, peppers, and mushrooms, and grill, brushing with marinade as they cook. (If you use bamboo skewers, soak them in water for several hours before skewering chicken and vegetables. This prevents them from burning as easily on the grill.)

*For hors d'oeuvres:* Skewer a bit of chicken and a mushroom on a wooden toothpick, brush with marinade, and broil in oven for 3 minutes, turning and cooking until chicken is cooked through. (Or nestle the bit of chicken directly in mushroom, brush with marinade, and broil for 5 to 6 minutes, until cooked through.)

*As a salad:* Combine leftover chicken teriyaki with oriental vinaigrette (page 217). Serve over shredded lettuce garnished with fresh bean sprouts and chopped salted peanuts.

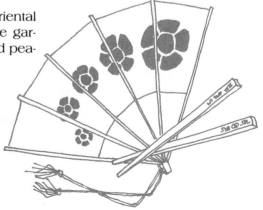

# SWISS CHICKEN

Memories of a summer spent as an *au pair* girl in Switzerland prompted Kathy Yurman to suggest that we prepare Gerschnitzeltes (which simply means little bits of meat) as a dinner special. It has remained on the menu ever since. Its simple goodness depends on the quality of the ingredients: Use the best chicken, butter, wine, and cream.

**Preparation and Cooking Time:**   1 hour

> 2½ pounds boned chicken breasts, cut into 1-inch strips
> ½ cup all-purpose flour, seasoned with 1 teaspoon each salt and pepper
> 6 tablespoons butter
> 4 to 5 cups sliced mushrooms (about 1 pound)
> 1 cup plus 2 tablespoons good dry white wine (chardonnay, sauvignon blanc, or whichever wine you prefer to drink)
> 1½ cups heavy cream
> Hot cooked rice or noodles
> ½ cup thinly sliced green onions, tops and bottoms

1. Dredge chicken in flour to coat each piece lightly.

2. Heat 3 tablespoons butter in a large, heavy-bottomed pan over medium-high heat. When butter is hot and foam begins to subside, add half the chicken to pan. Cook quickly, stirring, until lightly browned on all sides, but not cooked through. Using a slotted spoon, remove from pan and keep warm. Add 3 tablespoons butter to pan and when it is hot, cook second batch of chicken.

3. Return all chicken to pan and stir in mushrooms. Cook 1 to 2 minutes, until you can faintly smell aroma of mushrooms.

4. Add white wine and bring to a boil. Immediately add heavy cream. Bring back to a boil, then reduce heat to low. Cook gently until chicken is cooked through.

5. Line a large casserole with hot rice or noodles. When chicken is cooked through, use a slotted spoon to transfer it to casserole. Keep warm while finishing sauce.

6. Increase heat under sauce to high, stir in green onions, and cook briskly until sauce is reduced slightly and begins to thicken (about 5 minutes). Taste and correct seasoning.

7. Pour sauce over chicken and serve at once.

**Yield: 6 servings**

# FETTUCCINE GRETA GARBO

With a haunting, elusive smokiness, this simple, elegant pasta dish seems well named. (The recipe is easily halved if you want to be alone.)

**Preparation and Cooking Time:** 30 minutes

> "Just know your lines and don't bump into the furniture."
> —*Spencer Tracy*

    16 ounces fettuccine noodles
    6 tablespoons butter
    4 teaspoons minced fresh garlic (about 4 large cloves)
    9 ounces Alaskan-style smoked salmon, bones and skin removed, broken into pieces*
    1½ cups heavy cream
    1 cup (4 ounces) freshly grated Parmesan cheese
    1½ cups chopped green onions (2 ounces, 1 large bunch)

1. Bring a large pot of water to boil over high heat. When water is boiling, drop in pasta and boil until *al dente* (see page 122). Drain and set aside.

2. In a large pot over medium-high heat, heat butter and garlic. Stir and cook until butter has melted and garlic is aromatic.

3. Add cooked pasta and smoked salmon. Using a fork or pasta tongs, stir until pasta and salmon are hot and well mixed.

4. Add heavy cream. Cook, stirring frequently, until cream begins to thicken.

5. Stir in Parmesan cheese and green onions.

6. Transfer to a serving dish and serve at once, with additional cheese if you like.

**Yield: 6 servings as a main course; 12 as an appetizer**

**\*See mail-order sources, page 237.**

I vant to be alone

# LAMB CURRY

Scott Miller, a naturally gifted cook who guided the Fiddle-head kitchen for many years, devised this wonderful curry inspired by one he found in *The New York Times Cook Book*. In the tradition of many curries, it is essentially a casserole. Hot, but not too hot, this dish usually elicits the response "I never liked lamb until I tried this!"

**Preparation Time:** 30 minutes

**Cooking Time:** 1½ hours

> 3 tablespoons oil
> 2½ pounds lamb stew meat, trimmed of excess fat and cut into 1-inch cubes
> 1 cup large-diced onion (about 1 medium onion)
> 1 teaspoon minced garlic (1 large clove)
> ½ teaspoon crushed dried mint (or mint tea leaves)
> 1 teaspoon minced fresh ginger (or crystallized ginger)
> 1 tablespoon freshly squeezed lime juice
> ¼ teaspoon cayenne
> ⅔ cup milk or coconut milk (see note, page 129)
> 1 tablespoon curry powder
> 1½ teaspoons garam masala (page 208), or combine a bit of powdered cardamom, cumin, freshly ground pepper, ground clove, nutmeg, and cinnamon and toast lightly in a pan on low heat before adding to curry
> ½ cup freshly grated coconut, or ⅓ cup dried unsweetened coconut (available at health food stores as "desiccated coconut"*)
> ¾ cup heavy cream
> ¼ cup raisins

■ **Accompaniment**

> 6 to 7 cups hot rice

■ **Garnish**

> ½ cup plain yogurt
> ½ cup tomato chutney (page 228) or use a good-quality brand*

1. Preheat oven to 350°F if you would like to cook curry in oven. Heat oil in a large, heavy-bottomed pan over high heat. When oil is very hot, add lamb and stir to brown it on all sides. Add onion, stir, and cook until onion is transparent (about 5 minutes).

2. Stir in garlic, mint, ginger, lime juice, and cayenne. Cook 5 minutes.

3. Stir in milk, curry powder, and garam masala. Cover and reduce heat to low. Simmer (or bake) for 1 hour.

4. Uncover pot and add coconut, cream, and raisins. Simmer on top of stove for 10 to 15 minutes.

5. Line a serving dish with hot rice, spoon curry into center, top with dollops of yogurt and chutney, and serve at once.

**NOTE:**
**Curry can be made ahead through step 3 and frozen.**

**Yield: 5 to 6 servings**

**\*See mail-order sources, page 237.**

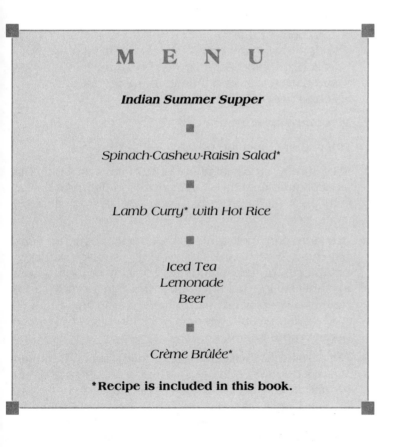

# M E N U

*Indian Summer Supper*

■

*Spinach-Cashew-Raisin Salad\**

■

*Lamb Curry\* with Hot Rice*

■

*Iced Tea*
*Lemonade*
*Beer*

■

*Crème Brûlée\**

**\*Recipe is included in this book.**

## Raspberry Vinegar

■ ■ ■

*The mild fruitiness that raspberry vinegar brings to a dish is worth the effort to find it. If you have a raspberry patch close by, make your own to give as gifts, or just to stock your own larder:*

**1.** *Sterilize bottles or jars for vinegar.*
**2.** *Combine 3 parts wine vinegar (red or white) with 1 part whole raspberries in a glass, enamel, or stainless steel bowl or pan. (If you tend to like sweeter things, add 1 to 2 tablespoons sugar for every cup vinegar.) Heat gently until almost boiling. Remove from heat. When cooled, pour through a funnel into bottles, seal, and store in a cool place until needed. (Strain raspberries out before using.)*

*Sprinkle raspberry vinegar into salads or over fresh fruit, or use it to baste roast chicken. We call for it in salmon Véronique (page 108) and smoked turkey and pasta salad (page 32). Try it as a change from everyday vinegar.*

# TURKEY SCALOPPINE WITH CRANBERRIES

Here is a deliciously quick and scrumptious alternative to the traditional holiday roast turkey. This dish is elegant enough for the most special occasion and yet the whole meal can be ready in 1 hour or less.

**Preparation and Cooking Time:** 45 minutes

> 2 to 2¼ pounds boneless, skinless fresh turkey breast
> ⅓ cup all-purpose flour, seasoned with 1 teaspoon each salt and pepper
> 3 tablespoons butter
> 6 tablespoons dry white wine (chardonnay or sauvignon blanc)
> 3 tablespoons raspberry vinegar*
> ¾ cup heavy cream
> 1½ cups fresh cranberries or red currants (substitute frozen, defrosted cranberries or currants; in summer, use salmonberries or raspberries)
> Salt and pepper as needed

■ **Accompaniment**

Hot rice or fettuccine noodles

**1.** Slice turkey breast almost horizontally into small thin steaks, or scaloppine, 2 to 3 inches in diameter and ½ inch thick. Lightly dredge each one in flour and set aside.

**2.** In a large pan, melt 2 tablespoons butter over medium-high heat. When foam is beginning to subside, add several pieces of turkey and cook quickly on both sides, just until sealed, but not cooked through. Remove from heat and keep warm while cooking remaining turkey. Add additional butter as needed, letting it get hot before adding more turkey.

**3.** Return all turkey to pan and add white wine and vinegar. When it bubbles, add cream. Bring almost to a boil and reduce heat. Add cranberries and simmer gently, uncovered, until turkey is cooked through, 3 to 5 minutes, depending upon thickness of turkey and how far you cooked it to begin with. Remove scaloppine and arrange on a serving platter.

**4.** Increase heat, stir, and let cranberries and cream bubble until sauce thickens slightly and is a light pink color.

Taste it and adjust seasoning with salt and pepper. Pour sauce over turkey and serve immediately with rice or buttered noodles.

**Yield: 6 servings**

**\*See mail-order sources, page 237.**

# BOONVILLE CHOPS

This is a quick and easy preparation for pork chops, based on a dish formerly served at the New Boonville Hotel in California.

**Marinating Time:**   1 to 4 hours

**Preparation and Cooking Time:**   20 minutes

■ **Marinade**

¼ cup tamari or soy sauce
1 tablespoon minced fresh ginger
¼ cup finely chopped fresh cilantro (there is no real substitute; use other fresh herbs such as basil or tarragon for a different and delicious flavor if you cannot locate fresh cilantro\*)
6 pork chops, about 1 inch thick

1. Combine marinade ingredients in a large flat-bottomed nonreactive (nonaluminum) container. Coat chops with marinade on both sides and let them marinate for 1 to 4 hours, covered and refrigerated.

2. Preheat broiler or barbecue. Broil or grill chops on high heat 7 to 10 minutes on each side, depending on thickness of meat. When meat is no longer pink (peek inside with tip of a knife), transfer chops to a serving platter and serve at once.

**Yield: 6 servings**

**\*See mail-order sources, page 237.**

NOTE:
The marinade is equally delicious with boneless pork loin or chicken.

# PORK SZECHUAN

This is hot stuff and not for the faint of heart, but if you are one of those who feel food is not properly seasoned unless it's painful to eat, then this is for you. Serve a side dish of lightly salted cucumbers (nature's fire extinguishers) with this and watch out! Things are going to get hot.

**Preparation Time:**  30 minutes

**Marinating Time:**  1 hour

**Cooking Time:**  15 minutes

## ▪ Szechuan Sauce

6-ounce can hot bean paste*
2 tablespoons oriental sesame oil*
2 tablespoons chopped fresh cilantro (no real flavor substitute)
1 tablespoon minced fresh garlic (about 3 large cloves)
1 tablespoon minced fresh ginger
1 tablespoon Chinese five-spice powder*
1 tablespoon Chinese hot oil*

## ▪ Pork

2 pounds boneless pork loin, cut into 2- by 1- by ¼-inch strips
¼ cup reserved Szechuan sauce
¼ cup Chinese rice wine or mirin*
¼ cup chicken stock
2 teaspoons cornstarch
1 teaspoon soy sauce
4 tablespoons corn or safflower oil
2 cups onions, thinly sliced stem to tip (2 medium)
4 cups carrots, cut in half lengthwise, then cut on the bias ⅛ inch thick (2 medium)
½ pound snow peas, stem and strings removed, cut in half diagonally
2 tomatoes, cut into wedges

## ▪ Accompaniment

Hot rice or oriental noodles

1. **To prepare Szechuan sauce:** Combine all sauce ingredients in a small nonreactive (nonaluminum) bowl. (Sauce can be stored tightly wrapped in the refrigerator for up to 1 month.)

2. **To prepare pork:** Place pork in a small nonreactive (nonaluminum) bowl and stir in ¼ cup Szechuan sauce. Cover and marinate, refrigerated, for 1 hour.

3. Combine rice wine, stock, cornstarch, and soy sauce in a small bowl. Cover and refrigerate until ready to use.

4. Heat 2 tablespoons oil in a large wok or pot over high heat. When oil is almost smoking hot, add onions and carrots. Stir and cook for 1 minute. Add snow peas, stir, and cook for 1 minute. Add tomatoes and stir. Cook for 1 minute, transfer to a bowl, and set aside.

5. Add 2 tablespoons oil to wok. When oil is quite hot, add pork. Stir and cook just until seared on all sides, about 3 minutes. Return vegetables to wok and stir. When vegetables are hot, move mixture to sides of wok to make a well and pour in rice wine mixture. Stir gently until it comes to a boil, thickens, and becomes clear. Stir vegetables and meat into sauce to combine flavors; remove from heat. Transfer to a serving dish and serve at once, accompanied by hot rice or Chinese noodles. (Or serve pork on top of rice or noodles, all in one dish.)

**Yield: 5 to 6 servings**

*Available in oriental grocery stores. For mail-order sources, see page 237.

*Available in oriental grocery stores. For mail-order sources, see page 237.

"People are like teabags: You never know how strong they'll be until they're in hot water."
   —*Rita Mae Brown*

**NOTE:**
Less calloused palates prefer to reduce the amount of hot bean paste and oriental hot oil by half. Know your limits.

# ALASKAN SEAFOOD

It is no surprise that Alaskan kitchens are famed for their seafood. Out of the icy cold waters off Alaska's 34,000-mile coastline come some of the best fish and shellfish in the world. Fishing supports our economy, lures tourists to the state, and keeps most Alaskans out on the water much of the year.

**Alaskan salmon**, prized for flavor, full of healthful nutrients, is the backbone of our fishing culture.

**King salmon** *Oncorhynchus tschawytscha*, also known as Chinook or Tyee, is the largest (up to 120 pounds) and most valuable of the five species of salmon that inhabit our waters. Rich in fat, firm and succulent, it is available fresh from October through April and again in June and July. Usually red-fleshed, the white-fleshed kings are preferred by many locals for their exceptional richness. King salmon is delicious grilled, poached, sautéed, baked, steamed, smoked, or in sushi.

**Sockeye** *O. nerka*, also known as red salmon, is a little leaner than king. It has a deep red-colored flesh and for many years was known best as canned salmon. It is available fresh from June through August. Its rich color and flavor make it especially pleasing at the table. Grill, poach, sauté, bake, steam, or smoke fresh sockeye. Canned sockeye is delicious in quiche, mousse, and casseroles, and more than adequately sees many families through the winter.

**Silver salmon** *O. kisutch*, or coho, is firm, orange-red fleshed, and full of fat. It is equally delicious fresh or smoked. Silver salmon head inland between July and October. Prepare silvers as you would kings.

**Pink salmon** *O. gorbusha*, also known as humpbacks or humpies, is the most plebeian of the salmon family. The smallest of the group, its flesh is light pink and delicately flavored. Most is canned, because it appears only briefly during mid to late summer. Cook pinks on the grill, or smoke or can them for winter.

**Chum** *O. keta*, also known as dog or silver bright, is a fall fish, available fresh from July through October. Its flesh is pink with a medium fat content. It is excellent fresh; prepare as you would kings or silvers, or can or smoke.

**Alaskan smoked salmon** is a kippered, hot-smoked fish. Usually brined with salt and sometimes sugar, it is drier than lox and usually darker in color. It is available vacuum-packed as full sides or fillets still on the skins. See the note on methods of smoking salmon on page 38.

Squaw candy is brined hot-smoked strips cut from the belly, which is the fattest part of the salmon.

Salmon harvests are strictly regulated and monitored to preserve the fish stocks. Fresh salmon of some variety is available almost all year, with occasional brief periods when commercial fishing is not permitted.

**King Crab** *Paralithodes camtschaticus* is prized around the world for its sweet succulence and amazing size, weighing up to twenty pounds.

**Dungeness Crab** *Cancer maenas* is sweet-flavored, tender, and flaky. Many locals prefer it to king crab.

**Tanner or Snow Crab** *Chionecetes tanneri, opilio, or bairdi* is the most difficult to catch because it inhabits very deep water. Many people like the tender, snowy white, delicately sweet meat best of the three varieties.

Crab seasons vary, based on the size of the crab populations. Ordinarily, harvests occur from early spring through early fall. In season, live crab is available directly from the fishing fleet and freshly steamed crab is available in stores. Other times of the year, find fresh frozen crab legs or frozen crabmeat at the store.

Absolutely the best way to eat crab is pulled right from the water, steamed, cracked, and dipped in melted butter with lots of fresh sourdough bread to catch the juices. (It may be worth the air fare to get here.) Defrosted frozen crab legs are good the same way. Add fresh or fresh-frozen crabmeat to soups, eggs, casseroles, quiche, salads, and sandwiches, or serve with a dip.

**Halibut** *Hippoglossus stenolepsis*, the largest member of the flounder family, is highly prized for its firm, mildly sweet, lean white meat. Often reaching sizes of 500 pounds or more, the best, most tender meat comes from fish in the 50-pound range. Grill, bake, sauté, braise, or steam fresh or fresh-frozen halibut, but best of all is beer-battered, deep-fried fresh halibut (see page 96).

Hot-smoked halibut fillets are moist and slightly salty. Use them when you might use smoked salmon or smoked haddock.

Fresh Alaskan halibut is available commercially for only a few days each year. The fishery is carefully regulated and monitored to prevent overharvesting of the stock.

**Petersburg shrimp** *Pandalus borealis* is a tiny sweet cocktail shrimp most commonly available cooked, peeled, and flash-frozen. Add to salads, pasta, soups, omelets, casseroles, and stuffings, or just eat out of the bag like popcorn.

**Spot prawns** *Pandalus platyceros* and **Side-stripe shrimp** *Pandalopsus dispar*, medium-size delicately flavored shrimp, are available fresh periodically throughout the year. Fresh-frozen are readily available any time. Grill, sauté, bake, or steam these as you would other prawns.

**Kodiak scallops** *Patinopecten caurinus*, or weathervanes, come from the Gulf of Alaska. The fishery is just developing, and these large, very sweet and succulent scallops are available in limited quantities throughout the year. Kodiak scallops are delicious sautéed, poached, or baked according to any recipe calling for sea or bay scallops.

**Pacific or True cod** *Gadus macrocephalus,* **Lingcod** *Ophiodon elongatus,* numerous **Rockfish** *Sebastes* species, and a variety of **Soles and flounders** appear fresh and fresh-frozen in markets throughout the year. These are all good in any recipe calling for red snapper, halibut, or other white fish. Their unassertive nature takes well to a variety of sauces and preparations.

**Oysters** are being cultivated south of Juneau, near Wrangell. The catch is as yet very limited and the oysters are generally available only by special request. However, they are extremely good (large in size, quite creamy, and delicate in flavor) and worth seeking out.

**Abalone** *Haliotis* is harvested by a small number of intrepid individuals in the Sitka area and is available intermittently during the year.

### ■ Tips on Cooking Seafood

1. Use only the best quality fish you can find and afford.

2. Fresh is best. Modern freezing techniques and improved transportation systems make it possible to enjoy good fish from around the world every day, but nothing compares with one you just pulled from the water.

3. Fresh fish does not smell fishy.

4. If you are buying whole fish, check to make sure that the eyes are clear rather than cloudy. The eyes of a fish become progressively cloudy the longer it is out of the water.

5. Seafood cooks very quickly, and overcooking causes it to be dry and tough. Never boil seafood; cook it gently and quickly.

6. The rule of thumb for cooking fish is 10 minutes for each inch in thickness, measured at the thickest part. Generally, the smaller the piece of fish, the higher the cooking temperature.

7. Remember Scott Miller's advice: "Great ingredients call for restraint more than help and great things can happen when you cook as if your life depended on it."

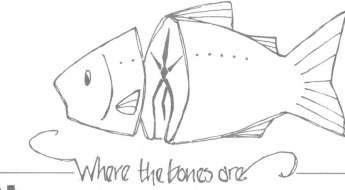

Where the bones are

# FIDDLEHEAD CADDY GANTY

Halibut Caddy Ganty is the ubiquitous Alaskan fish recipe. Everyone loves it, it's easy to prepare, works well with frozen fish, and can be made to feed the entire town. Sally Lesh of the Gustavus Inn first introduced us to the dish and we've loved it ever since. With the substitutions given, this becomes a heart-healthy dish.

**Marinating Time:** 1 to 2 hours

**Preparation and Cooking Time:** 30 minutes

> 3 pounds skinned halibut fillets, cut ¾ inch thick (substitute red snapper, cod, or other firm, white fish)
> 1 bottle dry white wine (such as chablis)

■ **Topping**

> ½ cup mayonnaise (substitute low-cholesterol mayonnaise)
> ½ cup seeded and coarsely chopped tomatoes
> 6 tablespoons coarsely chopped onion
> 2 tablespoons apple cider vinegar
> 2 tablespoons safflower oil
> 4 fresh parsley sprigs, washed and squeezed dry (about 1 tablespoon chopped)
> 1½ cups sour cream (substitute low-fat yogurt)
> 2 to 2½ cups dry sourdough French bread crumbs
> Paprika

1. Place halibut pieces in a deep bowl and add white wine to cover. Cover and refrigerate for 1 to 2 hours.

2. **To prepare topping:** Purée mayonnaise, tomatoes, onion, vinegar, oil, and parsley together in a blender or food processor. Transfer to a small bowl and fold in sour cream. Cover and refrigerate until ready to use.

3. Preheat oven to 500°F. Lightly oil a cookie sheet or two 13- by 9- by 2-inch glass baking dishes.

4. Drain halibut and pat dry with paper towels. Roll each piece in bread crumbs and place in baking pan(s), keeping pieces right next to each other.

5. Spread topping evenly over the fish. Lightly dust with paprika. Bake for 10 to 15 minutes, or until fish flakes easily and topping is golden brown. Transfer to a serving dish and serve at once.

**Yield: 8 servings**

NOTE:
Topping can be made 1 day ahead and kept refrigerated. It also makes a good vegetable dip.

NOTE:
This recipe can easily be doubled, tripled, quadrupled, or halved, depending on the crowd.

# Beer Batter

■ ■ ■

There are lots of reasons to avoid deep-frying: It's a messy operation, somewhat dangerous, no one knows what to do with the used cooking oil, and (because deep-fried food tastes so good) it probably is not good for you.

There is one very good reason to deep-fry at least once a year: beer-battered fresh halibut. It's incredibly good.

Nancy DeCherney's mother uses this recipe, which she got from her friend Jan McPhetres. The baskets full of golden, crispy, succulent, tender pieces of very fresh sweet halibut keep the fishing crew going back out for more.

>   1 cup all-purpose flour
>   2 teaspoons salad oil
>   1½ teaspoons salt
>   1 cup beer
>   2 egg whites
>   2 to 2½ pounds boneless, skinless halibut, cut into 2-inch cubes (substitute red
>       snapper, cod, flounder, or other firm, white fish)

**1.** In a large mixing bowl, whisk together flour, oil, salt, and beer. Cover loosely and let sit for at least 30 minutes.
**2.** In a separate bowl, whip egg whites to a firm but not stiff peak. Fold gently into batter.
**3.** Dip pieces of fish into batter and lower into 375°F* cooking oil. The pieces will float freely in the oil and be golden brown on all sides when ready.
**4.** Use tongs or a spider to remove fish from oil, set on several layers of absorbent towels, sprinkle lightly with salt, and serve at once.

**Yield: 4 big servings**

***Use higher temperatures for smaller pieces, lower for larger.**

Use this batter for deep-frying vegetables also. Proceed as above, using onion rings, whole mushrooms, broccoli or cauliflower florets, and thin slices of zucchini and carrot. Accompany cooked vegetables with a dip of equal parts honey and Dijon mustard.

# HALIBUT NIÇOISE

Inspired by memories of the Mediterranean, this is a good preparation for those who love fish and who also love red wine. The robust flavors of the dish are well matched with a sturdy red wine.

**Preparation and Cooking Time:**   30 minutes

  3 pounds skinless fresh halibut fillets, sliced into small steaks about 4 by 2 by ½ inch (substitute red snapper, flounder, or ling cod)
  ⅔ cup all-purpose flour, seasoned with 1 teaspoon each salt and pepper
  3 tablespoons mild olive oil
  ⅔ cup dry white wine (chardonnay or sauvignon blanc)
  3 teaspoons minced garlic (4 large cloves)
  3 cups peeled, seeded, and large-diced fresh tomatoes (4 or 5 tomatoes)
  3 tablespoons minced fresh basil (or 3 teaspoons dried)
  ¾ cup pitted and sliced black olives
  Salt and pepper

1. Preheat oven to 350°F. Lightly oil a 12- by 8- by 2-inch casserole.

2. Lightly dust pieces of halibut with flour.

3. Heat olive oil in a medium pan over medium-high heat. When oil is hot, add 4 or 5 pieces of fish and sauté 2 to 3 minutes on each side. Transfer to oiled casserole and cook remaining fish. Arrange fish neatly in casserole.

4. Add wine to sauté pan to deglaze it, then stir in garlic, tomatoes, and basil. Bring to a quick boil, stir in olives, and taste to correct seasoning. Pour sauce over fish.

5. Cover casserole and bake 5 to 10 minutes, until fish flakes easily. Remove from oven and serve at once.

**Yield: 6 servings**

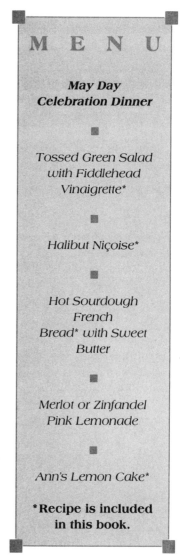

M E N U

*May Day
Celebration Dinner*

▪

*Tossed Green Salad
with Fiddlehead
Vinaigrette\**

▪

*Halibut Niçoise\**

▪

*Hot Sourdough
French
Bread\* with Sweet
Butter*

▪

*Merlot or Zinfandel
Pink Lemonade*

▪

*Ann's Lemon Cake\**

**\*Recipe is included
in this book.**

**NOTE:**
**To peel tomatoes, drop them into boiling water for 10 seconds, slip off skin, cut in half around the middle, and squeeze gently to remove the seeds.**

# HALIBUT SICILIAN

The flavors in this dish are fresh and simple and the sauce is very light. Don't save this recipe just for halibut season: It's good with almost any fish.

**Preparation and Cooking Time:** 45 minutes

3 pounds halibut fillets, skinned and cut into steaks about 1 inch thick (substitute snapper, cod, or other white fish, salmon fillets, or scallops)

½ cup all-purpose flour, seasoned with 1 teaspoon each salt and pepper

2 tablespoons olive oil

½ cup thinly sliced red onion, cut stem to tip (½ onion)

½ cup thin bias-cut celery slices (1 stalk)

2 tablespoons drained capers

1½ teaspoons minced garlic (2 cloves)

1 tablespoon red wine vinegar

½ cup dry white wine (chardonnay or sauvignon blanc)

2 tablespoons butter

1. Lightly dust pieces of fish with flour and set aside.

2. Heat olive oil in a large pan over medium-high heat. When oil is hot, add as many pieces of fish as will fit comfortably and cook on both sides until just lightly browned, but not cooked through. Remove fish and keep warm while you cook remaining pieces.

3. Add onion, celery, capers, and garlic to pan and pour in vinegar and white wine to deglaze pan. Reduce heat to low. Arrange browned pieces of fish on vegetables so they barely overlap in pan. Cover and simmer very gently until fish is cooked through and flakes easily, about 7 minutes.

4. Transfer fish to a serving platter, increase heat to high, and add butter to pan. Gently shake pan while butter melts to create a smooth sauce from juices, and pour sauce with vegetables at once over fish. Serve immediately.

*If you would like to finish fish in oven:*

1. Preheat oven to 350°F. Lightly dust fish with flour.

2. Heat olive oil in a large pan over medium-high heat. When oil is hot, brown pieces of fish on both sides and place browned fish in an oblong baking pan.

**Yield: 6 servings**

3. Add onion, celery, capers, and garlic to pan in which you browned fish, add vinegar and wine, bring to a boil, and pour mixture over fish. Set pan aside to use to finish sauce. Cover and bake for 10 minutes, until fish flakes easily.

4. Transfer fish to a platter and pour juices from baking pan into original pan over high heat. Add butter and gently shake pan while butter melts to create a smooth sauce. Pour sauce and vegetables at once over fish and serve immediately.

# SALMON RIESLING

A winter king salmon, richer than those caught at other times of the year, is especially succulent poached in this faintly sweet tarragon cream sauce.

**Preparation and Cooking Time:** 35 minutes

> 1¾ to 2 pounds fresh salmon fillets, skinned and cut into 4 portions
> 3 tablespoons all-purpose flour, seasoned lightly with salt and pepper
> 3 tablespoons butter
> ½ cup Riesling wine
> 1 teaspoon dried tarragon
> ½ cup heavy cream

■ **Accompaniment**

> Hot rice

1. Lightly dust salmon with flour.

2. Heat butter in a large pan over medium-high heat. When foam subsides, place salmon, skinned side down, in pan. Brown lightly on both sides.

3. Add wine and tarragon. Cover pan and reduce heat to a slow simmer. Poach fish very gently for 10 minutes (depending on thickness of fillets), until it flakes easily. Remove salmon from pan and place on a serving platter. Keep warm while you finish sauce.

4. Add heavy cream to pan and raise heat to high. Cook rapidly until sauce has thickened and reduced to ¾ to 1 cup. Pour sauce over fish and serve at once with rice.

**Yield: 4 servings**

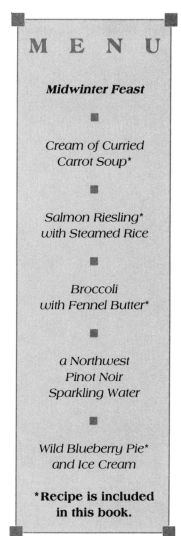

M E N U

*Midwinter Feast*

■

Cream of Curried
Carrot Soup*

■

Salmon Riesling*
with Steamed Rice

■

Broccoli
with Fennel Butter*

■

a Northwest
Pinot Noir
Sparkling Water

■

Wild Blueberry Pie*
and Ice Cream

*Recipe is included
in this book.

# GRILLED SALMON WITH LIME, SESAME, AND GINGER BUTTER

Long before people began grilling everything from eggplant to tortellini, it was the Alaskan's preferred method for cooking salmon. Grilling keeps the salmon moist and imparts a pleasant smoky flavor. The flavors of lime, sesame, and ginger gently enhance, without overwhelming, the flavor of the salmon. This marinade is based on an extremely versatile one in *The New York Times Cook Book*.

**Marinating Time:** 1 to 4 hours

**Preparation and Cooking Time:** 30 minutes

■ **Marinade**

> ½ cup olive oil
> ½ cup dry vermouth
> 1 tablespoon freshly squeezed lime juice (grate zest of 1 lime and squeeze juice, then set aside zest and remaining juice)
> ½ teaspoon salt
> 2 teaspoons dried parsley
> Pinch of dried thyme
> Dash of freshly ground pepper
> 6 salmon steaks or fillets (about 3 pounds)

■ **Butter**

> ¼ pound butter
> 1 tablespoon fresh lime juice
> 2 teaspoons oriental sesame oil (available in oriental groceries*)
> 2 teaspoons minced fresh ginger
> 1 teaspoon finely grated lime zest

1. **To prepare marinade:** Combine olive oil, vermouth, lime juice, salt, parsley, thyme, and black pepper in a large glass bowl or casserole. Add salmon and coat well on all sides. Cover and allow to marinate in refrigerator for 1 to 4 hours.

**NOTE:**
Butter can be made, wrapped well in plastic wrap, and frozen for up to 1 month.

2. **To prepare butter:** Using an electric mixer on high, cream butter until smooth. Add 1 tablespoon lime juice, sesame oil, ginger, and lime zest. Combine thoroughly, then wrap tightly and refrigerate until ready to use.

3. **To prepare salmon:** Preheat grill or broiler. When grill is hot, remove salmon from marinade and cook about 5 minutes on each side, depending on thickness of the fish: 10 minutes total cooking time for 1-inch-thick pieces. Fish should flake easily but not seem dry in the center. Transfer to a serving platter.

4. Remove butter from refrigerator and melt it in a small pan over medium heat. Pour over fish and serve at once.

**Yield: 6 servings**

*See mail-order sources, page 237.

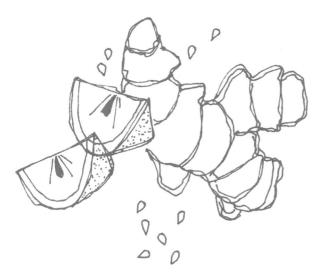

# POACHED SALMON DIJONNAISE

Lightly poached salmon is perfectly dressed in this delicate mustard cream sauce. Serve this beautiful and delicious dish for any special occasion.

**Preparation and Cooking Time:** 35 minutes

> 2¼ to 2½ pounds salmon steaks or fillets, cut into 6 portions (remove skin and as many bones as possible)
> ¼ cup all-purpose flour
> 4 tablespoons butter
> 2 cups thinly sliced mushrooms (about 12 ounces)
> 1 teaspoon minced fresh garlic (1 large clove)
> 1 cup dry white wine (chardonnay or sauvignon blanc)
> 4 teaspoons Dijon mustard
> 1 cup heavy cream
> 1 teaspoon salt
> ½ teaspoon freshly ground pepper

■ **Garnish**

> 1 cup Petersburg shrimp (optional)
> ¼ cup thinly sliced chives or green onions

■ **Accompaniment**

> Hot rice (aromatic Basmati rice is particularly good with this)

1. Preheat oven to 350°F and set rack in center. Lightly oil a 10- by- 7- by 2-inch ovenproof casserole and set aside. Lightly dust salmon pieces with flour and set aside.

2. Heat butter in a large pan over medium-high heat. When foam subsides, put in as many pieces of salmon as will fit comfortably. (Place fillets skinned side up.) Cook fish briefly on both sides until it is very lightly browned but not cooked through. Transfer fish to oiled casserole and keep warm while cooking remaining fish.

3. When all fish is browned and waiting in casserole, add mushrooms and garlic to pan. Stir and cook until softened. Add white wine and mustard. Stir to loosen bits from bottom of pan and pour mixture over fish. Set pan aside to use to finish sauce. Cover casserole and bake for 15 to 20 minutes, depending on thickness of fish.

4. While fish is cooking, bring cream to a boil in browning

pan over medium heat to allow it to begin to reduce slightly.

5. Remove fish from oven and test for doneness: It should flake easily but not seem dry in the center. Transfer fish to a serving platter and keep warm.

6. Raise heat under cream to high and pour juices from casserole into pan. Stir and bring to a boil. Add salt and pepper. Let sauce reduce to about 1½ cups, until it has thickened somewhat. Taste and correct seasoning, then pour sauce over fish, sprinkle with shrimp and chives, and serve at once, with hot rice.

**Yield: 6 servings**

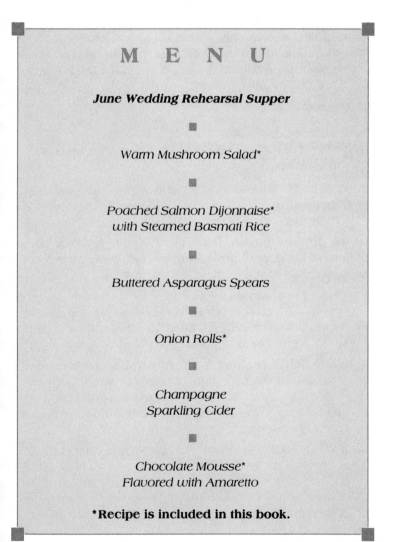

M  E  N  U

*June Wedding Rehearsal Supper*

*Warm Mushroom Salad\**

*Poached Salmon Dijonnaise\**
*with Steamed Basmati Rice*

*Buttered Asparagus Spears*

*Onion Rolls\**

*Champagne*
*Sparkling Cider*

*Chocolate Mousse\**
*Flavored with Amaretto*

**\*Recipe is included in this book.**

# SALMON MATISSE

Matisse? The pinks, creams, and muted reds of this dish bring to mind French Impressionists.

**Marinating Time:** 4 hours

**Preparation and Cooking Time:** 30 minutes

> Grilled salmon marinade (page 100)
> 6 salmon steaks or fillets, about 3 pounds (remove skin if you wish)

■ **Yogurt Sauce**

> 1 cup plain low-fat yogurt
> ½ tablespoon oriental sesame oil (available in oriental groceries or health food stores*)
> ½ tablespoon freshly squeezed lemon juice
> 1 to 2 tablespoons minced fresh herbs (tarragon is good), or substitute 1 teaspoon dried if fresh herbs are unavailable

■ **Garnish**

> 2 tablespoons butter
> 1 to 1½ cups thinly sliced red onion rings (1 medium red onion)

1. In a large, flat-bottomed, nonreactive (nonaluminum) container, marinate salmon in marinade, covered and refrigerated, for 4 hours.

2. **To prepare yogurt sauce:** Mix yogurt, sesame oil, ½ lemon juice, and tarragon in a small bowl. Refrigerate until ready to use.

3. **To prepare salmon:** Preheat broiler or barbecue. Broil or grill salmon for 5 minutes on each side (more or less, depending on thickness of fish: 10 minutes total cooking time for each inch of thickness).

4. **While fish is cooking, prepare garnish:** Heat butter in a large pan over medium-high heat. When foam subsides, add onion rings and cook until lightly browned on both sides and somewhat softened. Keep warm until ready to serve.

5. Just before fish is completely done, spread top side of each fillet or steak with yogurt sauce. When fish is cooked through (it will flake easily but still look moist in center), transfer to a serving platter and arrange sautéed onions impressionistically over the dish. Serve at once.

**Yield: 6 servings**

NOTE:
Yogurt sauce is delicious on grilled chicken as well as fish.

*See mail-order sources, page 237.

# SALMON ADRIATICA

This unusual combination of salmon and cheeses came about one day when we made a little more cannelloni filling than we needed and were wondering what to have for the dinner special. Would the marriage work? It has remained one of our most popular seafood specials.

**Preparation Time:** 15 minutes (can be done ahead)

**Cooking:** 25 minutes

### ▓ Filling

2 eggs, lightly beaten
1 pound ricotta cheese
½ pound frozen spinach, thawed, chopped fine, and squeezed dry
¼ pound feta cheese, rinsed and broken into pieces
2 tablespoons freshly grated Parmesan cheese
⅓ cup grated mozzarella cheese (1½ ounces)
½ teaspoon grated nutmeg
¼ teaspoon salt
¼ teaspoon pepper

### ▓ Salmon

8 6-ounce fresh salmon fillets, skin removed
½ cup dry bread crumbs

### ▓ Garnish
8 fresh lemon wedges

1. **To prepare filling:** Beat all filling ingredients together in a large mixing bowl. Taste and adjust seasoning as needed.

2. **To prepare salmon:** Preheat oven to 350°F and set rack in center. Lightly oil a large baking pan.

3. Place salmon fillets, skinned side down, on baking pan. Evenly cover each piece of fish with ½ cup filling. Sprinkle bread crumbs over filling and bake fish until cooked through. (It will flake easily but not be dry inside.) Baking time will vary with thickness of fish: Figure about 10 minutes for each inch of thickness.

4. Transfer fish to a serving platter and serve at once, garnished with fresh lemon wedges.

**Yield: 8 servings**

**NOTE:**
Filling can be made 1 day in advance and refrigerated until ready to use, or frozen for up to 1 month. Defrost in refrigerator.

# SALMON WELLINGTON

This recipe requires time and attention, but is well worth the effort. Beneath the layers of buttery pastry await a savory mushroom stuffing called *duxelles*, and tender baked salmon.

**Preparation Time:** 1 hour

**Cooking Time:** 30 minutes

### ▪ Duxelles

3 tablespoons butter
⅔ cup small-diced onion (1 small onion)
4 teaspoons minced fresh garlic (4 large cloves)
4 cups finely chopped mushrooms (about 1 to 1½ pounds)
½ cup dry red wine
2 tablespoons chopped fresh parsley
1 teaspoon salt
½ teaspoon dried thyme
½ teaspoon ground black pepper

### ▪ Salmon Wellington

4 pounds salmon fillets, skinned and all bones carefully removed (if possible, use tail fillets, which have no bones) and cut into 8 portions
1 tablespoon corn oil
½ pound (8 to 10 sheets) phyllo dough (if dough is frozen, defrost it in refrigerator; phyllo dough is available in the frozen foods section of many grocery stores*)
¼ pound plus 4 tablespoons butter, melted

1. **To prepare duxelles:** Heat butter in a large pan over medium heat. When it begins to foam, add chopped onion, garlic and mushrooms.

2. As soon as the mushrooms begin to give up their juices, stir in wine, parsley, salt, thyme, and pepper. Reduce heat to low and cook, stirring occasionally, until all moisture has evaporated. Remove from heat and allow to cool.

3. Preheat oven to 350°F and set rack in center. Lightly oil 2 cookie sheets.

4. Arrange salmon fillets on 1 cookie sheet and bake 10 minutes, until salmon is just barely cooked. (It will flake easily but seem moist in the center. It is better to have

**NOTE:**
Finely chop onion, garlic, and mushrooms together in a food processor fitted with a steel blade if you have one.

**NOTE:**
Duxelles can be made 1 day ahead and kept refrigerated until ready to use, or it can be frozen for up to 1 month.

**NOTE:**
Salmon can be baked up to 1 day ahead and kept refrigerated until ready to prepare Wellingtons.

fish slightly underdone at this point.) Chill salmon until you are ready to assemble Wellingtons.

5. To assemble Wellingtons: Gently unroll phyllo dough and place 1 sheet in front of you. (Keep remaining dough covered loosely with a cloth.) Generously brush melted butter over whole sheet.

6. Place 1 piece of salmon in center of phyllo. Spread ¼ cup duxelles evenly on top of salmon. Fold lower third of dough up over fish and duxelles. Brush dough on top of fish with butter. Fold top third of phyllo down over salmon, and brush that part with butter. Carefully fold left side of dough over fish, brush with butter, and then finish package by folding right side over all, and brushing with butter. Place package on second lightly oiled cookie sheet. Repeat process with each remaining piece of fish.

7. Bake for 15 to 20 minutes, until phyllo is puffed and golden brown. Transfer to a serving platter and serve at once.

**Yield: 8 servings**

*See mail-order sources, page 237.

NOTE:
Wellingtons can be made up to 2 hours ahead through step 6 and kept refrigerated, tightly wrapped, until ready to bake.

---

### Beach Asparagus

■ ■ ■

*The plant is called beach asparagus by Alaskans, pousse-pied by the French, and sea bean, sea asparagus, samphire, sandfire, salicornia, chicken claws, crowfoot, or glasswort by the rest of the English-speaking world. Common in the Pacific Northwest, it's found almost everywhere the soil is alkaline. For a gourmet foraging experience, look in the Seattle freight yards for pousse-pied.*

*In Alaska, beach asparagus grows in wetlands that are flooded at high tides. A red variety is common in some areas, such as near Anchorage's water treatment plant. July is the best month to collect beach asparagus in Alaska; before then the plants are barely up, and later they are stringy.*

*Beach asparagus's chief virtues are its crunchiness, salty tang, and exotic appearance. Traditional cooks boil it and eat it with butter, purée it into a green sauce, or pickle it for winter use. Modern chefs use beach asparagus as a garnish, salad ingredient, or stuffing for fish. It also makes a beautiful sea-green bed for baked or poached seafood.*

*See mail-order sources, page 237.*

# SALMON VÉRONIQUE

In classical French cuisine, "Véronique" indicates that the dish is prepared with white grapes. We have adapted the preparation to salmon and red flame seedless grapes.

**Preparation and Cooking Time:** 35 minutes

>  6 salmon fillets, 2½ to 3 pounds altogether, skin removed
>  ¼ cup all-purpose flour, seasoned with 1 teaspoon each salt and pepper
>  2 tablespoons butter
>  ½ cup dry white wine (chardonnay or sauvignon blanc)
>  1 teaspoon raspberry vinegar (see note, page 88)*
>  1 teaspoon Dijon mustard
>  1 cup heavy cream
>  1½ cups seedless green or red grapes, halved

■ **Accompaniment**

Hot rice or fresh croissants

1. Preheat oven to 350°F and set rack in center. Lightly butter a 13- by 9- by 2-inch casserole.

2. Lightly dust each piece of salmon with flour.

3. Heat butter in a large pan over medium-high heat. When butter is hot and foam subsides, add as many pieces of salmon as will comfortably fit, skinned side up. Brown very lightly on both sides, then remove to casserole. Keep warm while cooking remaining salmon.

4. When all fish has been browned and is waiting in casserole, pour white wine into pan, whisk in vinegar and mustard, and bring to a boil. Pour mixture over fish and set pan aside to use when finishing sauce. Cover casserole and bake for 10 to 20 minutes, depending on thickness of fish.

5. While salmon is baking, pour heavy cream into browning pan and simmer over medium heat.

6. When salmon is cooked through (it will flake easily but not seem dry in the center), place it on a serving platter to keep warm while you finish sauce. Add juices from casserole and grapes to cream and raise heat to high. Stir and bring to a boil. Cook vigorously until reduced to about 1½ cups and slightly thickened. Pour over fish and serve at once with hot rice.

**Yield: 6 servings**

---

**Fireweed**

■ ■ ■

*Like a fiddlehead fern that holds the promise of spring in its tight coil, fireweed holds the plenitude of summer in its elegant spire. Salmon spawning in their ancient rivers, berries ripening on the hillsides, the sun giving its warmth to the earth; each summer day is counted by the opening of a new fireweed blossom on its tall stalk. When "the fireweed is halfway up the stalk," summer is at its best.*

*Wherever you see its magenta spires coloring the relentless green of forest or beach fringe, you can be sure that nature or a human hand disturbed the earth underneath. Warm summer breezes carry clouds of fluffy fireweed seeds to every vacant spot of earth. By next season, the barren land is thickly blanketed in rose-pink blossoms.*

*So esteemed was the plant that areas of fireweed near Haida Indian villages were often owned by noble families. The young shoots were eaten at springtime feasts, and also used as a womanly beauty aid.*

# WHOLE POACHED (OR BAKED) SALMON WITHOUT BONES

Bountiful, luxurious, impressive, and delicious, the classic whole poached salmon embodies the magnificence of Alaska. You'll find it as the centerpiece on the table at every Alaskan celebration.

To prepare it you will need:

■ 1 fresh, cleaned, whole, unmarred salmon with head and tail on

■ 1 to 3 quarts court bouillon (page 225)

■ An oven or pot large enough to cook a really big fish whole, and then some place to refrigerate the fish overnight

■ One large cookie sheet or a board covered with foil or plastic wrap

■ A large, attractive platter on which to serve the fish

■ Aspic, herbed mayonnaise, flowers, or whatever you'd like to decorate the fish

Plan to cook the whole fish the day before you wish to serve it, and refrigerate it until you are ready to decorate it.

For excellent instructions on poaching and decorating a whole fish, refer to *James McNair's Salmon Cookbook*, Jacques Pepin's *La Technique*, or A. J. McClane's *The Encyclopedia of Fish Cookery*.

1. We have found that the average Alaskan salmon is too big to poach on top of the stove (we know people who wrap the fish tightly and run them through the dishwasher, but let's not do that!), so it is necessary to bake it. Preheat oven to 350°F.

2. Neatly remove head and tail from fish and set aside. The fish will look nicer if the head and tail are cooked separately from the body and, given the size of most Alaskan salmon, it is necessary to remove them just to fit the fish into the oven.

3. Seam several sheets of heavy-duty foil together tightly and place on the back of 1 or 2 cookie sheets. Lay fish on foil and fold up edges. Pour in about ½ inch court

bouillon, then crimp edges of foil together so fish is enclosed in an envelope.

4. Bake fish for 10 minutes for every inch of thickness, measured at the thickest part, plus an additional 10 minutes to give envelope a chance to heat up. Place some foil on rack below fish, in case your envelope leaks.

5. While fish is baking, gently poach head and tail in court bouillon in a large pot on top of stove until meat in head is opaque. (Take care to lay head so that it faces the same way the body is facing in the oven.) Remove head and tail from poaching liquid and refrigerate. (Keep them facing the right direction.) Strain and refrigerate poaching liquid separately, if you plan to use it in an aspic.

6. Remove fish from oven, carefully unwrap it (don't let steam burn you) and check for doneness by probing horizontally along backbone. (Don't poke directly down through top of fish and mar the appearance.) The flesh should be opaque all the way to the bone. Drain off liquids to use in an aspic, and slide fish onto a clean tray. (Remember to keep the same side up.) Cover lightly and refrigerate overnight.

7. The next day, take fish out of refrigerator. Neatly cut off all fins and set them aside. (Remember where they came from so your fish will be anatomically correct when you present it!) Place the fish top side down on a large cookie sheet or flat board covered with foil or plastic. Carefully pull off skin and discard.

8. Very carefully, using a large chef's knife or long boning knife, cut horizontally along back of fish, starting at head end and staying on upper side of backbone. When you have cut the full length of the fish, using a broad spatula, lift off upper fillet and place it on serving platter skinned side down. If it must be removed in two or three large sections, that is OK, just fit them back together neatly.

9. Using needle-nose pliers or large tweezers, remove perpendicular bones found in dorsal, or top half, of fillet, and all ribs from lower half of fillet. Lift backbone from remaining fillet and use tweezers to pick out all bones from that fillet.

10. Now comes the tricky part: You need to flip the top fillet (which is sitting on cookie sheet) in one piece onto bottom fillet (which is waiting on serving platter). Line

up the two halves on their respective trays so they are mirror images of each other, right next to each other. Bravely, with no hesitation, turn tray holding top fillet right on top of bottom fillet waiting on serving platter. Remove top tray and gently line up the fillets.

11. Peel skin from top fillet and, using a thin sharp knife, carefully cut away gray layer of meat. (It is edible, just not pretty.) Arrange head and tail so that they appear to be connected to the fish, and put the fins back in place. (It may be necessary to trim head and tail a bit to make them fit nicely. A little mayonnaise piled decoratively around the neck does wonders.)

You are now ready to begin decorating the fish as whimsically and artistically as you like. One thing to remember: If you are applying overlapping surrogate scales (use sliced almonds or thin slices of cucumber or lemon), begin placing them from the tail, so that they point in the right direction when you are done. (Otherwise your fish will have a hard time swimming upstream!)

Present fish chilled and accompany it with crackers and herbed mayonnaise.

**Yield: A 20-pound king salmon will serve 30, for a buffet dinner, and up to 75 people at a cocktail reception**

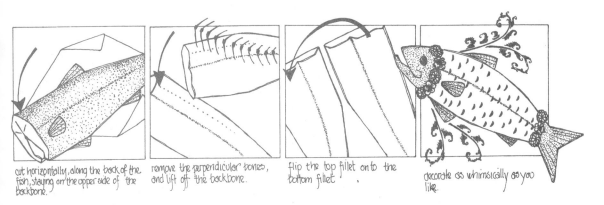

cut horizontally, along the back of the fish, staying on the upper side of the backbone.

remove the perpendicular bones, and lift off the backbone.

flip the top fillet onto the bottom fillet.

decorate as whimsically as you like.

# SEAFOOD FETTUCCINE

People love this combination of fish and tomatoes in a light cream sauce. The recipe comfortably accommodates the season and your resources: It works well with almost any combination of fresh or freshly cooked seafood.

**Preparation and Cooking Time:**  1 hour 15 minutes

> 1 pound fettuccine noodles
> 2 cups heavy cream
> 1½ to 2 pounds skinned and boned fish, cut into 1½-inch pieces (preferably a combination of seafood such as shrimp, scallops, halibut, salmon, and snapper)
> 1 teaspoon minced garlic (1 large clove)
> 3 cups peeled, seeded, and large-diced tomatoes (3 to 4 large tomatoes)
> ½ cup dry white wine (chardonnay, fumé blanc, or substitute chicken or vegetable stock)
> ¾ cup thinly sliced green onions (tops and bottoms, about 6)
> ¾ cup freshly grated Parmesan cheese
> 1½ teaspoons salt, or to taste
> 1½ teaspoons ground black pepper

**NOTE:**
Cooked fish may be substituted.

**NOTE:**
To peel and seed tomatoes, drop them into boiling water for 10 seconds, slip off skin, cut in half, and squeeze gently to remove seeds.

**NOTE:**
If you substitute all cooked seafood for fresh, in step 4 cook tomatoes and garlic in butter, then add wine and cream. Cook sauce over high heat until it thickens, and then add seafood. Toss together with hot cooked fettuccine, green onions, cheese, and seasonings. Serve as above.

1. Bring a large pot of water to a boil over high heat. Add fettuccine and cook until *al dente* (see page 122). Drain and set aside in a large bowl to keep warm.

2. **While fettuccine is cooking:** Place cream in a large pot over high heat and boil until reduced to 1½ cups.

3. Heat butter in a large pot over medium heat. When butter begins to foam, add seafood* and garlic. Stir gently to coat fish with butter and cook briefly until opaque on the outside but not cooked through. Add tomatoes and wine. Reduce heat and simmer gently until seafood is cooked through, about 2 minutes, depending on type of fish. (Do not overcook.) With a slotted spoon, remove fish and set aside to keep warm.

4. Add cream to juices in pan, raise heat to high, and cook until sauce begins to thicken (3 to 5 minutes).

5. Using spaghetti tongs or a large fork, gently stir in noodles until most of sauce is absorbed.

**6.** Gently stir in cooked seafood, green onions, cheese, salt, and pepper. Taste and adjust seasoning, transfer to a serving dish, and serve at once.

**Yield: 6 servings**

\*Add Petersburg or small cocktail shrimp or previously cooked seafood in step 7 to avoid overcooking it.

---

### Black Seaweed

■ ■ ■

*Black seaweed (also called red laver, Porphyra perforata) has long been a staple of Northwest Coast natives. Adeline St. Clair, a Tlingit Indian from the village of Hoonah, prepares it this way: Go to the beach during the lowest tide in May and roll the seaweed off the rocks by hand. Spread the sea-leaves on a sheet in the sun to dry. When they are half dry, grind them in a meat grinder and add clam or cockle juice to taste. Spread out again on the sheet and dry thoroughly, turning occasionally. If the day is warm and windy, the seaweed should be dry by 4 P.M. It may take a week to dry if the weather is bad.*

*Adeline's two sons, Aaron and Earl St. Clair, have been transforming our customers' eating habits with their creative blending of traditional Tlingit foods and the best of modern ingredients. They frequently offer specials, such as seafood sauté, garnished with crumbled black seaweed. See mail-order sources, page 237.*

# PRAWNS OREGANATE

Scott Miller, the chef who created so many of our best dishes, took one of our favorite foods, prawns, and sprinkled it with an herb usually associated with another one of our favorites, pizza. The result is a simple, robust dish full of flavor. If you can find it, use fresh oregano here. If you have garden space, plant your own. In spite of its popularity in the Mediterranean countries, oregano grows very well in cool climates and will winter over even in southeast Alaska. You will have a regular source of the fresh herb and, as a bonus, the plant produces lovely purple flowers that dry beautifully.

**Preparation and Cooking Time:**   30 to 40 minutes

> 2 pounds Alaskan spot prawns (or other large shrimp), peeled and deveined
> ¼ cup all-purpose flour, seasoned with 1 teaspoon each salt and pepper
> 2 tablespoons olive oil
> 2 tablespoons butter
> 2 cups seeded large-diced fresh tomatoes (cut 2 large tomatoes around the middle and squeeze gently to remove seeds)
> 3 tablespoons finely chopped fresh oregano (substitute 2 teaspoons dried)
> 1 tablespoon minced fresh garlic (3 to 4 large cloves)
> ¼ cup dry white wine (such as chardonnay), or substitute chicken or vegetable stock
> 3 tablespoons freshly squeezed lemon juice
> 4 ounces feta cheese, crumbled
> 1 cup thinly sliced green onions, including tops (10 to 12 green onions)
> ½ teaspoon salt
> ¼ teaspoon pepper

■ **Accompaniment**

Hot rice or sourdough bread

1. Lightly dust prawns with flour.

2. Heat oil and butter in a large pot over medium-high heat. When foam subsides but butter is not yet brown, add prawns to pan. Stir to coat prawns evenly with oil and cook briefly, stirring frequently, until they are white on the edges but not cooked through.

3. Add tomatoes, oregano, garlic, wine, and lemon juice. Lower heat to medium and cook until prawns begin to

curl and are opaque all the way through. (Take care not to overcook.)

4. Immediately stir in cheese, green onions, salt, and pepper. Taste and correct seasoning. Transfer to a serving dish and serve at once, accompanied by rice or crusty sourdough bread.

**Yield: 5 to 6 servings**

**Peeling and Mincing Garlic**

■ ■ ■

*To peel garlic quickly and easily:*

1. *Break a head of garlic apart into individual cloves.*
2. *Place one clove innocently on a cutting board.*
3. *Holding a broad-bladed knife, such as a Chinese cleaver or 10-inch chef's knife, gently lay it flat, with the blade facing away from you, directly on top of the little clove of garlic.*
4. *Smash your free hand down onto the the broad side of the blade, crushing the defenseless little garlic clove.*
5. *Easily remove the peel from the bruised garlic clove. Set garlic aside.*

*When you have peeled all the garlic cloves you need:*

6. *Chop garlic cloves fine. If salt is called for in your recipe, sprinkle it onto garlic, and use broad side of knife blade to press garlic into a purée. (You can use a food processor to mince large quantities of garlic, but the purée will not be as smooth as doing it by hand.)*
7. *Set puréed garlic aside until you are ready to add it to the dish you are preparing.*
8. *To remove garlic flavor from your cutting board, chop parsley on the spot where you minced the garlic, or sprinkle cutting board with salt and lemon juice. Let it sit for a minute and clean it off.*

*Smashing garlic is a very satisfying pastime, particularly after a stressful day: Do a whole head of garlic at one time and store the purée until you need it.*

*To store puréed garlic:*

*Place garlic in a glass jar, cover it with olive oil, and refrigerate until needed. Drain garlic before you use it and use the oil in salad dressings. Another method is to place purée on a sheet of plastic wrap, roll up into a tube, and twist ends. Wrap tube with foil or another layer of plastic and freeze. Cut off bits of garlic as you need it. A third method is to whip garlic together with butter and freeze it in a double-wrapped tube, to use in cooking, on garlic bread, or melted over vegetables.*

# SCAMPI PROVENÇAL

Lots of garlic and lemon juice accent this simple dish of shrimp and tomatoes, which keeps out the cold on those days one dreams of wintering in the south of France.

**Preparation and Cooking Time:** 30 minutes

> 1 pound Alaskan spot prawns (8 to 10 per person) or substitute other large shrimp, peeled and deveined
> ¼ cup all-purpose flour, seasoned with 1 teaspoon each salt and pepper
> 4 tablespoons butter
> 2 teaspoons minced fresh garlic (3 to 4 large cloves)
> 1⅓ cups peeled, seeded, small-diced tomatoes (1½ medium tomatoes)
> ⅓ cup homemade chicken stock (see page 226) (substitute unsalted commercial chicken broth)
> 3 tablespoons freshly squeezed lemon juice
> ⅔ cup thinly sliced green onions, tops and bottoms (5 or 6)

■ Accompaniment

Hot rice

1. Lightly dust prawns with flour.

2. Heat butter and garlic in a large pan over medium heat. When butter is hot and still foamy, add prawns to pan. Cook them quickly on both sides, until edges begin to turn white. Don't overcook.

3. Add tomatoes, stock, and lemon juice. Reduce heat to low and simmer gently until prawns begin to curl (2 minutes). Stir in green onions.

4. Cook briefly until prawns are opaque through the center and sauce is slightly thickened. Line a serving dish with hot rice, pour prawns over top, and serve at once.

**Yield: 4 servings**

NOTE:
Drop tomatoes into boiling water for 10 seconds, remove, slip off skins, cut in half, and squeeze gently to remove seeds.

# SHRIMP FRIED RICE

It's fast, delicious, versatile, the kids like it, and it's good for you: Do you need any more excuses to make it tonight?

**Preparation and Cooking Time:**   50 minutes (30 minutes if rice is already made)

    2½ tablespoons cooking oil
    4 eggs, beaten
    1½ cups large-diced onion (1 large onion)
    1½ cups large-diced green peppers (2 medium
        peppers)
    1½ cups sliced fresh mushrooms (about 6 ounces)
    1 pound Petersburg shrimp or small cocktail shrimp
        (substitute diced cooked chicken, pork, or other
        seafood)
    2 tablespoons soy or tamari sauce
    2 teaspoons minced fresh garlic (2 large cloves)
    6 to 7 cups cooked brown rice (page 209)

**1.** Heat 1½ teaspoons oil in a large wok or deep pan over medium-high heat. When oil is hot, pour in beaten eggs. Cook gently, stirring, until softly scrambled. Remove, and set aside. If eggs stuck to pan at all, clean it out before continuing.

**2.** Heat remaining 2 tablespoons oil in wok or pan over high heat. When oil is almost smoking, add onion, peppers, and mushrooms. Stir to coat evenly with oil and continue to stir and cook quickly until vegetables begin to soften, but not brown.

**3.** Add shrimp, soy, and garlic and stir for 30 seconds. Add cooked rice. (If rice is cold, stir in and cook until heated through.) Stir in cooked scrambled eggs.

**4.** As soon as mixture is piping hot, transfer to a serving dish and serve at once.

**Yield: 6 to 7 servings**

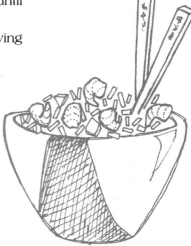

the Governor's House
Calhoun Street, Juneau Alaska

The Governor's House—Construction on the Governor's House was completed in time for New Year's 1913, and the territorial governor, Walter J. Clark, opened the house on that day to the community. Each governor since then has continued that tradition, and the house is opened every year at Christmastime for caroling and refreshments.

# Vegetarian Entrées

# FRESH VEGETABLE SAUTÉ

This dish has been on our menu since the restaurant opened and is loved for its simple, tasty, wholesomeness. Try it after a busy day at work.

**Preparation and Cooking Time:** 1 hour (less if you have cooked rice on hand)

## ▍ Vegetable Mix

1½ cups thinly sliced carrots, diagonally cut (about 4 medium carrots)
1½ cups thinly sliced onion, cut stem to tip (1 large onion)
1½ cups zucchini, cut in half lengthwise, then thinly sliced on the diagonal (1 large)
1½ cups 2-inch broccoli florets and thinly sliced peeled stems (½ medium head)
1½ cups 2-inch cauliflower florets (⅓ medium head)
1 cup thinly sliced green pepper (1 pepper)
6 mushrooms, quartered

## ▍ Vegetable Sauté

3 tablespoons cooking oil
¼ cup dry white wine
1 tablespoon tamari or soy sauce
3 cups grated Cheddar cheese (½ pound)
¾ cup chopped raw almonds
6 cups hot steamed brown rice (page 209)

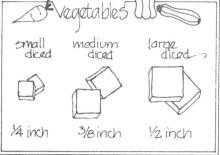

1. **To prepare vegetable mix:** Cut all vegetables and combine in a large container. Use immediately, or wrap tightly and keep overnight.

2. **To prepare vegetable sauté:** Heat oil in a wok or large pan over high heat. When oil is very hot, add vegetables, stirring to coat evenly. Stir and cook for 1 minute.

3. Add wine and tamari, stir, and cover. Reduce heat to medium and steam for 3 to 4 minutes. Check vegetables for doneness: We like them still a little crisp, just beginning to soften. Cook a little longer if you like them a little softer.

4. Spoon hot rice into a large serving bowl and make a well in center. Sprinkle rice with 1 cup grated cheese. Pour vegetables into center of rice and cheese and sprinkle with remaining cheese and chopped almonds. Serve at once.

**NOTE:**
Use eggplant, celery, snow peas, parsnips, bok choy, or any other vegetables you like: For 6 servings you need 9 cups altogether.

**Yield: 6 servings**

# EGGPLANT PARMIGIANA

Lightly battered and fried slices of eggplant substitute beautifully for noodles in this variation of lasagne. This is a great casserole for parties: The recipe doubles easily and can be made well ahead and frozen.

**Preparation Time:** 2 hours, including preparing marinara sauce

**Baking Time:** 1 hour

■ **Eggplant**

> 1¾ pounds fresh eggplant (1 large)
> 2 tablespoons olive oil
> 2 tablespoons corn or safflower oil
> ¾ cup all-purpose flour, seasoned with 1 teaspoon each salt and ground black pepper
> 3 or 4 eggs, beaten with 3 tablespoons water

■ **Parmigiana**

> ½ cup red wine (optional)
> 6 cups marinara sauce (page 224)
> 1½ pounds mozzarella cheese, grated (about 6 cups)
> 8 ounces Jack cheese, grated (about 2 cups)
> ¼ cup freshly grated Parmesan cheese

1. **To prepare eggplant:** Slice eggplant into ⅛-inch slices. If you are using 1 large eggplant, cut it in half or in quarters lengthwise so that slices are no more than 3 inches in diameter. Place slices in a single layer on a cookie sheet lined with absorbent towels and sprinkle with salt. Cover with towels and repeat until all eggplant is salted. Allow to sit at room temperature for 30 minutes. Rinse slices well and pat dry.

2. Combine olive oil and cooking oil. Heat 1 tablespoon of mixed oils in a large pan over medium heat. Dip eggplant slices first in seasoned flour, then in beaten eggs, and fry in oil until golden brown on each side. Remove when tiny beads of moisture begin to appear on surface of cooked slices. Place on absorbent towels while cooking remaining slices.

3. **To assemble casserole:** Preheat oven to 350°F and set rack in center. Lightly oil a 13- by 8- by 2-inch casserole.

4. Stir red wine into marinara sauce. Dip slices of eggplant in sauce and place them in a single layer on bottom of casserole. Spread ¾ cup sauce over eggplant and evenly sprinkle with a third of the grated mozzarella and half the Jack cheese. Make a second layer of eggplant, sauce, and cheeses. Top with remaining eggplant, sauce, and mozzarella, and sprinkle with Parmesan cheese.

5. Bake for 45 minutes, until golden brown on top and bubbly throughout. Let it rest for 15 to 20 minutes before cutting into portions.

**Yield: 8 servings**

**NOTE:**
Casserole can be prepared to this point and kept refrigerated for up to 2 days.

**NOTE:**
This dish is good made ahead (it's excellent boat food) and can be frozen baked or unbaked for future use. Freeze in individual portions to have homemade TV dinners!

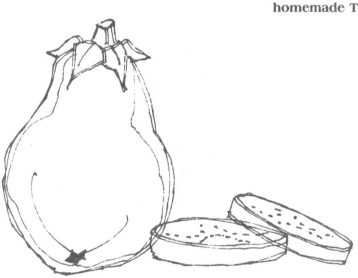

**NOTE:**
Substitute 1¼ pounds fresh pasta or 1 pound dried fettuccine noodles and skip to step 6 of the instructions.

■ 122 ■

# FETTUCCINE ALFREDO

When Susan Kirkness worked in the kitchen and managed the restaurant for years, she inspired us to make our own pasta for this classic Roman dish. The delicate noodles and creamy cheese sauce go deliciously with most white wines (although we have friends who prefer it with Coca-Cola).

**Preparation Time:** 30 minutes (about 10 minutes if you use commercial noodles)

**Resting Time:** 20 minutes (only if you make your own noodles)

**Cooking Time:** 20 minutes

### ■ Homemade Fettuccine

2 cups semolina flour, available in most grocery stores or health food stores* (substitute all-purpose flour only in direst of emergencies; it lacks the protein necessary to make good pasta)
2 eggs
2 teaspoons olive oil
(Optional: Add ¼ cup tomato paste; ½ cup freshly steamed, well-drained, puréed spinach; or ¼ cup puréed carrots** to dough)
4 tablespoons water (only as needed to bind dough)
1½ cups rice flour (to dust pasta and work surface), available in oriental markets or health food stores*

### ■ Fettuccine Alfredo

¼ pound plus 4 tablespoons butter
2 teaspoons freshly minced garlic (2 large cloves)
1½ cups heavy cream
1 cup freshly grated Parmesan cheese (about 5 ounces; use the best quality you can find)
¾ cup thinly sliced green onions (12 medium)

1. **To prepare fettuccine:** Combine semolina, eggs, olive oil, and water in a large bowl and knead until dough changes from light yellow in color to almost white. (This is easiest in an electric mixer fitted with a dough hook or in a food processor fitted with a metal blade.)

2. Let dough rest, covered, on a lightly floured surface for 10 to 20 minutes.

3. Cut dough into 8 equal parts. Keep them covered as you work.

4. Lightly dust work surface with rice flour. Roll out each bit of dough until very long and thin ($\frac{1}{32}$ inch), using a pasta machine, if you have one, or by hand. Hang strips of pasta from racks to dry while rolling out remaining dough. (Use the rack from your oven. Put a clean tray or waxed paper under rack in case dough falls.)

5. When all dough has been rolled out, check strips for stickiness. When they are no longer tacky but are not yet brittle, take first strip and cut into ¼-inch fettuccine noodles using pasta machine; or gently and loosely roll toward the center, beginning at opposite ends, and slice by hand. Slip a long knife, such as a slicer, down the middle and lift with back edge. Noodles will drape over knife. Dust cut noodles with rice flour and hang to dry briefly.

6. **To prepare fettuccine Alfredo:** Heat a large pot of water to boiling and drop in pasta. Boil until cooked through (it takes only a few minutes), drain, and set aside. (Dried pasta will take longer to cook.)

7. Melt butter with garlic in a large pot over medium-high heat. As soon as butter begins to bubble, carefully stir in cooked fettuccine. Using spaghetti tongs or a large fork, toss gently to mix thoroughly.

8. Add heavy cream and bring to a boil. Gently stir in Parmesan cheese and green onions. When thoroughly mixed, transfer to a serving dish and serve at once. Pass additional cheese if you like.

**NOTE:**
To make ahead, wrap loosely and refrigerate to use within 1 day, or freeze unwrapped, then place in airtight bags for use later.

**Yield: 5 to 6 servings**

**\*See mail-order sources, page 237.**

**\*\*Use a good-quality baby food.**

"No man can be wise on an empty stomach."
    *—George Eliot*

# SAAG PANIR

This classic Indian dish was adapted for the restaurant by the longtime Fiddlehead manager and Indian food fan, Susan Kirkness. Colorful, wholesome, and delicious, this is an intriguing change of pace for a special gathering.

**Preparation and Cooking Time:** 1 hour 45 minutes

■ **Panir**

> 1 gallon of milk
> ½ cup fresh lemon juice

■ **Spinach**

> 3 pounds fresh spinach, thoroughly washed, stems removed (substitute 3 pounds frozen spinach, defrosted and well drained; skip step 4 and add some of the whey from the panir to the spinach when you pureé it in step 5)
> 4 teaspoons minced fresh garlic (4 large cloves)
> 1 jalapeño, quartered and seeds removed*
> ½ teaspoon cayenne
> ½ teaspoon salt

■ **Saag Panir**

> 1 tablespoon butter
> 1 tablespoon oil
> 1½ teaspoons coriander seed
> 1 teaspoon cumin seed
> 1 teaspoon turmeric
> 3 cups small-diced onions (3 medium onions)
> 3 cups seeded and medium-diced tomatoes (about 3 large)
> 6 to 7 cups hot steamed brown rice (page 209)

■ **Garnish**

> ¾ cup plain nonfat yogurt
> ¼ cup tomato chutney (page 228) or use any other good-quality chutney**

**NOTE:**
One tablespoon of garam masala (page 208) can be substituted for all three spices.

**NOTE:**
To peel and seed tomatoes, drop them into boiling water for 10 seconds, remove from water, slip off skins, cut in half, and squeeze gently to remove seeds.

1. **To prepare panir:** Line a colander with 2 layers of damp cheesecloth and set it over a deep bowl or pan.

2. Bring milk to a boil in a 2-gallon stainless steel or enamel pot (or do it in two batches) over medium-high heat. Remove from heat, stir in lemon juice, and let sit for 10 minutes, until curds and whey begin to separate. Pour into lined colander so that whey is collected in bowl.

Allow to drain for 5 minutes, then set a weighted plate on top of curds and let sit for 30 minutes.

3. Refrigerate or freeze whey for other uses, reserving 1 cup if you are using defrosted frozen spinach. (Use whey in place of water when preparing soups, bread, vegetables, etc.) Remove curds from cheesecloth and cut into ¼-inch cubes. Wrap and refrigerate until ready to use.

4. **To prepare spinach:** Steam spinach in a large pot over medium-high heat just until it begins to wilt. (Omit this step if you are using frozen spinach.)

5. Purée garlic, jalapeñö, cayenne, and salt with spinach in a blender or food processor. (If you are using frozen spinach, add whey as needed to make a smooth purée.) Set aside spinach mixture.

6. **To prepare saag panir:** Heat butter and oil in a large pot over medium-high heat. When butter and oil are hot, stir in coriander, cumin, and turmeric (or garam masala) and cook until aromatic. Add onions and cook until they begin to soften. Stir in tomatoes and cook until softened.

7. Stir in spinach purée. Add additional whey, if necessary, to make a smooth mixture the consistency of very thick pea soup. When mixture is heated throughout, stir in cheese cubes. Heat through.

8. Line a large serving dish with hot rice. Spoon spinach into center of dish and serve, garnished with a dollop of yogurt and chutney. Serve additional yogurt and chutney on the side.

**Yield: 6 servings**

*Be extremely careful to avoid touching your face with your hands while working with hot peppers. Immediately after you finish with them, thoroughly wash your hands, knife, and work surface. The hot oils in the peppers will irritate your skin.

**See mail-order sources, page 237.

**See mail-order sources, page 237.

"Think globally, eat locally."
—*The Chef*

**NOTE:**
Cheese can be prepared 1 to 2 days ahead.

**NOTE:**
Spinach mix can be prepared 1 day ahead and kept covered and refrigerated until ready to use.

# SHERRIED BLACK BEANS AND RICE

Black beans are favorites in the Caribbean and South America, and in southeast Alaska we love them too. These earned a compliment from a Cuban guest, who said our beans were the best he'd had since he'd left home.

**Soaking Time:** overnight

**Preparation Time:** 45 minutes

**Cooking Time:** 3 hours

> 2 cups dried black beans
> 2 cups large-diced onions (1 medium onion)
> 1 cup seeded and large-diced green pepper (1 medium pepper)
> ½ cup large-diced celery (1 large rib)
> 2 teaspoons salt
> ½ teaspoon pepper
> 1 bay leaf
> 2 teaspoons minced garlic (1 to 2 large cloves)
> 2 teaspoons dried thyme
> 1 teaspoon dried oregano
> ¼ to ½ teaspoon cayenne (depending on your outlook on life)
> 1 tablespoon chopped fresh cilantro (sorry, no flavor substitute; even dried won't work)
> ¼ cup sherry (dry to medium dry)
> 1 tablespoon miso (red or brown)
> 1 tablespoon freshly squeezed lime juice

## ■ Accompaniment

> 8 cups hot cooked brown rice (page 209)

## ■ Garnish

> 1 cup large-diced fresh tomatoes (1 medium)
> ½ to ⅔ cup sour cream
> 6 lime wedges
> 6 avocado wedges
> ½ cup thinly sliced green onions (8 medium)

1. Wash and soak beans in 5 cups water overnight.

2. Drain beans, place in a large pot, and add 6 cups water. Add onions, peppers, celery, salt, pepper, bay leaf, garlic, thyme, oregano, and cayenne. Bring to a boil

over high heat and allow to cook for 10 minutes. Reduce heat to low, cover, and simmer gently until beans are tender and almost mushy (2½ to 3 hours, depending upon age of beans). Remove and discard bay leaf. Using a wooden spoon, beat beans briefly to mash them slightly.

3. Stir in cilantro, sherry, miso, and lime juice and cook briefly, just to heat through.

4. Line a large serving bowl with hot rice and ladle beans into center. Garnish with chopped tomatoes, sour cream, lime wedges, avocado, and green onions. Serve at once.

**Yield: 6 servings**

**NOTE:**
Cooked black beans can be frozen in airtight containers at this point. Thaw and proceed as follows.

# SPICY PEANUT PASTA

A friend writes: "This would be a great dish to build a cooking party on. Invite everyone to come with cutting board, knife, and their favorite ingredient. What a great party!" And what a great idea! You make up the sauce and noodles ahead and enjoy the festivities while everyone joins in the fun.

**Preparation and Cooking Time:**  45 minutes, including preparing hot peanut sauce

> 1 pound buckwheat soba* or fettuccine noodles
> 2 tablespoons cooking oil
> 1½ to 2 cups thinly sliced onion, cut stem to tip (1 large onion)
> 1½ cups thinly sliced green pepper (1 medium)
> 1 to 1½ cups carrots, cut in half lengthwise, then thinly sliced on the diagonal (2 medium)
> 1 to 1½ cups zucchini, cut just like the carrots (2 medium)
> 1 to 1½ cups broccoli florets and thinly sliced trimmed stems (½ small head)
> ½ medium eggplant, cut into 1½- by ½- by ½-inch sticks (optional, but really good)
> 1 cup hot peanut sauce (page 223)
> ½ to ¾ cup unsweetened coconut milk (available in the frozen juice section of many grocery stores; see page 129) or water

■ **Garnish**

> ½ cup thinly sliced green onions (8 green onions)
> ½ cup chopped cocktail peanuts

1. Bring a large pot of water to a boil over high heat. Add pasta and cook until *al dente* (see page 122). Drain and set aside.

2. Heat 2 tablespoons oil in a wok or large fry pan over high heat until very hot. Add vegetables and stir to coat evenly with oil. Stir and cook for 2 minutes. Cover wok and cook for another 2 minutes. Vegetables should be softened but still a bit crisp.

**3.** Add 1 cup peanut sauce and ½ cup coconut milk. Stir to combine, then add noodles. Using spaghetti tongs or a large fork, mix everything well. If it seems dry, add additional coconut milk. As soon as mixture is quite hot, transfer to a large serving dish. Sprinkle green onions and chopped peanuts over all and serve at once.

**Yield: 6 servings**

**\*See mail-order sources, page 237.**

---

### Coconut Milk

■ ■ ■

*Coconut milk is the creamy liquid squeezed from grated fresh coconut meat or from re-constituted dried (desiccated) coconut. It adds an unmistakable flavor and richness to Southeast Asian and South American dishes.*

*Look for coconut milk in the oriental section or frozen juice department of your supermarket. If it is unavailable, you can easily make it at home:*

*1. Put 2 cups unsweetened desiccated coconut\* in a blender with 2½ cups very hot water. Blend on high for 30 seconds, then strain through cheesecloth or a fine-mesh strainer into a bowl, reserving liquid.*
*2. Squeeze out all moisture in pulp.*
*3. Return coconut to blender and add 2½ cups hot water. Blend for 30 seconds, strain, and squeeze dry, discarding pulp and reserving this liquid with liquid from first straining (step 1).*

*Use the same method to extract milk from fresh coconut: Put small chunks of fresh coconut meat into blender with hot water and blend until smooth. Strain and repeat as you would with dried coconut.*

*If a recipe calls for the richest milk, use only the first squeezing and save the second for soups, curries, or other dishes. (Rice is wonderful cooked in coconut milk.)*

**\*Unsweetened desiccated coconut is available in most health food stores. For mail-order sources, see page 237.**

# CANNELLONI

This cannelloni is made from delicate French crepes filled with a light savory mixture of spinach and ricotta cheese. Although this seems to be a complicated and time-consuming dish, it is actually one of the easiest filled pastas to make. It can be made in advance, the recipe doubles easily, and it holds well, making it a great choice for large supper parties.

**Preparation Time:** 2 hours 30 minutes (including making sauces)

**Cooking Time:** 1 hour

■ **Crepes**

4 eggs
1⅓ cups flour
1½ teaspoons salad oil
¼ teaspoon salt
1⅓ cups milk
½ to ¾ cup water

■ **Filling**

4 eggs
2 pounds ricotta cheese
1 pound frozen spinach, thawed, chopped fine, and
    squeezed dry
⅓ cup freshly grated Parmesan cheese (about 1½
    ounces)
¾ cup grated mozzarella cheese (3 ounces)
1 teaspoon grated nutmeg
½ teaspoon salt
½ teaspoon pepper
2 cups marinara sauce (page 224; can be made
    several days ahead)
¼ teaspoon grated nutmeg
1½ cups béchamel sauce (page 219; can be made 2
    days ahead)
¼ cup freshly grated Parmesan cheese (about 1
    ounce)

1. **To prepare crepe batter:** Place 4 eggs in a large bowl and whisk until thoroughly mixed but not foamy.

2. Add flour, oil, salt, and milk. Mix thoroughly and add water to bring to consistency of heavy cream.

3. Cover and allow to rest in refrigerator for 1 hour. (While batter is resting, prepare filling, marinara, and béchamel.)

4. **To prepare filling:** In a large mixing bowl, combine 4 eggs, ricotta cheese, spinach, ⅓ cup Parmesan cheese, mozzarella cheese, nutmeg, salt, and pepper; mix thoroughly. Cover and keep refrigerated until you are ready to fill crepes.

5. **To cook crepes:** Lightly oil a well-seasoned 8-inch crepe pan or small nonstick skillet and heat over high heat. (If pan is well-seasoned or nonstick, it should not be necessary to oil it between each crepe; otherwise, oil pan lightly as needed.)

6. When pan is quite hot, ladle or pour in about 1 ounce (2 tablespoons) batter, quickly tilting pan to cover bottom evenly with a very thin coat of batter. Cook briefly, just until set, then carefully flip and cook briefly until slightly browned on other side. Remove from pan and repeat until all batter is used.

7. **To fill crepes:** Place ¼ cup filling in center of each crepe. Fold bottom edge up over filling, fold each side edge in, then roll over onto remaining edge to form a neat oblong package.

8. **To assemble:** Preheat oven to 350°F and set rack in center.

9. Place filled crepes in a buttered 15- by 10-inch ovenproof casserole. Spread marinara sauce evenly over crepes. Stir nutmeg into béchamel and pour sauce down center of dish. Sprinkle with ¼ cup Parmesan cheese.

10. Bake for 45 minutes, or until bubbly and heated through. Remove from oven and serve at once.

**Yield: 6 to 8 servings**

**NOTE:**
Filling can be refrigerated for up to 2 days, or wrapped well and frozen at this point.

**NOTE:**
Unfilled crepes may be well wrapped and frozen for future use at this point.

**NOTE:**
Crepes may be filled and frozen at step 7. However, don't freeze crepes filled with previously frozen filling.

**"The first blini is always a mess."**
**—Russian Proverb**

# PART 2

# FROM THE BAKERY

Bald Eagles

Bald Eagles—Just ninety miles north of Juneau, in the Chil-kat Valley, is one of the world's largest nesting grounds for the bald eagle. Eagles are common sights in the Juneau area, soaring high above the coastline.

# BREADS

(INCLUDING YEAST AND QUICK BREADS, COFFEE CAKES, AND MUFFINS)

## From the Bakery

■ ■ ■

*I was fortunate to be one of the founders of the Fiddlehead Restaurant and Bakery when it opened in the summer of 1978. The Fiddlehead R&B was rather hit and miss that summer, but it was in those earliest months that our old standbys were created . . . those delicious specialties that I can still find when I visit the restaurant more than ten years later: ginger crinkles, chocolate mousse, fantasy cookies, honey-oatmeal bread, and more. Some measure of success certainly lies in the thirteen-year history of these goodies. I remember dedicated early patrons whose compliments and suggestions bestowed on us the highest of honors: Our breads and pastries were becoming habit-forming!*

*We were filling an often rainy and sometimes dismal corner of the earth with crusty breads, chewy cookies, and a warm place to duck into on a wet fall afternoon for a bowl of hearty soup and a chunk of fresh bread. Then there were rare crystal-blue hot summer days when we were young enough to close the doors and hang a "gone fishing" sign out, in order to swim and play on Juneau's beautiful beaches.*

*I have moved on to another occupation in the intervening years, but there are times when working through the wee hours of the night with warm living breads pressing their way —round and brown—out of the pans, seems enviable and is missed, as are those early fellow occupants of the night kitchen: Peg Malone Strader, Martha Covington Hopson, and Laura Lucas. It is good to be able to visit the wonderful place where all of this began, to sit and have a pot of tea and a Fantasy.*

—Lydia Marshall

# ON MAKING BREAD

Bread is such an elemental food that it has come to symbolize health, happiness, prosperity, and even life itself. Making bread satisfies as surely as eating bread does: The leisurely uncomplicated pace soothes and calms the mind while the physical process exercises the body. The aroma of baking bread warms as well as a wood stove in December, and a freshly baked loaf with butter makes a meal.

### ▉ The Basics of Bread Baking

Simple bread is made from four ingredients:

**For 1 loaf**
Yeast  1 tablespoon dry yeast
Water  1 to 1½ cups
Salt  1 to 2 teaspoons
Flour  3 to 3¾ cups, depending on the flour

All other ingredients are embellishments.

**Yeast** makes the bread rise. It is alive, made of tiny organisms that consume starches and sugars to produce carbon dioxide, which leavens the bread, and alcohol, which evaporates.

Yeast is available in compressed or dried forms, which are different strains of the same species, or as sourdough, which is closely related but not the same. (See the notes on sourdough on page 230.) Dried and compressed yeasts keep well frozen or in the refrigerator.

Like all living things, yeast does its best if it is well treated:

▉
    Reconstitute it in warm water between 105°F and 110°F. Temperatures over 115°F will kill it, below 100°F will slow it down.

▉
    Give it starches and sugars to eat. Just a teaspoon of honey or sugar mixed with the water will greatly encourage it.

▉
    Let bread dough rise at about 80°F. Yeast works faster at higher temperatures, but also produces some unpleasant aromas and flavors, and makes the dough stickier and harder to work.

**Water** combines with the starches and proteins in flour to give bread elasticity.

The amount and type of minerals found in your water will affect your bread, usually not significantly.

Many people save the water from boiling potatoes to use when making bread because of the extra starch it contains.

**Salt** gives bread flavor. It also controls the activity of the yeast, preventing it from going wild, and interacts with the flour to strengthen the dough. While too much salt results in a dense, tough loaf, no salt causes a loose, poorly textured, and flavorless loaf.

**Flour** gives bread its substance and character. Wheat flour is unique because, combined with water, its proteins develop into gluten, the substance that enables a dough to capture and stretch with the gases produced by the yeast. Of all the grains, only wheat forms gluten strong enough to support raised breads.

White flour makes the lightest, most finely textured raised bread. Bread made from 100 percent whole wheat flour rises slowly and not so loftily as bread made from white flour because the germ and bran of the grain, included in whole wheat flour, interfere in the development of gluten.

Wheat flours vary in the amount of protein, starch, and moisture they contain because of variations in strains of wheat and growing conditions, and therefore in the way they react as part of the bread dough. Most recipes give an approximation of the amounts needed: Because of the inexact nature of flour, it is very difficult to say precisely how much you'll need. For this reason, add the last bit of flour gradually to a dough, just until the right consistency is reached.

## ■ The Embellishments

**Shortening, butter, or oil** enriches a bread, giving it tenderness, flavor, and moistness.

Improve a simple loaf of bread with just a tablespoon of oil or butter. Dinner rolls call for almost 1 tablespoon of butter for each cup of flour, and breakfast pastries such as brioche, croissant, or Danish have as much as 4 tablespoons of butter for every cup of flour.

**Milk** gives bread a finer, richer quality and adds nutritional value.

Substitute milk for water in a bread recipe or stir in powdered milk solids. Scald the milk to alter the milk proteins, which affect the flour proteins, and cool it, to avoid killing the yeast, before adding it to the dough.

**Eggs** add richness, flavor, and nutritional value, and give color to bread.

When you calculate how much flour you will need for a loaf, remember that the water in the egg will contribute to the amount of liquid in the dough. A *rough* equivalent is that 1 large egg adds 2 to 3 tablespoons (sometimes up to ¼ cup) of liquid.

**Sugar** speeds the activity of the yeast (although too much will inhibit it), keeps the loaf moist, adds flavor, and makes the crust brown.

Add a tablespoon or so of honey, granulated sugar, brown sugar, or molasses, depending upon the flavor you prefer.

Because sweetened doughs brown more quickly, bake them at a slightly lower temperature (depending upon the amount of sweetening, anywhere from 350°F to 375°F) to be sure they are completely baked before they are overly brown.

**Different flours** give the bread texture, flavor, nutritional value, and character. Experiment!

If you want to use predominantly a low-gluten flour in your bread, use the *sponge method* (explained below) for making the bread. Add any white flour or gluten flour called for in the recipe to the sponge and beat very well at that point to develop as much gluten as possible. After the sponge has risen, add the low-gluten flour and avoid kneading the dough at that point to minimize damage to the gluten developed from the white flour.

Flour that has had all the starch removed, called gluten flour, is available. You can add a small amount (¼ cup for every loaf) to whole wheat breads or others made from primarily low-gluten flours to give the bread lightness.

## Making Bread

In the process of making bread, you must do three things:

1. Activate the yeast and give it plenty of opportunity to multiply and develop throughout the dough, creating lots of gases to leaven the bread.

2. Thoroughly knead the dough to distribute the yeast and create the three-dimensional structure that captures, and expands with, the gases the yeast produces.

3. Bake the bread at the right temperature so the dough solidifies at the same time the gases expand to their greatest volume.

**The sponge method** gives the yeast a head start: Soften yeast in the liquid and knead in a small amount of flour to create a very soft "sponge." Let the sponge rise, giving the yeast an opportunity to multiply rapidly and become lively and well distributed throughout the dough. After the dough has doubled, add remaining ingredients to finish the dough, then let it rise once or twice more.

**The straight method** is faster: Soften yeast, then add all remaining ingredients and knead thoroughly. Allow dough to rise at least once, twice if you can.

Both methods work well. We recommend using the sponge method for breads with lots of whole wheat flour or other low-gluten flours such as rye, buckwheat, or oat.

**Kneading** aerates the dough and develops the gluten in the flour. This creates the sturdy gridwork of protein strands that expands and holds the gases produced by the yeast. A well-kneaded dough is springy, smooth, and only slightly sticky to the touch. Kneading is accomplished efficiently in 10 minutes by an electric mixer fitted with a dough hook; kneading by hand takes longer—15 to 30 minutes—but is more intimately satisfying.

It is possible to overknead a bread dough, breaking down the gluten structure and resulting in a soggy mess. It's not likely this will happen if you are kneading by hand, but if you use a food processor or electric mixer to knead the dough, do not be over-zealous.

While good bread requires lots of kneading, pie crusts, cakes, biscuits, and cookies should be light, tender, and delicate. Too much mixing or kneading develops the gluten, making them tough and chewy.

**Rising** is the time for the yeast to do its work. Choose a draft-free, warmish (80°F) spot, such as the top of your refrigerator, or an oven that has been preheated to warm and turned off, with a cup of water on the bottom to make it a little steamy. (Is the television always on at your house? That's a good spot too.) Let the yeast multiply and produce carbon dioxide.

The dough has finished rising when it does not spring back when you poke it gently to a depth of ½ to 1 inch. Punch it down and let it rise again if you have the time, or form it into loaves. (The second rising will be much faster than the first, because there is more yeast at work in the dough.)

Allowing the dough to rise more than once distributes the yeast through the dough more thoroughly, creating a finer, more delicately textured bread.

Once you have formed the loaf, allow it to "proof," or rise, until doubled in size, but not to its limit: The loaf will rise in the oven and needs room to accommodate that expansion.

**Baking** kills the yeast, expands the gases, cooks the dough, and gives you the best, most basic, and wonderful of foods: homemade bread.

Plain doughs bake best at 400°F to 425°F, sweet doughs at 350°F to 375°F. Traditionally, the baker is instructed to tap the bottom of the loaf to test for doneness. If it sounds hollow, the loaf is ready. Trust yourself to know this sound. An underbaked loaf will feel heavy and soggy, and when tapped will sound dull and thick because, in fact, it is still liquid in the center. The fully baked loaf will feel light, the crust will look crispy, and the sound will seem to travel right through the loaf. If you are unsure, bake the bread just a little longer.

There are those who recommend letting freshly baked bread cool before slicing it. This is practical advice, but not sensible: Get out the butter!

---

### Flour

■ ■ ■

*We use organically grown, naturally aged, unbleached, non-bromated flours for all our baked goods. While you will obtain good results from the all-purpose flours available around the country, if you become a baking enthusiast, you will probably notice and appreciate the differences in flours. We heartily recommend searching out sources for high-quality, freshly milled flours, for your breads especially. Our customers seem to agree.*

---

# HERB BREAD

This bread makes *wonderful* grilled cheese sandwiches.

**Preparation and Kneading Time:**  30 minutes

**Rising Time:**  1 hour 30 minutes to 2 hours

**Baking Time:**  35 minutes

> 2 tablespoons chopped green onions (2 small) or fresh chives
> 3 tablespoons minced fresh parsley (or 3 teaspoons dried)
> 1½ teaspoons dried basil
> 1 teaspoon dried oregano or marjoram
> 1½ cups warm water (110°F)
> ½ cup milk, scalded and cooled to room temperature
> 2 tablespoons honey
> 2 tablespoons dry yeast (2 packages)
> 4 cups unbleached white flour (plus up to ½ cup as needed)
> 1 cup whole wheat flour
> 2 tablespoons safflower oil
> 1 tablespoon olive oil
> 1 tablespoon salt

1. Combine green onions, parsley, and dried herbs. Chop them together until fairly uniformly sized, then set them aside.

2. In a large mixing bowl or the bowl of an electric mixer fitted with a dough hook, combine warm water, milk, honey, and dry yeast. Allow to sit, or "bloom," for 5 minutes, until yeast is bubbling.

3. Add mixed herbs, white flour, whole wheat flour, oils, and salt to yeast mixture. Stir well and knead for 10 minutes. (If necessary add a little additional white flour until dough comes cleanly away from bowl or work surface and is just slightly sticky to the touch.)

4. Place in a large, well-oiled bowl, turning dough so that it becomes lightly oiled on all sides. Cover loosely and set in a warm spot to rise until doubled in bulk and dough does not spring back when lightly touched.

5. Punch down. If you have time, allow dough to rise until doubled again. (It will take half the time of the first rising.)

6. Cut dough into two equal parts. Knead each into a smooth ball and allow to rest for 5 minutes.

7. Lightly oil two 8- or 9-inch bread pans. Preheat oven to 375°F and place rack in lower third of oven.

8. Flatten each ball into a 12- by 8- by 1½-inch rectangle. Beginning from narrow ends, roll up tightly, jelly-roll fashion, tuck in ends, pinch seams together, and place, seam down, in oiled bread pans. Cover loosely and let dough rise in a warm place until doubled in bulk, or until slightly higher than edge of pan.

9. Bake for 30 to 35 minutes, until golden brown on top and hollow sounding when tapped on bottom.

10. Remove from oven, turn out onto racks to cool, or serve at once. When cooled, wrap any uneaten bread and store at room temperature for 1 or 2 days, or freeze to eat later.

**Yield: 2 loaves**

---

### Mincing Parsley

■ ■ ■

*Parsley contains large amounts of chlorophyll, a natural breath freshener, which is why it is welcome after highly seasoned meals. When you chop parsley to sprinkle over a dish or to dry for later use, the chlorophyll is released and makes the minced leaves stick together in clumps. To mince parsley and clean it so it is fluffy and pretty:*

*1. Separate parsley leaves from stems; freeze stems to use in stocks.*
*2. Using a chef's knife, chop leaves until they are very fine. You can do this in a food processor if you are pressed for time, but the results will not be as fine as hand-chopped parsley.*
*3. Place minced leaves in center of a clean white cotton napkin or several layers of cheesecloth and bring up the corners to create a little pouch with parsley inside.*
*4. Run cold water through pouch, squeezing water out, until it runs almost clear. This removes most of the chlorophyll.*
*5. Remove from running water and squeeze pouch as dry as possible, open, and transfer fluffy minced parsley to a small container.*
*6. If you will not use the parsley within a couple of days, spread it on a cookie sheet lined with waxed paper and set in a warm, undisturbed place (on top of your refrigerator or in a warm oven) overnight to dry. To dry in a microwave, spread on paper towels and cook on full power, uncovered, for about 4 minutes. Store in jars.*

# HONEY-BUTTER-OATMEAL BREAD

The honey in this bread keeps it moist, the butter makes it tender, and the oats fill it with goodness. We love it for sandwiches, toast, or just plain bread and butter.

**Preparation and Kneading Time:** 30 minutes

**Rising Time:** 2 hours to 2 hours 30 minutes

**Baking Time:** 30 to 35 minutes

> 1 cup buttermilk
> 1 tablespoon dry yeast (1 package)
> 3 tablespoons honey
> 2 tablespoons butter, melted
> 1½ teaspoons salt
> ⅔ cup old-fashioned rolled oats
> 2½ cups unbleached white flour
> 1 tablespoon butter, melted (optional)

1. Warm buttermilk to lukewarm and place in a large mixing bowl or bowl of an electric mixer fitted with a dough hook. Add yeast and honey. Allow it to sit, or "bloom," for 3 to 5 minutes, until yeast is bubbling and active.

2. Add remaining ingredients and mix thoroughly, kneading for 10 minutes. If necessary, add small amounts of additional flour until dough forms a soft ball that comes cleanly away from edges of bowl, or no longer sticks to your hands.

3. Place dough in a large well-oiled mixing bowl, turning dough so that it becomes lightly oiled on all sides. Cover loosely and let sit in a warm spot until doubled in bulk and dough does not spring back when lightly touched.

4. Punch down. If you have time, allow dough to rise until doubled again. (It will take half the time of the first rising.)

5. Turn out dough onto a very lightly floured surface and knead into a smooth ball. Allow to rest 5 minutes.

6. Preheat oven to 375°F and place rack in lower third of oven. Oil an 8- or 9-inch loaf pan.

7. Flatten dough, by hand or with a rolling pin, into a 12- by 8- by 1½-inch-thick rectangle. Beginning from narrow end, roll up tightly, tuck in ends, pinch seam to-

gether, and place, seam down, in oiled loaf pan. Cover loosely and let dough rise in a warm place until doubled in bulk, or until slightly higher than edge of pan.

8. Optional: Using a sharp knife or razor, make a ¼-inch cut the length of the loaf and pour 1 tablespoon melted butter in cut.

9. Bake for 30 to 35 minutes, until golden brown on top and hollow sounding when tapped on bottom.

10. Remove from oven and turn out onto a rack to cool. When cooled, wrap well and store at room temperature or freeze to eat later.

**Yield: 1 loaf**

NOTE:
This recipe can be doubled, but not tripled. The amount of flour may vary.

If thou of fortune be bereft,
And in thy store there be but left
Two loaves—sell one, and with the dole
Buy hyacinths to feed the soul.
    —*James Terry White*

# ONION BUNS

It's worth baking these for the aroma alone. These make terrific hamburger buns or dinner rolls: Just shape the dough to suit your needs.

**Preparation and Kneading Time:**  30 minutes

**Rising Time:**  2 hours

**Baking Time:**  20 minutes

    2½ cups warm water
    2 tablespoons dry yeast (2 packages)
    ¼ cup honey
    4 cups unbleached white flour
    2 cups whole wheat flour
    ½ cup small-diced onions (½ medium onion)
    ¼ cup safflower oil
    1 tablespoon salt
    1 to 1¼ additional cups white flour only as needed
    Cornmeal
    2 eggs, beaten well
    ¼ cup untoasted sesame seeds

1. In a large mixing bowl or the bowl of an electric mixer fitted with a dough hook, combine water, yeast, and honey. Allow to sit for 3 to 5 minutes until active and bubbly.

2. Stir in 4 cups white flour, whole wheat flour, onions, oil, and salt. Knead for 10 minutes, until dough forms a smooth, springy ball that comes away from edges of bowl cleanly or no longer sticks to your hands. Add additional white flour only as needed to bring dough together into a ball.

3. Place in a large, well-oiled bowl, turning dough so that it becomes lightly oiled on all sides. Cover loosely and set in a warm spot to rise until doubled in bulk and dough does not spring back when lightly touched. Punch down. If you have time, allow dough to rise until doubled again. (It will take half the time of the first rising.)

4. Lightly oil 3 cookie sheets. Dust with cornmeal if you like.

5. Turn dough out onto a lightly floured surface and knead into a smooth ball. Cover loosely and let rest for 5 minutes. To make hamburger buns, roll into a long rope and cut into 18 equal pieces. Knead each piece into a

smooth ball. Using a rolling pin or your hand, flatten each ball to a ¾-inch pancake, and place on cookie sheets. These may also be formed into your favorite dinner roll shape.

6. Preheat oven to 350°F. and place racks in upper and lower thirds of oven.

7. Let buns rise until doubled, then brush with beaten egg, and sprinkle with sesame seeds. Bake for 15 to 20 minutes, until golden brown and hollow sounding when tapped on bottom.

8. Remove from oven and arrange in baskets to eat immediately, or transfer to racks to cool. Wrap tightly and store at room temperature or freeze for later use.

**Yield: 18 3-inch burger buns or 24 dinner rolls**

"God is in the details."
—*Mies van der Rohe*

# ORANGE-MACE-RAISIN BREAD

Toasted and spread with cream cheese, this bread is *so* good. Full of whole wheat goodness, scented with oranges and mace, and sweetened with plump raisins, this is a bread for special days.

**Preparation and Kneading Time:**   30 minutes

**Rising Time:**   2 to 2½ hours

**Baking Time:**   35 minutes

   2 tablespoons molasses
   1⅓ cups warm water
   1 tablespoon dry yeast (1 package)
   ½ cup raisins
   ¼ teaspoon powdered mace
   ½ teaspoon freshly grated orange peel
   1⅓ cups whole wheat flour
   ¾ cup unbleached white flour
   1½ teaspoons salt
   2 tablespoons safflower oil
   1 to 1⅓ cups whole wheat flour

1. In a large bowl or the bowl of an electric mixer fitted with a dough hook, dissolve molasses in warm water, stir in yeast, and allow to sit, or "bloom," for 5 minutes.

2. When yeast is bubbly and active, stir in raisins, mace, and orange peel. Beat in 1⅓ cups whole wheat flour and ¾ cup white flour. Beat for 10 minutes.

3. Cover loosely and let sit in a warm place for ½ hour.

4. Add salt, oil, and 1 cup whole wheat flour. Knead until dough forms a smooth ball that comes cleanly away from edges of bowl or no longer sticks to your hands. (Add remaining ⅓ cup whole wheat flour only as needed to finish dough.)

5. Place in a large well-oiled bowl, turning dough so that it becomes lightly oiled on all sides. Cover loosely and set in a warm, draft-free spot to rise until doubled in bulk. (Rising time will vary depending upon the type of yeast you use and how warm the dough is. Plan on 1 to 1½ hours for the first rising.)

6. Punch down. If you have time, allow dough to rise until doubled again. (It will take half the time of the first rising.)

7. Turn out dough onto a lightly floured surface and knead into a neat ball by pressing edges into center. Turn ball upside down and allow to rest for 5 to 10 minutes.

8. Preheat oven to 375°F and place rack in lower third of oven. Lightly oil an 8- or 9-inch bread pan.

9. Using your hand or a rolling pin, flatten dough into a 12- by 8- by 1½-inch-thick rectangle. Beginning from narrow end, roll up tightly, tuck in ends, pinch seam together, and place, seam down, in oiled bread pan. Cover loosely and let dough rise in a warm place until it is about an inch above the rim of the pan (about ½ hour).

10. Bake for 35 minutes, until browned on top and hollow sounding when tapped on bottom when removed from pan. Remove from oven and place on a rack to cool. Serve at once, or keep tightly wrapped at room temperature and use to make great toast. The loaf may be frozen to eat later.

**Yield: 1 loaf**

# DARK PUMPERNICKEL BREAD

Dark, chewy, and savory with caraway, this loaf goes well with a bit of ham and mustard, a selection of good cheeses, and some fresh fruit.

**Preparation and Kneading Time:** 30 minutes

**Rising Time:** 2 hours to 2 hours 30 minutes

**Baking Time:** 35 minutes

> 1½ cups warm water
> 6 tablespoons molasses
> 1½ tablespoons dry yeast (1½ packages)
> 3 tablespoons unsweetened cocoa
> 1¾ cups rye flour
> 1 cup unbleached white flour
> ¾ cup whole wheat flour
> 1½ tablespoons oil
> 1½ tablespoons caraway seeds
> ¾ tablespoon salt
> 2 tablespoons finely chopped onion (optional)
> ⅓ to ½ cup cup unbleached white flour as needed
> Cornmeal
> 1 egg
> 1 tablespoon water

1. Place water in a large mixing bowl or the bowl of an electric mixer fitted with a dough hook and dissolve molasses in it. Add dry yeast and allow to sit, or "bloom," for 3 to 5 minutes, until it is bubbling and active.

2. Stir in cocoa, then add rye flour and 1 cup white flour. Beat until smooth and allow to rise for 30 minutes in a warm spot.

3. Add whole wheat flour, oil, caraway seeds, salt, and optional onion. Knead for 10 minutes, until dough forms a smooth, spongy ball, slightly sticky to the touch. Add additional white flour only as needed to bring dough together. Place in a large well-oiled bowl, turning dough so that it becomes lightly oiled on all sides. Cover loosely and let sit in a warm spot until doubled in bulk and dough does not spring back when lightly touched.

4. Punch down. If you have time, allow dough to rise until doubled again. (It will take half the time of the first rising.)

5. Turn out dough onto a very lightly floured surface and

knead into a smooth ball. Cover loosely and let rest for 5 minutes.

6. Lightly oil a large cookie sheet. Sprinkle with cornmeal. Preheat oven to 350°F.

7. Roll or pat dough into a 12- by 8- by 1½-inch-thick rectangle. Beginning from narrow end, roll up tightly, tuck in ends, pinch seam together, and roll lightly to even out the loaf. Place loaf, seam down, on cookie sheet. Cover loosely and let rise in a warm spot until doubled in bulk.

8. Beat egg with water and brush over loaf. Using a very sharp knife or kitchen shears, make 3 diagonal cuts in top of loaf. Bake for 35 to 40 minutes, until loaf is crusty and hollow sounding when tapped on bottom. Remove from oven and place on a rack to cool. Wrap tightly and store at room temperature or freeze to eat later.

**Yield: 1 loaf or 2 cocktail loaves**

---

### Swirl Bread

■ ■ ■

*Charm your children with sandwiches made of bread that looks like a pinwheel:*

**1.** *Make doughs of honey-butter-oatmeal bread (page 142) and of dark pumpernickel bread (opposite).*

**2.** *When doughs are ready to be shaped into loaves, cut each in half. Knead all four lumps into smooth balls and allow to rest for 5 minutes.*

**3.** *Preheat oven to 375°F and place rack in lower third of oven. Lightly oil two 8- or 9-inch bread pans.*

**4.** *Using a rolling pin, roll out each ball of dough into a 12- by 8- by ¾-inch-thick rectangle.*

**5.** *Mix 1 egg with 1 tablespoon water and brush lightly onto honey-butter-oatmeal rectangle. Set dark pumpernickel dough on top of honey-butter-oatmeal dough and pat gently to join the two doughs. Beginning from narrow end, roll up tightly, jelly-roll fashion, pinch seam together, and place, seam down, in oiled bread pan. Repeat procedure with remaining two balls of dough.*

**6.** *Refrigerate remaining egg mixture.*

**7.** *Cover loaves loosely and allow to rise until doubled in bulk, or until about 1 inch higher than edge of pan (about ½ hour). Brush tops of loaves with reserved egg mix and bake until crusty and brown, 35 to 40 minutes. Remove from oven, turn out onto racks to cool, wrap tightly, and store at room temperature or freeze to eat later.*

**Yield: 2 loaves**

# SOURDOUGH FRENCH BREAD

Set the starter the evening before you plan to bake. If you use fast-acting yeast to supplement the action of the starter, the bread will be ready in 3 hours. If you rely on sourdough starter alone, start the bread in the morning in order to finish by supper. Rising times depend on how vigorous your starter is and how warm the dough is.

**Starter Time:** overnight

**Preparation and Kneading Time:** 30 minutes

**Rising Time:** 2 to 2½ hours (4 to 5 hours if you omit the dry yeast)

**Baking Time:** 30 minutes

### ■ Bread Starter

¼ cup sourdough starter (recipe and notes page 230)
1 cup unbleached white flour
1 cup warm water

### ■ To Replenish Starter Pot

½ cup sourdough starter (recipe and notes page 230)
1 cup water
1 cup unbleached white flour

### ■ Bread Dough

1 teaspoon dry yeast (⅓ package)
¼ cup warm water
1 teaspoon honey
1 teaspoon salt
2 cups plus ⅓ cup unbleached white flour
½ cup whole wheat flour
Cornmeal
1 egg
1 tablespoon water
Sesame or poppy seeds

**NOTE:**
Omit ¼ cup warm water, yeast, and honey if you want to rely on your sourdough starter alone to raise the bread. Skip step 4.

1. **To start bread:** Combine ¼ cup starter, 1 cup white flour, and 1 cup warm water in a large glass, ceramic, or clean wooden bowl. Stir to mix well.

2. **To replenish starter pot:** Combine ½ cup starter, 1 cup water, and 1 cup white flour in your starter pot and mix well.

3. Cover both bread starter and starter pot and allow to sit at room temperature overnight. Refrigerate starter pot in the morning.

4. **To complete bread:** In a large mixing bowl or the bowl of an electric mixer fitted with a dough hook, dissolve yeast in ¼ cup warm water. Add honey. Allow to sit for 2 to 5 minutes, until it has "bloomed" and is actively bubbling.

5. Stir in bread starter. Add salt, 2 cups white flour, and whole wheat flour. Knead until dough forms a soft, springy ball that comes cleanly away from bowl or table. (This dough may seem a little stickier than other bread doughs.) Add additional white flour only as needed. Knead for 10 minutes.

6. Liberally oil a large mixing bowl and place dough in it, turning dough so that it becomes lightly oiled on all sides. Cover loosely and let sit in a warm, draft-free spot until doubled in bulk, or until dough does not spring back when lightly touched.

7. Punch down. If you have time, allow dough to rise until doubled again. (It will take half the time of the first rising.)

8. Turn out dough onto a lightly floured surface and knead into a smooth ball. Allow to rest for 5 minutes.

9. Preheat oven to 400°F and place rack in lower third of oven.

10. Lightly oil a cookie sheet and dust with cornmeal. Pat dough into a 12- by 8- by 1½-inch-thick rectangle. Beginning from narrow end, roll up tightly, pinch seam together, and place, seam down, on cookie sheet. Cover loosely with a clean cloth, place in a warm spot, and allow to rise until doubled.

11. Whisk together egg and 1 tablespoon water. With a sharp knife, razor, or kitchen shears, cut 3 diagonal slices in top of loaf. Brush loaf with beaten egg and sprinkle with sesame or poppy seeds.

12. Bake for 20 to 30 minutes, until crusty brown on top and bottom, and hollow sounding when tapped on bottom. Remove from oven, transfer to a rack to cool, and wrap well. Store at room temperature for up to 2 days, or freeze to store longer.

**Yield: 1 loaf**

# SUNFLOWER-MILLET BREAD

Inspired by *The Tassajara Bread Book*, Joan Daniels of Bird Creek created this wonderful bread for the Bread Factory in Anchorage. Deborah Marshall loved it so much she brought the recipe with her when she opened the Fiddlehead. We love this whole wheat bread and serve it every day at the Fiddlehead. It takes a little longer to rise than other breads, but the result is a light, chewy, flavorful loaf studded with sunflower seeds and tiny golden grains of millet. Toast it, serve it with cheese or soup, or use it for sandwiches: Its nutty goodness makes even the simplest meal quite satisfying.

**Preparation Time:** 30 minutes

**Rising Time:** 3 hours

**Baking Time:** 30 to 35 minutes

> 2 tablespoons dry yeast (2 packages)
> 2 cups warm water (100–115°F)
> ¼ cup honey
> ½ cup millet (available in health food stores*)
> ½ cup unsalted sunflower seeds (available in health food stores*)
> 1 cup unbleached white flour
> 2 cups whole wheat flour
> 1 tablespoon salt
> 3 tablespoons safflower oil
> 2½ cups plus ½ cup whole wheat flour

1. In a large mixing bowl or the bowl of an electric mixer fitted with a dough hook, sprinkle yeast over warm water. Allow to "bloom" for 5 minutes, until yeast is active and bubbly.

2. Add honey, millet, sunflower seeds, and white flour. Mix thoroughly until batter is smooth. Add 2 cups whole wheat flour and beat for 10 minutes.

3. Cover loosely with a clean, damp towel. Set in a warm, draft-free place and allow to rise until doubled in bulk, about 30 minutes.

4. Add salt, oil, and 2½ cups whole wheat flour. Knead together until dough forms a smooth, springy, soft ball that comes cleanly away from bowl or table. Add additional flour by tablespoons only as needed.

5. Liberally oil a large bowl and place dough in it, turning dough so that it becomes lightly oiled on all sides. Cover

loosely and let sit in a warm spot until doubled in bulk and the dough does not spring back when lightly touched.

6. Preheat oven to 400°F and place rack in lower third of oven. Oil two 8- or 9-inch loaf pans.

7. Punch down dough. Turn out onto a lightly floured surface and cut in half. Form each half into a smooth ball by gently kneading outer edges into center. Allow to rest 5 minutes. Form each ball into a loaf by flattening dough into a 12- by 8- by 1½-inch-thick rectangle. Beginning from narrow end, roll up tightly, pinch seam closed, and place, seam down, in loaf pan. Cover loosely and allow to rise until doubled in bulk, or until slightly higher than edges of pans.

8. Bake for 30 minutes, until golden brown and hollow sounding when tapped on bottom. Remove from oven and turn out onto racks to cool. When cooled, wrap tightly and store at room temperature for up to 2 days, or freeze for future use.

**Yield: 2 loaves**

**\*See mail-order sources, page 237.**

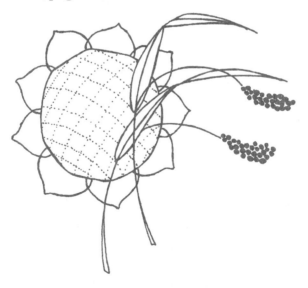

# WHOLE WHEAT—BRAN BREAD

Terrie Sollie, a talented Fiddlehead baker, perfected this good chewy bread. The sponge method of bread making gives this loaf extra lightness.

**Preparation and Kneading Time:** 30 minutes

**Rising Time:** 2 hours to 2 hours 30 minutes

**Baking Time:** 35 minutes

> 1 tablespoon molasses
> 1⅓ cups warm water
> 1 tablespoon dry yeast (1 package)
> 1⅓ cups white flour
> 1 teaspoon salt
> 1 tablespoon safflower oil
> 1 cup whole wheat flour
> ¼ cup unbleached white flour
> ¼ cup bran

1. In a large mixing bowl or the bowl of an electric mixer fitted with a dough hook, dissolve molasses in warm water and add dry yeast. Allow to "bloom" for 5 minutes, until yeast is active and bubbly.

2. Add 1⅓ cups flour and beat for 10 minutes.

3. Cover loosely and set in a warm place for ½ hour.

4. Add salt, oil, whole wheat flour, white flour, and bran. Mix together and knead until dough forms a smooth ball that comes cleanly away from bowl and is no longer sticky to the touch. Try to knead as little as possible after adding bran. (Add additional flour slowly if needed.)

5. Generously oil a large bowl and place dough in it, turning dough so that it becomes lightly oiled on all sides. Set in a warm, draft-free place and allow to rise until doubled in bulk and the dough does not spring back when lightly touched.

6. Punch down dough. If you have time, allow bread to rise until doubled again. (It will take half the time of the first rising.)

7. Turn out dough onto a lightly floured work surface and knead into a smooth ball. Allow to rest 5 minutes.

8. Preheat oven to 350°F and place rack in lower third of oven. Lightly oil an 8- or 9-inch loaf pan.

9. Flatten dough, by hand or with a rolling pin, into a 12- by 8- by 1½-inch-thick rectangle. Beginning from narrow end, roll up tightly, pinch seam together, and place, seam down, in loaf pan.

10. Allow dough to rise until doubled, until it no longer springs back enthusiastically when gently poked.

11. Bake for 35 minutes, or until hollow sounding when tapped on bottom. Remove from oven, turn out of pan, and cool on a rack. If you have managed to avoid eating the bread immediately, store the loaf tightly wrapped in plastic at room temperature. If you will be unable to eat the bread within 2 days or so, wrap it well and freeze to eat later in the week.

**Yield: 1 loaf**

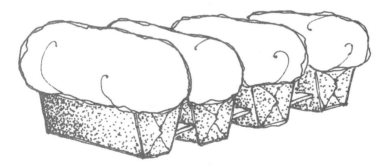

# HONEY-YOGURT SCONES

Claudia Coyner, a gracefully artistic Fiddlehead baker, perfected these delightfully buttery and delicious scones.

**Preparation Time:** 15 minutes

**Baking Time:** 15 minutes

    4 tablespoons butter
    1 tablespoon honey
    ½ cup plain yogurt (substitute sour cream or
        buttermilk if necessary)
    1 egg
    1¾ cups unbleached white flour (for delicious nutty
        flavor, decrease to 1½ cups flour and add ¼ cup
        graham flour)
    ½ teaspoon baking powder
    ½ teaspoon baking soda
    ¼ teaspoon salt
    ¼ cup dried currants, dried cherries,* pecans, or
        raisins
    1 egg, beaten (optional)

1. Preheat oven to 400°F and place rack in center of oven.

2. Melt together butter and honey in a small glass bowl in microwave, or in a small pan on stove over medium heat. Remove from heat and whisk in yogurt and egg.

3. In a medium-size mixing bowl, sift together flour, baking powder, baking soda, and salt. Stir in currants.

4. Pour egg mixture over flour mixture and, using a fork, very gently cut together just until dough is beginning to come together but is not quite completely combined.

5. Turn out onto a lightly floured surface and gently pat into a 6-inch circle. Fold dough in half and pat out again. Repeat two to three more times, taking care not to overwork or knead dough.

6. Pat into a 1-inch-thick circle (about 6 inches in diameter) and cut into 6 wedges.

7. Place on an ungreased baking pan. Brush lightly with beaten egg (optional) and bake for 12 to 15 minutes, until puffed and golden brown.

8. Remove from oven and serve immediately with lots of butter and homemade jam.

**\*See mail-order sources, page 237.**

**Yield: 6 scones**

# SOUR CREAM–BLUEBERRY COFFEE CAKE

Honey and sour cream combine to make a delectably moist and rich-tasting cake. The wild blueberries add a touch of sweet tartness.

**Preparation Time:** 30 minutes

**Baking Time:** 1 hour

> 1 cup honey
> ½ pound butter
> 6 eggs
> 1 cup sour cream
> 1 teaspoon vanilla extract
> 4 cups unbleached white flour
> 1 tablespoon baking powder
> ½ teaspoon baking soda
> ½ teaspoon salt
> 2 cups fresh wild blueberries (substitute fresh domestic berries, or frozen berries, defrosted and drained)

1. Preheat oven to 350°F and place rack in lower third of oven. Lightly coat a tube cake pan with butter and dust with flour. It is preferable to use one with a removable bottom.

2. In a large mixing bowl, and with an electric mixer set on high, cream honey and butter together until light and fluffy. Add eggs and beat well. Add sour cream and vanilla and beat well. (The batter will seem curdled.)

3. Sift together flour, baking powder, baking soda, and salt. Gently stir into butter mixture.

4. Fold in blueberries. Stir just to combine.

5. Spoon into cake pan, smoothing top of batter with a spatula. Bake for 1 hour, until a knife comes out clean when inserted into center of cake.

6. Remove from oven, run a knife around edge of cake, and remove from pan. Cool briefly on a rack before slicing. Serve warm with butter, or cool, wrap well, and store at room temperature overnight.

**Yield: 16 slices**

### Nagoonberries

■ ■ ■

*If you are hiking near Juneau in August, look carefully in the moss for a tiny, ankle-high plant bearing a single iridescent red raspberry. You may just find a nagoonberry, the jewel of all Alaskan berries.*

*They are virtually unknown outside Alaska and Scandinavia, where they are called honey berry, nectar berry, or arctic brambleberry; but within these northern borders the delicate taste of Rubus arcticus has inspired legends— and fantastic prices. Nagoonberry jelly, when you can get it, fetches up to ten dollars a jar in Juneau. (For mail-order sources, see page 237.)*

*Nagoonberries rarely fruit abundantly even though they are common throughout the circumpolar countries. Scientists have spent years probing their mysterious likes and dislikes, but so far the plants have defied all attempts at domestication. We hope they remain untamed forever.*

# CARDAMOM COFFEE CAKE

Riches untold! With this much butter, it has to be good. To the delight of our customers, we borrowed this spiced coffee cake from *The Moosewood Cookbook*, by Molly Katzen, and with her kind permission, share the recipe with you.

**Preparation Time:** 30 minutes

**Baking Time:** 1 hour 15 minutes

### ■ Nut Mixture

½ cup chopped walnuts
¼ cup brown sugar
1 tablespoon ground cinnamon

### ■ Cake

1 pound butter
2 cups granulated sugar
4 eggs
2 teaspoons vanilla extract
4 cups unbleached white flour
2 teaspoons baking soda
1½ teaspoons baking powder
1½ teaspoons ground cardamom
½ teaspoon salt
2 cups sour cream

1. Preheat oven to 350°F and place rack in lower third of oven. Lightly coat a tube or bundt cake pan with butter and dust with flour. (Don't use your angel food pan: The oil will ruin any future angel food cakes.)

2. **To prepare nut mixture:** Stir together walnuts, brown sugar, and cinnamon in a small bowl. Set aside.

3. **To prepare cake:** In a large mixing bowl, cream together butter and 2 cups sugar until light and fluffy. Beat in eggs and vanilla.

4. Sift together white flour, baking soda, baking powder, cardamom, and salt. Add to butter mixture alternately with sour cream. Stir just until mixture is combined, but do not overbeat. Dough will be soft and sticky.

5. Spoon one third of batter evenly into prepared pan. Sprinkle half of nut mixture over batter. Add one third more of batter and sprinkle with remaining nut mixture. Top with remaining batter. Smooth top of cake with a spatula.

**NOTE:**
On a visit to Vermont, we ate breakfast in a small café that served slices of this cake grilled in butter and drizzled with real maple syrup. Sheer decadence!

**6.** Bake for 1 hour 15 minutes, until a probe comes out clean and cake is golden brown. Remove from oven and cool for 10 minutes in pan. Run a knife around edge to loosen cake, then turn out onto a rack to cool. Serve slightly warm, or at room temperature. Store tightly wrapped, unrefrigerated.

**Yield: 16 pieces**

# RAISIN-BRAN MUFFINS

Enjoy these honey- and molasses-sweetened muffins in minutes every morning. The mix can be made up and kept in the refrigerator for up to a week.

**Preparation Time:** 15 minutes

**Baking Time:** 20 minutes

1¾ cups whole wheat pastry flour (available in health food stores*), or substitute whole wheat flour or whole wheat with a little white flour)
1¼ cups bran
1 tablespoon baking powder
¼ teaspoon baking soda
¼ teaspoon salt
5⅓ tablespoons butter or margarine, melted (⅓ cup)
1 egg
1¼ cups buttermilk (if you use powdered buttermilk, add ¼ cup dry buttermilk to flour, and 1¼ cups water with wet ingredients)
¼ cup honey
3 tablespoons molasses
¾ cup raisins

**1.** Preheat oven to 375°F and place rack in center of oven. Line a muffin tin with paper liners.

**2.** Whisk together flour, bran, baking powder, baking soda, and salt in a large bowl.

**3.** Whisk together butter, egg, buttermilk, honey, and molasses in a small bowl and pour over dry ingredients. With a few strokes of a spoon, stir together, then add raisins. Stir just until ingredients are combined. Avoid overbeating.

**4.** Spoon batter into muffin tins and bake 20 minutes, until puffed and lightly browned. Remove from oven and serve at once with butter and homemade jam.

NOTE:
**This muffin batter can be made in advance and kept refrigerated up to 1 week, until ready to bake.**

**Yield: 12 muffins**

**\*See mail-order sources, page 237.**

# FRUIT MUFFINS

This is the only muffin recipe you'll ever need: It is simple, good with almost every variety of fruit or nut, and delicious. As an added bonus, the basic mix makes a nice cobbler topping. Keep this recipe in your emergency file for those panic occasions when you need a quick and easy breakfast treat, lunch box snack, or dessert.

**Preparation Time:** 15 minutes

**Baking Time: (Muffins) 20 minutes**
**(Cobbler) 30 minutes**

■ **Basic Muffin Mix**

1¾ cups unbleached white flour (substitute ¼ cup
  graham or whole wheat flour for ¼ cup white flour if
  you like)
¼ to ½ cup granulated sugar (depending on your
  preference and whether this is dessert)
2 teaspoons baking powder
½ teaspoon salt
4 tablespoons butter, melted
2 eggs
¾ cup milk
2 to 2½ cups fruit (see following suggestions)

■ **Fruit Muffins**

1. Preheat oven to 400°F and place rack in center of oven.
   Line a muffin tin with 12 paper cups.

2. Sift together flour, sugar, baking powder, and salt in a
   large bowl. (Measure sugar to match your taste and
   intentions.)

3. Whisk together butter, eggs, and milk in a small bowl.
   Pour liquid ingredients into dry ingredients. Stir together
   with as few strokes of the spoon as possible, just until
   most of the dry ingredients are wet. (The batter will
   seem kind of lumpy.)

4. Add 2 to 2½ cups fruit and the flavoring you'd like. (Combinations are suggested below.) Stir just to combine
   and spoon into 12 lined muffin cups. Bake for 20 minutes, until muffins are lightly golden brown and a probe
   comes out clean. (Baking time may vary with amount
   and type of fruit you add.)

5. Remove from oven and serve at once with butter.

**Yield: 12 muffins**

### Peach Muffins

2 to 2½ cups peeled, sliced peaches (unsweetened canned and drained will work)
1 pinch of mace

### Blueberry Muffins

2 cups wild blueberries
¼ teaspoon lemon zest (optional)

### Strawberry Muffins

2 cups wild strawberries (cut large ones into ½-inch pieces)
¼ teaspoon grated fresh orange zest
(use ¼ cup sugar rather than ½ cup)

### Poppy Seed Muffins

¼ cup fresh poppy seeds (keep poppy seeds frozen to ensure freshness)
1 tablespoon dry sherry

### Fruit Cobbler

1. Preheat oven to 400°F and place rack in center of oven. Lightly coat a 9- by 9-inch baking pan with butter.

2. Combine 3 to 3½ cups fruit with about ¼ cup sugar. (Use peaches, nectarines, Italian prunes, plums, or blueberries. Try apples sprinkled with a little brown sugar and cinnamon.)

3. Fill baking pan with fruit and spoon basic fruit muffin batter over top.

4. Bake for 25 to 30 minutes, until cobbler is bubbly and cake is cooked through. Remove from oven and serve warm with ice cream.

**Yield: 8 servings**

# CRANBERRY MUFFINS

A regular customer gave us this muffin recipe to use. Unlike most muffins, these are still terrific the second day, and they freeze well. (Pop one still wrapped and frozen in the microwave for 45 seconds and it's breakfast time.)

**Preparation Time:** 20 minutes

**Baking Time:** 20 minutes

> 2 cups unbleached white flour
> 2 teaspoons baking powder
> ½ teaspoon salt
> 1 cup granulated sugar
> 1 egg, beaten
> ½ cup milk
> 4 tablespoons butter, melted
> ½ cup orange juice
> 1½ teaspoons freshly grated orange zest (the bright orange part of the peel)
> 1½ cups chopped fresh cranberries (substitute red currants)
> ½ cup chopped pecans or walnuts

**1.** Preheat oven to 400°F. Line a muffin tin with 12 paper cups.

**2.** Sift together flour, baking powder, salt, and sugar.

**3.** In a small bowl, beat egg and stir in milk, melted butter, and orange juice.

**4.** Stir egg mixture into dry ingredients with a few quick strokes.

**5.** Fold in orange zest, cranberries, and pecans.

**6.** Spoon into lined muffin cups and bake for 20 minutes, until a tester comes out clean. Remove from oven and serve at once with butter and homemade jam.

**Yield: 12 muffins**

**NOTE:**
If highbush cranberries are available, run them through a food mill and substitute the juice for the orange juice.

**NOTE:**
The recipe can be doubled.

Northern Lights

Northern Lights—The aurora borealis dances across the skies over Juneau on crisp clear nights from August to April. (The rest of the year it is too light at night to see this luminous phenomenon.)

# DESSERTS

(INCLUDING COOKIES, CHEESECAKES, CAKES, AND PIES)

## Extra Egg Yolks?

■ ■ ■

*Here are some recipes that call for yolks alone:*

*Crème brûlée (or custard) (page 201)*
*Hollandaise (page 40)*
*Mayonnaise or salad dressings (page 40)*
*Holiday cookies (page 173)*
*Avogolemono soup or other cream soups or sauces*
*or mix a yolk with a bit of water to use as a glaze for dinner rolls*

*You can freeze yolks, mixed with a pinch of sugar or salt, and use them later in either sweet or savory dishes.*

# COCONUT MACAROONS

This confection of almonds, coconut, and chocolate melts in your mouth.

**Preparation Time:**  30 minutes

**Baking Time:**  12 to 15 minutes

## ■ Macaroons

6 egg whites
½ teaspoon salt
2 cups sifted confectioners' sugar
2 teaspoons almond extract
1 teaspoon vanilla extract
4 cups unsweetened coconut (use desiccated coconut found at health food stores*)
2 cups very finely ground almonds (use either a food processor fitted with a steel blade, or a blender, and process until fine-meal consistency)
⅓ cup unbleached white flour
4 tablespoons butter, melted

## ■ Icing

½ cup heavy cream
4 ounces semisweet chocolate chips (⅔ cup)

1. **To prepare macaroons:** Preheat oven to 350°F and arrange racks so they are evenly spaced in oven. Lightly oil 2 cookie sheets.

2. In a large mixing bowl and using an electric mixer (if possible), whip egg whites and salt until frothy. Gradually add sugar and whip until shiny and stiff. Fold in almond and vanilla extracts.

3. Gently fold in coconut, almond meal, flour, and butter.

4. Using an ice cream scoop, scoop dough onto cookie sheets. (You can also spoon or pipe the dough into 2-inch lumps about the size of a large egg: The scoop makes nice round macaroons.)

5. Bake 12 to 15 minutes, until very lightly browned on top and fairly firm to the touch. (Break one open: There should be no darker damp part in the middle.) Remove from oven and immediately transfer cookies to wire racks to cool.

6. **To prepare icing:** In a small pan over high heat, bring cream to a boil. Remove from heat and immediately

add chocolate chips. Whisk until smooth and dark. Set aside until ready to use, but keep warm enough to pour.

7. When macaroons are cool, dip half of each cookie into icing. Set on racks over a clean cookie pan to drip.

8. Store at room temperature well wrapped for up to 5 days. (They will soften as they sit.)

**Yield: 24 cookies**

**\*See mail-order sources, page 237.**

■　　　　　■　　　　　■

# CAROLYN'S COOKIES

Carolyn Peterson, one of our most regular customers, created this incredibly chocolaty cookie and gave us the recipe. It is a chocophile's dream come true.

**Preparation Time:** 20 minutes

**Baking Time:** 12 minutes

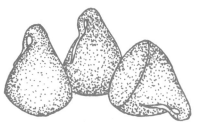

¼ pound plus 4 tablespoons butter
¾ cup granulated sugar
¾ cup packed brown sugar
1 egg
6 tablespoons unsweetened cocoa
2 tablespoons milk
1½ teaspoons vanilla extract
1¼ cups unbleached white flour
½ teaspoon baking powder
¼ teaspoon salt
1⅓ cups (8 ounces) semisweet chocolate chips

1. Preheat oven to 375°F and place racks so they are evenly spaced in center of oven.

2. In a large mixing bowl, cream butter until smooth. Add sugar and brown sugar and cream together thoroughly. Add egg and beat in well. Carefully stir in cocoa, milk, and vanilla.

3. Sift together flour, baking powder, and salt and stir gently into butter mixture. Add chocolate chips and stir until combined evenly.

4. Drop by teaspoonfuls onto ungreased cookie sheets and bake for 10 to 12 minutes.

5. Remove from oven and allow to cool slightly on cookie sheets, then transfer to racks to cool. Store tightly wrapped at room temperature for several days.

**NOTE:**
The dough freezes well: Form into cookies, freeze uncovered until solid, then wrap well in an airtight bag and keep frozen until you are ready to bake. Defrost on cookie sheets and bake as above.

**Yield: 36 cookies**

# FANTASY COOKIES

Martha Hopson, a baker with a flair, devised the characteristic flower shape for these cookies, which makes them easy to share or savor bite by bite.

**Preparation Time:** 30 minutes

**Baking Time:** 15 to 20 minutes

½ pound butter (substitute ¼ pound butter and ¼ pound margarine but not all margarine; the butter is important for flavor)
½ cup honey
1½ teaspoons vanilla extract
1 cup finely ground almonds (to the consistency of coarse meal)
2½ cups sifted unbleached white flour
⅓ cup carob chips (available in health food stores*), or substitute semisweet chocolate chips

1. Preheat oven to 350°F and arrange racks so they are evenly spaced in center of oven.

2. In a large mixing bowl, using a wooden spoon or electric mixer set on high, cream together butter and honey until light and fluffy. Beat in vanilla.

3. With a spoon, gently cut almonds and flour into butter and honey mixture using short, straight strokes, as if making pie crust. (Do not beat or knead at this point: The delicate shortbread-like texture of the cookie would be lost.)

4. Just before completely combined, add carob chips. Mix lightly, just until dough comes together in one ball. Do not overmix.

5. Form dough into 1½-inch balls. (An ice cream scoop works well for this purpose.) Place on ungreased cookie sheets. To give cookies the characteristic "Fiddlehead Fantasy Cookie" shape, flatten each cookie with a rosette iron form. (Any cookie press, the tines of a fork, or the back of a table knife will work just as well.)

6. Bake for 15 minutes, or until lightly golden and slightly puffed in center. Remove cookie sheets from oven; remove cookies from sheets and place on a wire rack to cool. To store, place cooled cookies in an airtight container and keep at room temperature for (it is rumored) up to 1 week.

**NOTE:**
The cookies will be crunchy when they are first made, then soften the second day.

**Yield: 36 cookies**

*See mail-order sources, page 237.

# REALITY COOKIES

In spite of our best intentions, the fact remains that granulated sugar and white flour make really good cookies. These celebrate that reality with brightly colored candies sprinkled like confetti through the dough.

**Preparation Time:** 30 minutes

**Baking Time:** 20 minutes

¾ pound butter
⅓ cup plus 1 tablespoon granulated sugar
⅓ cup plus 1 tablespoon packed brown sugar
1 cup finely ground almonds
2½ cups unbleached white flour
½ cup M & M's

1. Preheat oven to 275°F and arrange racks so they are evenly spaced in center of oven.

2. In a large mixing bowl or the bowl of an electric mixer fitted with a paddle, beat butter until fluffy. Add white and brown sugars and continue to beat until light and fluffy.

3. Add almonds and flour. Stir gently until almost completely combined.

4. Add M & M's and stir just until dough comes together. If you are using a mixing machine, dough will begin to come away from sides of bowl.

5. Shape dough into Ping-Pong-size balls and place on an ungreased cookie sheet. Lightly flour bottom of a small glass, a cookie press, or palm of your hand and flatten each cookie to about ½ inch thick. Place an M & M in center of each cookie and bake until very lightly golden brown and beginning to puff slightly in center (about 20 minutes).

6. Remove from oven and transfer to racks to cool. Store in an airtight container at room temperature for up to 2 days.

**Yield: 32 cookies**

NOTE:
This dough can be frozen and baked when needed: Place balls of dough on a cookie sheet and freeze uncovered. When frozen solid, transfer to airtight bags and store in freezer. To bake, place frozen balls of dough on a cookie sheet, allow to come to room temperature, and proceed as in step 5.

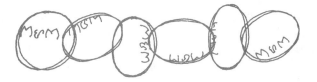

# HERMITS

A friend writes that in her household these have become known as "Klondike Cookies" as they are often taken on the Klondike Road Race over the Chilkoot Trail from Skagway to Whitehorse. She notes they freeze (and travel) well.

**Preparation Time:**  30 minutes

**Resting Time:**  overnight (at least 1 hour anyway)

**Completion Time:**  45 minutes

> 3 cups unbleached white flour
> 1½ teaspoons ground cinnamon
> 1½ teaspoons powdered ginger
> 1½ teaspoons baking soda
> ¾ teaspoon ground allspice
> ¾ teaspoon salt
> 1¼ cups sugar
> ¼ pound margarine or butter
> 1 egg
> ⅓ cup molasses
> ½ cup milk
> 1½ cups raisins
> ½ cup chopped walnuts

■ **Glaze**

> 2 tablespoons milk
> ⅔ cup sifted confectioners' sugar

1. Sift together flour, cinnamon, ginger, baking soda, allspice, and salt. Set aside.

2. In a large mixing bowl, cream sugar and margarine until light and fluffy.

3. Add egg and molasses and beat until well blended.

4. Stir in milk, raisins, and nuts.

5. Carefully add sifted flour mixture and stir just until combined.

6. Divide dough into 4 balls, wrap tightly, and refrigerate overnight (or at least an hour).

7. Preheat oven to 375°F. Lightly oil two 13- by 18-inch cookie sheets.

8. Form each ball of dough into a long snake, the length of the cookie sheet. Place two snakes on each sheet, flatten slightly with your hand until they are about 3 inches wide and ½ inch thick, and bake for 12 to 15

"I couldn't help it. I can resist everything except temptation."
—Oscar Wilde

minutes. (They will begin to puff and finely crack on top, and change to a slightly more golden color, but will still seem soft in the center. Underbake rather than over-bake.)

9. In a small bowl, whisk together milk and sugar. When cookies come out of oven, brush lightly with glaze. Cut into bars, transfer to racks to cool, and store at room temperature in an airtight container.

**Yield: 32 cookies**

# PEANUT BUTTER COOKIES

Just a little bit chewy, just a little bit crunchy, these are just about perfect.

**Preparation Time:** 20 minutes

**Baking Time:** 12 minutes

> ¼ pound plus 4 tablespoons butter
> ¾ cup granulated sugar
> ¾ cup well-packed brown sugar
> 1 egg
> ¾ teaspoon vanilla extract
> ¾ cup crunchy peanut butter
> 2¼ cups unbleached white flour
> 1 teaspoon baking soda
> ¾ teaspoon salt

1. Preheat oven to 350°F and arrange racks so they are evenly spaced in oven.

2. In a large mixing bowl, cream butter until soft. Add white and brown sugars and beat until fluffy.

3. Add egg and beat until smooth, then add vanilla and peanut butter. Beat well.

4. Sift together flour, baking soda, and salt and add to butter mixture. Stir until completely combined.

5. Spoon walnut-size balls onto an ungreased cookie sheet and flatten slightly with lightly floured tines of a fork.

6. Bake for 12 minutes, until lightly golden brown. Remove from oven and transfer to racks. When cooled, store tightly wrapped at room temperature for up to 2 days.

**VARIATION: Add 1 cup chocolate chips to dough.**

**Yield: 36 cookies**

# GINGER CRINKLES

This cookie wins the award as "The Most Requested Recipe." Ginger crinkle fans are a dedicated and faithful cadre who fall into two camps: those who prefer their ginger cookies soft in the center and those who want them crisp. This recipe pleases both.

**Preparation Time:**  30 minutes

**Baking Time:**  13 minutes

> ½ pound butter
> 1¾ cups granulated sugar
> 1 egg
> ⅓ cup molasses
> 2¾ cups unbleached white flour
> 1¼ teaspoons baking soda
> 1¾ teaspoons cinnamon
> 1¾ teaspoons powdered ginger
> ½ teaspoon salt
> ⅓ cup granulated sugar

1. Preheat oven to 350°F and arrange racks so they are evenly spaced.

2. In a large mixing bowl, cream together butter and 1¾ cups sugar until fluffy.

3. Beat in egg and molasses.

4. Sift together flour, baking soda, spices, and salt. Carefully stir flour mixture into butter mixture.

5. Form dough into walnut-size balls, dip in ⅓ cup sugar, and place on an ungreased cookie sheet, sugar side up.

6. Bake for 12 to 13 minutes. If you like these cookies soft in the center, remove from oven when cookie is puffed, very light golden brown, and cracked on top. If you prefer crisp ginger cookies, bake 2 to 3 minutes more, until puffed cookie has fallen and is golden brown.

7. Remove from oven and allow cookies to rest for 2 minutes before removing from cookie sheet. Cool on racks and store tightly wrapped at room temperature for several days.

**Yield: 36 cookies**

# OATMEAL-RAISIN COOKIES

Everyone likes the chewy goodness of oatmeal cookies.

**Preparation Time:**  20 minutes

**Baking Time:**  12 minutes

½ pound butter
⅔ cup granulated sugar
⅔ cup packed brown sugar
1 egg
1½ teaspoons vanilla extract
1 tablespoon milk
1¾ cups unbleached white flour
½ teaspoon baking soda
½ teaspoon baking powder
½ teaspoon salt
¼ teaspoon cinnamon
1 cup old-fashioned rolled oats
¾ cup raisins (chocolate chips make a great
   substitution)

1. Preheat oven to 350°F and arrange racks so they are evenly spaced in center of oven.

2. In a large mixing bowl, cream together butter and sugars until light and fluffy.

3. Add egg and beat until thoroughly combined. Stir in vanilla and milk.

4. Sift together flour, baking soda, baking powder, salt, and cinnamon.

5. Gently add sifted ingredients and rolled oats to sugar mixture. Stir until almost completely combined.

6. Add raisins and stir until dough is evenly mixed.

7. Scoop or spoon dough into egg-size lumps (use an ice cream scoop to make evenly shaped cookies) and place on ungreased cookie sheets.

8. Bake for 10 to 12 minutes, or until slightly puffed in center.

9. Remove from oven and transfer to a rack to cool. Store in an airtight container at room temperature for several days.

**NOTE:**
**You can freeze the lumps at this point and keep them in airtight bags to bake as needed. Defrost on cookie sheets before baking.**

**Yield: 24 cookies**

# OLD-FASHIONED CHOCOLATE CHIP COOKIES

The whole world loves chocolate chip cookies. These are full of chocolate and nuts, a perfect combination.

**Preparation Time:**  30 minutes

**Baking Time:**  15 minutes

> ½ pound butter
> ¾ cup granulated sugar
> ¾ cup packed brown sugar
> 2 eggs
> 2 teaspoons vanilla extract
> 2 cups unbleached white flour
> 1 teaspoon baking soda
> ½ teaspoon salt
> 1½ cups semisweet chocolate chips
> 1½ cups chopped walnuts

1. Preheat oven to 350°F and arrange racks so they are evenly spaced in oven.

2. In a large mixing bowl, cream together butter and sugars until light and fluffy. Add eggs and vanilla and continue to beat until fluffy.

3. Sift together flour, baking soda, and salt. Carefully add to butter mixture and stir gently until combined.

4. Stir in chocolate chips and walnuts until evenly mixed.

5. Scoop by tablespoon or small ice cream scoop onto an ungreased cookie sheet. Bake for 12 to 15 minutes, until golden brown and slightly puffed in center. Remove from oven and transfer to racks to cool. Can be stored tightly wrapped at room temperature for several days.

**Yield: 36 cookies**

**NOTE:**
Freeze cookies at this point, then wrap well to be baked as needed. Defrost on cookie pans at room temperature and proceed.

# HOLIDAY COOKIES

Award your littlest angel a buttery golden star; send your Valentine a big sweet heart; or leave Santa a crispy Christmas bell. These simple, versatile butter cookies are perfect for all occasions.

**Preparation Time:** 30 minutes

**Baking Time:** 10 minutes

¾ pound butter
2 cups sifted confectioners' sugar
2½ cups unsifted unbleached white flour
1 egg white (you can substitute 2 egg yolks, which
   will create a very delicate cookie)
1½ teaspoons vanilla or almond extract

1. Preheat oven to 350°F and arrange racks so they are evenly spaced in center of oven.

2. Cream butter in a large mixing bowl until fluffy. Add sugar and continue to beat until light.

3. Add flour and stir until almost completely combined. Add egg white and flavoring and mix until smooth, but do not overbeat.

4. Shape at once using a cookie gun, or roll out on a lightly floured surface and cut into fancy shapes with cookie cutters. (Optional: Brush with beaten egg, sprinkle with colored sugar, turbinado sugar, toasted almonds, or cinnamon sugar.)

5. Bake cookies on ungreased cookie sheets for 5 to 10 minutes (depending on shape and thickness of dough), until lightly browned around edges.

6. Remove from oven and transfer to racks to cool. Decorate as you like to fit the occasion. Store well wrapped at room temperature for up to 2 days. The cookies can be well wrapped and frozen either baked or unbaked.

**NOTE:**
These cookies are delightful dipped in ganache (page 208), sandwiched with preserves or buttercream, or left plain. They freeze well and make great Christmas trees, Valentine hearts, Easter bunnies, wedding bells, Fourth of July stars, or autumn leaves.

**NOTE:**
**Dough can be frozen at this point.**

# LINZER TORTE

This wonderfully nutty, slightly spiced giant cookie shows off homemade jams and preserves as nothing else. Use the same dough to make charming little filled hearts or stars to celebrate your favorite holiday.

**Preparation Time:** 30 minutes

**Baking Time:** 30 minutes

> ½ pound butter, softened
> 1 cup granulated sugar
> 1 tablespoon freshly grated orange zest (grate 1 orange, or substitute 1 teaspoon dried)
> 1 teaspoon freshly grated lemon zest (½ lemon)
> 1 egg
> 1 tablespoon kirsch (optional)
> 1½ cups unbleached white flour
> ½ teaspoon baking powder
> 1 teaspoon ground cinnamon
> ½ teaspoon ground cloves
> ¼ teaspoon salt
> 1 firmly packed cup finely ground almonds, skinned hazelnuts,* or walnuts, or any combination
> 1 cup raspberry jam (or other tart preserves or jams*)
> 1 tablespoon kirsch (optional)

1. In a large mixing bowl, cream butter with sugar until light and fluffy. Beat in orange and lemon zest, egg, and 1 tablespoon kirsch.

2. Sift together flour, baking powder, spices, and salt.

3. Carefully stir the flour mixture into butter mixture and stir in ground nuts.

4. If dough is quite soft, cover and refrigerate for 30 minutes.

5. Preheat oven to 350°F and place rack in center of oven. Divide dough into 2 parts, one slightly larger than the other. Pat the larger into a 9-inch cake pan (preferably with a removable bottom) to a thickness of about ¼ inch, and slightly up the sides.

6. In a small bowl, stir together raspberry jam and 1 tablespoon kirsch. Spoon into center of cake, spreading evenly to within ½ inch of edge of dough.

7. Divide remaining dough into 2 parts. Roll out 1 part on a lightly floured surface to about 8 inches in diameter and ¼ inch thick. Carefully cut dough into ½-inch-wide

strips. Using a long thin spatula, carefully lay 4 or 5 strips evenly across torte, then lay 4 or 5 strips at 45-degree angles across first, to create a lattice top.

8. Roll remaining dough into a long rope ¾ inch in diameter. Cut off ¾-inch pieces and roll into small balls. Use your thumb to press balls around edge of torte to seal jam and lattice strips in place.

9. Bake for 30 minutes, until jam seems bubbly in center. Remove from oven and cool in pan on a rack. (If you are using a pan with a removable bottom, slip torte out of pan, but leave it on bottom until almost completely cooled.) When torte is cooled, slide it off spring-form bottom onto a serving plate, or set a plate on top of pan and flip it over to release torte, then flip it right side up onto a cake plate. (If torte refuses to come out of pan, set it directly on a hot burner for several seconds to soften butter.)

10. Dust torte with confectioners' sugar and serve in small wedges. Store tightly wrapped at room temperature for several days.

**Yield: 10 to 12 servings**

**NOTE:**
This makes a good gift to mail to the kids in college or to other people you miss: It is quite sturdy and improves with age.

# LINZER COOKIES

You need 2 cookie cutters the same shape but different sizes.

1. Preheat oven to 350°F and arrange racks so they are evenly spaced in center of oven.

2. Roll out dough on a lightly floured surface and cut into shapes with the larger cookie cutter. Place on 2 ungreased cookie sheets.

3. Using smaller cookie cutter, remove center from cookies on 1 cookie sheet.

4. Bake for 10 to 12 minutes (the cookies without centers will bake faster than the others), until golden brown. Remove from oven and transfer to racks to cool. Spread whole cookies with jam** and place a cookie without center on top. Dust liberally with confectioners' sugar. Serve at once.

**Yield: 18 2-inch cookies**

*See mail-order sources, page 237.

**A friend suggests spreading them first with chocolate buttercream and then with jam.

# FIDDLEHEAD BROWNIES

Good and gooey, richly chocolaty, these have tempted customers and staff for years. This recipe makes a bunch because they freeze well (and you probably can't eat just one).

**Preparation Time:** 20 minutes

**Baking Time:** 30 minutes

> ½ pound butter (or ¼ pound butter and ¼ pound margarine)
> 6 ounces unsweetened chocolate
> 7 eggs
> ½ teaspoon salt
> 3½ cups granulated sugar
> 2 teaspoons vanilla
> 2 cups unbleached white flour
> 2 cups chopped walnuts

1. Preheat oven to 325°F and place rack in center of oven. Lightly oil and flour a 17- by 12- by 1-inch jelly roll pan (or two 13- by 8- by 2-inch pans).

2. In a small pan over low heat, or in a covered glass bowl in the microwave, melt together butter and chocolate. Cool slightly.

3. In a large bowl with an electric mixer set on high, beat eggs and salt until foamy. Add sugar slowly while beating. Beat until very light and fluffy (batter will be a pale lemon color). Add vanilla.

4. Using a large spoon or spatula, stir chocolate mixture into eggs until batter is marbled in appearance.

5. Begin to stir in flour with a few strokes of the spoon, then add walnuts and mix just until completely blended. (Don't overmix!)

6. Pour into prepared jelly roll pan and spread evenly with a spatula. Bake for 30 minutes until a knife inserted in center of brownies comes out clean, and edges are slightly puffed and cracked. (These are best if they are not overbaked.)

7. Remove from oven and cool for 10 minutes in pan, then run a knife around edges, and cut into 2-inch squares. Use a spatula to remove each brownie from pan and arrange on plates to eat at once, or wrap well and store at room temperature for up to 2 days, or freeze for later.

**Yield: 48 brownies**

NOTE:
These are very good topped with ice cream and hot fudge sauce, and they work quite well in Baked Alaska: Top with ice cream, coat with meringue, freeze, then brown in a 500°F oven and serve.

# ESPRESSO-CHOCOLATE CHEESECAKE

We adapted this recipe from one served at La Belle Pomme cooking school in Columbus, Ohio.

**Preparation Time:** 30 minutes

**Baking Time:** 1 hour 40 minutes

**Cooling Time:** 6 hours or, best, overnight

## ■ Crust

1 cup finely ground graham cracker crumbs
1 cup finely ground toasted almonds
2 tablespoons granulated sugar
5 tablespoons butter, melted

## ■ Filling

4 tablespoons instant espresso coffee
⅓ cup warm water
1 pound cream cheese, at room temperature
1 cup sugar
3 ounces semisweet chocolate, melted and cooled
   but still pourable
1¼ cups sour cream
4 eggs, lightly beaten

1. Preheat oven to 350°F and place rack in center of oven.

2. **To prepare crust:** Combine crumbs, almonds, and 2 tablespoons sugar in a 9½-inch springform pan. Mix in butter and pat mixture over bottom and part way up sides of pan. Chill while preparing filling.

3. **To prepare filling:** Dissolve espresso in water. Set aside.

4. In a large mixing bowl with an electric mixer set on high, beat cream cheese until smooth. Blend in sugar and beat until smooth. Add espresso and melted chocolate and mix just until smooth. Beat in sour cream and then eggs.

5. Pour mixture into crust and bake for 35 to 40 minutes, then turn off oven and let cake cool for 1 hour in oven with door cracked open.

6. Remove from oven, run a knife around edge of pan to loosen cake, and remove cake from ring. Cover loosely and refrigerate for 6 hours before serving.

"Between two evils, I always pick the one I never tried before."
—*Mae West*

NOTE:
This cake keeps well. The flavors improve if you can bear to let it sit overnight.

**Yield: 1 9-inch cake, 10 to 12 servings**

# HONEY CHEESECAKE

Just a hint of honey sweetens this creamy smooth cheese-cake. Wonderful alone, it is incredible topped with a wild blueberry or raspberry sauce.

**Preparation Time:** 30 minutes

**Baking Time:** 40 minutes

**Cooling Time:** 6 hours or, best, overnight (so much better if you can wait!)

■ **Crust**

> 1½ cups finely crushed honey graham cracker crumbs
> ¾ cup finely ground almonds
> 4 tablespoons butter, melted
> 3 tablespoons honey
> ¼ teaspoon almond extract

■ **Filling**

> 1½ pounds cream cheese
> 3 eggs
> ½ to ⅔ cup fireweed or other mild honey (depends upon type of honey and how sweet you like cheesecake)
> 3 tablespoons freshly squeezed lemon juice
> 1½ teaspoons vanilla extract

■ **Topping**

> 1 cup sour cream
> 1 tablespoon honey
> 1 teaspoon vanilla extract

1. Preheat oven to 350°F and place rack in center of oven.

2. Combine crust ingredients in a 9- or 10-inch springform pan and press evenly into bottom of pan and about 1 inch up sides. Set aside while preparing filling.

3. **To prepare filling:** In a large mixing bowl with an electric mixer set on high, beat cream cheese with eggs, honey, lemon juice, and vanilla for 10 minutes, until very smooth and light. Pour into crust and bake for 30 minutes, until lightly puffed almost all the way through. (The center should still seem a little soft, but not runny. It is better to underbake rather than overbake cheesecake.) Remove from oven and cool briefly while you prepare topping.

4. **To prepare topping:** In a small bowl, whisk together sour cream, 1 tablespoon honey, and 1 teaspoon vanilla. Pour evenly over baked cake and return to oven. Bake for 10 minutes. Turn off oven and crack the door open. Let cheesecake cool for 1 hour in oven, then refrigerate overnight. (You can cool cheesecake at room temperature instead of in oven if you need to use oven, but it may crack across the top.)

5. Run a knife around edge of cake to loosen it and remove springform ring. Cut with a hot knife and serve.

## VARIATIONS

### ■ Wild Blueberry Sauce

2 cups fresh wild blueberries (substitute fresh cultivated or frozen unsweetened berries that have been defrosted; reduce amount of honey if you use cultivated berries)
¼ to ⅓ cup honey
1 teaspoon fresh lemon juice
2 teaspoons cornstarch
2 teaspoons apple juice or water

1. In a large pot over medium-high heat, bring blueberries, honey, and lemon juice to a boil.

2. Whisk together cornstarch and juice or water and add to berries. Cook for 1 minute and remove from heat. Cool to room temperature and spread over cooled cheesecake.

### ■ Raspberry Topping

(not a honey-sweetened topping)

2 cups fresh raspberries, or 12 ounces defrosted unsweetened frozen berries
½ cup water
½ cup granulated sugar
1 teaspoon fresh lemon juice
1 tablespoon cornstarch
1 tablespoon water

1. In a medium pot over medium-high heat, combine raspberries and water and bring to a boil.

2. Add sugar and lemon juice. Boil for 2 minutes.

3. Combine cornstarch and water in a small cup and pour into raspberries. Stir and cook for 1 minute. Remove from heat.

4. Cool to room temperature, then spread over cooled cheesecake.

### Fireweed Honey

*Fireweed is a stately plant that carpets hundreds of acres of land in Alaska. Beekeepers move their hives to these areas so their bees can forage exclusively on the magenta-pink blossoms during July and August. Under the right conditions, Alaskan bees can make honey that is 99 percent pure fireweed nectar and virtually colorless.*

*Fireweed honey has a delicate floral sweetness with no aftertaste. Because the purest fireweed honey is nearly transparent, it can be used where a dark color would be objectionable. We can't think of a more delicious use for ambrosial, ethereal, fireweed honey than this heavenly cheesecake.*

*Honey has been enjoyed as "nature's health food" for many years. Unfortunately, infants under one year of age may have an adverse reaction to it, so keep the honey jar away from Baby!*

# ANN'S LEMON CAKE

Delicate, refreshing, and, in the French style, not overly sweet, this cake reflects pastry chef Ann Foster's graceful influence in the bakery.

**Preparation Time:**  1 hour (can all be done ahead)

**Baking and Cooling Time:**  1 hour

**Completion Time:**  30 minutes

### ■ Cake

> ⅔ cup unbleached white flour
> 4 tablespoons cornstarch
> 4 eggs
> ½ cup granulated sugar
> 2 tablespoons butter, melted
> ½ teaspoon vanilla extract

### ■ Lemon Curd Filling

> 2 lemons: grate rind to equal 2 teaspoons and
>    squeeze juice to equal 6 tablespoons
> ½ cup confectioners' sugar
> ½ cup granulated sugar
> 4 tablespoons unsalted butter
> 3 eggs, beaten

### ■ White Wine Syrup

> ¼ cup water
> ¼ cup granulated sugar
> ½ lemon
> 1 tablespoon dry white wine (such as chardonnay)

### ■ Icing

> 1 cup heavy cream
> 2 tablespoons granulated sugar
> 1 teaspoon vanilla extract

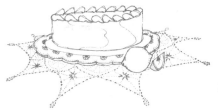

1. Generously coat a 9-inch cake pan with butter and dust with flour. Preheat oven to 350°F and place rack in center of oven. Prepare a double boiler set over simmering water.

2. **To prepare cake:** Sift together flour and cornstarch and set aside.

3. In a large mixing bowl with an electric mixer set on high, beat 4 eggs and ½ cup granulated sugar until they are fluffy and very light in color.

4. Sift flour mixture over eggs and fold in very gently. When flour is incorporated, add melted butter and ½ teaspoon vanilla. Fold in with as few strokes as possible.

5. Pour batter into pan, smooth top, and bake for 30 to 35 minutes, until a probe inserted in center of cake comes out clean. Remove from oven, cool cake briefly in pan, then turn out onto a rack to cool completely.

6. While cake is baking, **prepare lemon curd**: Place lemon rind, juice, confectioners' sugar, ½ cup granulated sugar, and butter in top of simmering double boiler. Stir gently until butter has melted. Pour beaten eggs through a wire strainer into mixture and, using a wooden spoon, stir for 10 minutes, until mixture is smooth and thickened to consistency of soft mayonnaise. Remove from heat and refrigerate until ready to use.

7. **To prepare syrup:** Bring water and ¼ cup sugar with ½ lemon to a boil in a small pan over high heat. Reduce heat to low and simmer for 5 minutes. Remove from heat and stir in white wine. Strain through a small wire-mesh strainer into a small jar and set aside.

8. **To prepare whipped cream icing:** Whip cream with 2 tablespoons sugar and 1 teaspoon vanilla until stiff. Refrigerate while you assemble cake.

9. **To assemble cake:** Place cooled cake top side down on back of a 9-inch cake pan. Using a serrated knife, very carefully slice cake into 3 thin layers. Gently set aside top 2 layers.

10. Brush remaining layer generously with one third of the syrup, then spread with half the lemon curd. Top with middle layer of cake and repeat sequence. Place top layer on cake and brush with remaining syrup. Smooth whipped cream icing over entire cake and decorate as you like. Using 2 large spatulas, carefully transfer cake to a cake plate and serve at once, or refrigerate and serve later in the day.

NOTE:
The cake may be made 1 day ahead and kept tightly wrapped, after it has cooled, at room temperature. It is best eaten within 1 day, however.

NOTE:
The lemon curd can be made up to 2 weeks in advance and kept tightly covered in refrigerator. It is delicious in tarts, on toast, over ice cream. The recipe doubles easily.

NOTE:
The syrup can be made 1 week in advance and stored, covered and refrigerated, until ready to use.

**Yield: 1 9-inch layer cake**

*Decorating idea:* Smooth icing evenly over entire cake, then pipe rosettes of icing around rim. Set a curl of lemon peel or chocolate, or a candied rose petal, into each rosette. If you do not have a pastry bag, use a knife to create voluptuous swirls over the cake and dust center with finely grated lemon zest or chocolate. Fresh flowers look nice tucked alongside or in center. Let your imagination guide you.

# EIGHTEEN-CARAT CAKE

Dazzle them with this jewel. Of all the carrot cakes we've tried and liked, this one, given to us by Fiddlehead hostess and office manager Nancy Huebschen, who said her sister calls it the "California Mission Cake," is the best.

**Preparation Time:** 40 minutes

**Baking and Cooling:** 1 hour

**Icing:** 20 minutes

### ■ Cake

1½ cups small-diced carrots (3 medium, 8 to 10 ounces)
2½ cups unbleached white flour
1½ to 2½ cups granulated sugar
2 teaspoons ground cinnamon
2 teaspoons baking soda
1 teaspoon salt
1¼ cups safflower oil
4 eggs
1 tablespoon vanilla extract
1 cup chopped walnuts
1 cup unsweetened finely flaked dried coconut (available in health food stores as "desiccated"*)
¾ cup drained, canned, crushed unsweetened pineapple (drink the juice)

### ■ Icing

8 ounces cream cheese
5⅓ tablespoons unsalted butter at room temperature (⅓ cup)
2½ cups sifted confectioners' sugar
1 teaspoon vanilla extract
½ cup orange marmalade (optional)
1 cup finely chopped walnuts

1. **To prepare cake:** Generously coat two 9-inch cake pans with oil and dust with flour. Preheat oven to 350°F and arrange racks so they are evenly spaced in center of oven.

2. Place carrots in a small glass bowl with 1 tablespoon water. Cover tightly with plastic and microwave on high for 6 to 7 minutes, until quite tender (or steam on top of stove in a small pot with water). Using a food processor or food mill, purée carrots. You should have 1 cup of purée. Set aside.

3. Sift together flour, sugar, cinnamon, baking soda, and salt in a large mixing bowl.

4. In a smaller mixing bowl, whisk together oil, eggs, and vanilla. Gently stir egg mixture into sifted ingredients. Just before batter is fully combined, add walnuts, coconut, pineapple, and carrot purée. Fold together until evenly mixed, but avoid overbeating.

5. Divide batter between cake pans and bake for 30 to 35 minutes, until a probe inserted in center of cake comes out clean. Remove from oven and allow to cool briefly in pans. Turn out onto racks to cool completely.

6. **To prepare icing:** Cream together cheese and butter until smooth. Gently stir in confectioners' sugar and vanilla until smooth. The icing should be creamy and somewhat firm. If it looks moist and seems to be separating into tiny moist grains, add a little more sugar until it is smooth and creamy.

7. **To assemble cake:** Place one layer of cake, top side down, on back side of a cake pan. Spread top with ⅔ to ¾ cup icing. Set next layer on cake, also top side down. Ice cake, filling in between the two layers. (Optional: Spread orange marmalade over top of cake.) Using a pastry bag, pipe any remaining icing around top or decorate as you like. Carefully pat chopped nuts around bottom inch of cake. Chill cake briefly to set icing, then, using a large spatula, transfer to a cake plate. Serve at once, or store refrigerated for several days.

**Yield: 1 9-inch, 2-layer cake**

*See mail-order sources, page 237.

NOTE:
Carrot cake freezes very well, iced or not.

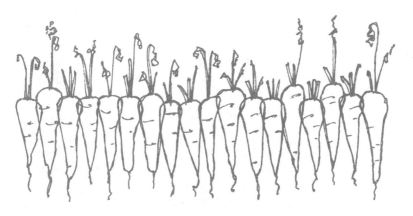

# CHOCOLATE-AMARETTO CAKE

This is a simple cake, moist, chocolaty, and impressive looking. Karen Terrell, one of the Fiddlehead's original staff, created it while she worked in the bakery, and it gets rave reviews.

**Preparation Time:**  30 minutes

**Baking and Cooling Time:**  1 hour 45 minutes

**Completion Time:**  15 minutes

■ **Cake**

> 2 cups granulated sugar
> 1¾ cups unbleached white flour
> ¾ cup sifted unsweetened cocoa
> 2 teaspoons baking soda
> 1 teaspoon baking powder
> 1 teaspoon salt
> ¾ cup very finely ground almonds, the texture of coarse meal
> ¾ cup sour cream
> ¾ cup buttermilk (substitute ¾ cup water and ¼ cup dry buttermilk)
> ½ cup mayonnaise
> 4 eggs (1 cup) beaten
> ¼ cup Amaretto
> 1 teaspoon almond extract

■ **Icing**

> ¼ cup heavy cream
> ⅓ cup semisweet chocolate chips

■ **Garnish**

> 2 tablespoons sliced almonds

1. Preheat oven to 350°F and place rack in lower third of oven. Lightly brush a 10-inch tube cake pan with oil and dust with flour. (Don't use your angel food cake pan; the oil will ruin future angel food cakes.) Set aside.

2. Sift together sugar, flour, cocoa, baking soda, baking powder, and salt. Set aside.

3. In a large bowl, mix almond meal, sour cream, buttermilk, mayonnaise, eggs, Amaretto, and almond extract until smooth. Add sifted dry ingredients and fold together by hand just to combine.

4. Pour into prepared tube pan and bake for 50 to 55 minutes without opening oven door. (A probe inserted into center of cake will come out clean when done.) Remove from oven and cool for 10 minutes. Remove from pan, then cool on a cake rack, bottom side up.

5. **To prepare icing:** Heat heavy cream in a small pan (or a small bowl in microwave) to the boiling point and add chocolate chips. Whisk until smooth. Cool to room temperature, until thickened but still pourable.

6. **To decorate cake:** Place cake, bottom side up, on a cake plate. Spoon icing onto the very top, smooth with the spoon and let icing drip decoratively down sides. Arrange sliced almonds around top.

7. Serve when cooled completely. Store tightly wrapped at room temperature.

**Yield: 12 to 16 slices**

# NORTH DOUGLAS CHOCOLATE CAKE

Chocolate lovers go out of control around this cake. It is the perfect old-fashioned birthday layer cake; it's always welcome at an office potluck, tastes very good at the beach, and seems right for a boat launching. There are sure to be several reasons you need to go make one right now. Linda Zagar, our gifted baker from North Douglas, is the cause of it all.

**Preparation Time:** 30 minutes

**Baking and Cooling Time:** 1 hour

**Completion Time:** 30 minutes

## ■ Cake

> 1 cup water
> ¼ pound butter
> ½ cup safflower or corn oil
> 3½ tablespoons sifted Dutch process dark cocoa*
> (other cocoas produce a lighter, sweeter cake and icing, more like milk chocolate)
> 2 cups unbleached white flour
> 2 cups granulated sugar
> 1 teaspoon baking soda
> ½ teaspoon salt
> 2 eggs
> ½ cup buttermilk
> 1 teaspoon vanilla extract

## ■ Icing

> ¼ pound plus 4 tablespoons butter
> 4 cups sifted confectioners' sugar
> ½ cup sifted Dutch process dark cocoa*
> 3 tablespoons milk
> 1½ teaspoons vanilla extract

1. **To prepare cake:** Preheat oven to 375°F and arrange racks so they are evenly spaced in oven. Generously coat two 8- or 9-inch cake pans with butter and dust with flour.

2. Combine water, butter, oil, and cocoa in a small pan and bring to a boil.

3. While butter and water are coming to a boil, sift together flour, sugar, baking soda, and salt in a large mixing bowl. Set aside.

4. Whisk together eggs, buttermilk, and vanilla in a small bowl and set aside.

5. When butter and water are boiling, pour over sifted flour. Stir just until combined. Add egg mixture and gently fold together. Pour into prepared cake pans.

6. Bake for 20 to 25 minutes (8-inch pans will take a little longer than 9-inch pans). Remove from oven when a probe inserted in center of cake comes out clean. Allow to rest briefly in pans, then turn out onto racks to cool completely.

7. **To prepare icing:** In a medium bowl, beat butter until smooth. Add confectioners' sugar and cocoa and stir gently until they are partially combined. Stir in milk and vanilla. Beat until smooth and spreadable. (It may be necessary to add additional sifted confectioners' sugar if mixture seems too soft.)

8. **To assemble cake:** Place first layer, top side down, on bottom of an inverted cake pan. Spread with ¾ cup icing. Place second layer on top of first, top side down. Spread with 1 cup icing, allowing a little to go over the sides. Using a straight-sided metal spatula, ice sides of cake, filling crack between layers with icing. Smooth out top of cake and use remaining icing to decorate cake as you like. Chill cake briefly to firm icing.

9. Using a large spatula, transfer cake to a cake plate. Serve at once, or cover and store at room temperature.

**Yield: 1 8- or 9-inch, 2-layer cake**

**\*See mail-order sources, page 237.**

**"Imagination is more important than knowledge."**
  *—Albert Einstein*

### When to Add Baking Soda

■ ■ ■

*Some older recipes, this one included, often call for adding the baking soda to a liquid before adding to the mixture. Inquiry reveals that this is because baking soda used to harden and it was necessary to dissolve it in liquid in order to disperse it evenly in a mix. These days, baking soda has been treated so it no longer forms hard lumps and is easily sifted with the flour.*

*We've baked this cake both ways, and find that sifting the soda with the dry ingredients results in a more tender and finer crumb, with fewer large air bubbles.*

# ORANGE-WINE CAKE

A visit to Williamsburg inspired this all-American cake.

**Preparation Time:**  30 minutes

**Baking and Cooling Time:**  1 hour

**Completion Time:**  30 minutes

## ■ Cake

3½ cups unbleached white flour
2 teaspoons baking soda
½ teaspoon salt
½ pound butter
1¼ cups granulated sugar
4 eggs
1 cup raisins, coarsely chopped
1 cup chopped walnuts
2 tablespoons freshly grated orange rind (grate rind
   from 1 large orange, then squeeze juice and reserve
   it for icing)
1½ cups buttermilk

## ■ Icing

¾ pound butter
5 to 5½ cups confectioners' sugar, sifted
¼ cup freshly squeezed orange juice
3 tablespoons medium-dry sherry

1. **To prepare cake:** Preheat oven to 350°F and arrange racks so they are evenly spaced in oven. Lightly coat three 9-inch cake pans with butter and dust them with flour. Set aside.

2. Sift together flour, baking soda, and salt. Set aside.

3. In a large mixing bowl, cream ½ pound butter until smooth, then add sugar and beat until fluffy. Beat in eggs, one at a time, until smooth, then stir in raisins, walnuts, and orange rind.

4. Gently fold in one third of flour mixture, then half the buttermilk mixture, then flour, buttermilk, and remaining flour.

5. Divide batter equally among prepared cake pans and bake for 20 to 25 minutes, until a probe inserted in center of one cake comes out clean.

6. Remove from oven and allow to rest 5 to 10 minutes in pans. Turn cakes out onto racks to cool completely.

7. **To prepare icing:** Cream ¾ pound butter until smooth. Add sugar and cream until almost smooth. Stir in orange juice and sherry and beat until smooth.

8. **To ice cake:** If tops of layers are extremely rounded, use a serrated knife to shave off a bit so cake is easier to assemble. Place first layer, top side up, on back side of a 9-inch cake pan. Spread with ⅔ to ¾ cup icing. Place second layer bottom side up and spread with ⅔ to ¾ cup icing. Place last layer on top of middle layer, bottom side up. Spread top and sides of cake decoratively with remaining icing.

9. Using two broad spatulas, carefully move decorated cake to a cake plate. Serve at once, or store, wrapped in plastic, at room temperature for 1 to 2 days.

**Yield: 1 9-inch, 3-layer cake, 12 to 16 servings**

# CHOCOLATE–PEANUT BUTTER PIE

Peanut butter rises from the commonplace to the astral in this pie. Incredibly rich, absolutely wonderful, this pie sends peanut butter fans into ecstasy.

**Preparation Time:**  45 minutes

**Baking Time:**  15 minutes

**Chilling Time:**  4 hours (you can cheat on this a little)

■ **Crust**

> 2 ½ cups finely crushed graham cracker crumbs (substitute chocolate wafers)
> ⅓ cup packed brown sugar
> ¼ pound butter, melted

■ **Ganache**

> ¼ cup heavy cream
> 2 ounces semisweet chocolate chips

■ **Filling**

> 5 ounces cream cheese
> 1½ cups sifted confectioners' sugar
> ⅓ cup milk
> 1½ cups smooth peanut butter
> 1 tablespoon vanilla extract
> 2 cups chilled heavy cream

■ **Garnish**

> Chocolate shavings, crushed peanuts, or whipped cream (or make a little extra ganache and drizzle that over the top)

1. **To prepare crust:** Preheat oven to 350°F and place rack in center of oven.

2. Combine cracker crumbs, brown sugar, and melted butter in a 9-inch pie pan. Press evenly into pan and bake for 10 to 15 minutes. Chill crust.

3. **To prepare ganache:** Bring ¼ cup heavy cream to a boil in a small pan over medium-high heat, or microwave for 2 minutes, and pour over chocolate chips. Whisk together until smooth. Pour into cooked and cooled pie shell and spread evenly over bottom. Refrigerate.

4. **To prepare filling:** In a large mixing bowl, with an electric mixer set on high, whip cream cheese and sugar until smooth. Add milk, peanut butter, and vanilla. Beat until well mixed.

5. In a separate bowl, whip chilled cream until stiff and fold into peanut butter mixture. Spoon gently into chilled crust, using a spatula to smooth surface of pie, and refrigerate for at least 4 hours.

6. Garnish with chocolate shavings, crushed peanuts, or whipped cream and serve at once. (Rumored to be even better the second day.)

**Yield: 1 9-inch pie, 10 to 12 servings**

### Glacier Ice Cream

■ ■ ■

*One of the joys of camping in Glacier Bay National Park is that, even on the longest trips, we can have ice cream every night. The only equipment necessary is a large coffee can with a plastic lid (also useful for picking wild berries), a long-handled wooden spoon, and a bucket.*

*We make up the ice cream mixture at home (any recipe is fine) and carry it in the can with the lid securely taped down. When we have a craving for ice cream, we camp on a beach that has a good selection of stranded icebergs, or tow one to shore if we have a kayak. The best bergs for making ice cream are those that have been beached for a day or two —they readily crumble into nuggets or flakes of ice when struck.*

*A few inches of glacier ice nuggets go into the bottom of the bucket, and then the coffee can is placed on top. The can is completely surrounded with more ice and salt (about a handful of salt to every three handfuls of ice) and seawater is poured into the ice-salt mixture. Everything is wrapped in a sleeping bag for about 20 minutes, or until ice crystals form on the inside of the can. Then we punch a hole in the lid, insert the spoon, and spin the can, adding more ice and salt as it melts. When we can't stir anymore, the ice cream is done and ready for a topping of wild berries. No need to worry about leftovers—there won't be any.*

# ICE CREAM PIE

Simple, good, and just right when you need a dessert you can make in advance, this pie hits the spot every time.

**Preparation Time:** 1 hour

**Baking Time:** 10 minutes

**Chilling Time:** 1 hour

### ■ Crumb Crust

2 cups granola (substitute finely ground graham cracker, chocolate wafer, or cookie crumbs, or a combination of any of them)
4 tablespoons butter, melted
¼ cup packed brown sugar

### ■ Filling

5 cups ice cream (choose your favorite flavor or combination of flavors)

### ■ Chocolate Mousse

1 ounce unsweetened chocolate, chopped
1 ounce semisweet chocolate, chopped
1 tablespoon butter
½ cup heavy cream
½ cup egg whites (3 to 4)
¼ cup granulated sugar
1½ teaspoons dark rum (optional)

### ■ Chocolate Topping

½ ounce unsweetened chocolate
1½ tablespoons butter
2 tablespoons corn syrup
2 tablespoons heavy cream
2 tablespoons chopped walnuts

1. **To prepare crust:** Preheat oven to 350°F and place rack in center of oven.

2. Combine crumbs, butter, and brown sugar in a 9-inch pie pan and evenly line pan. Bake for 10 minutes. Remove from oven and chill thoroughly 10 to 15 minutes.

3. Using an electric mixer fitted with a paddle, soften ice cream to a thick spreading consistency. Working very quickly, fill chilled pie crust with softened ice cream. Smooth top with a spatula and freeze while preparing mousse.

4. **To prepare mousse:** In a small bowl in the microwave or in a small pan over a double boiler, heat 1 ounce unsweetened chocolate and 1 ounce semisweet chocolate with 1 tablespoon butter until they are melted. Stir until smooth and cool slightly.

5. In a large mixing bowl, whip ¼ cup heavy cream until stiff and set aside. Warm remaining ¼ cup cream and, working quickly, stir it into chocolate until combined. Gently whisk into whipped cream.

6. In a separate bowl, whip egg whites until frothy and, while continuing to whip, gradually add sugar. Whip until they form stiff peaks.

7. Fold egg whites into chocolate whipped cream and add dark rum, folding just until combined.

8. Take pie out of freezer and, using a spatula, spread with mousse, sculpting gentle swirls evenly around pie. Return to freezer.

9. **To prepare chocolate topping:** In a small bowl in the microwave or in a small pot over a double boiler, melt together ½ ounce unsweetened chocolate and 1½ tablespoons butter and the syrup. Stir in heavy cream. Cool to room temperature.

10. Remove pie from freezer and drizzle chocolate topping over it. Sprinkle top with walnuts and freeze pie until you are ready to serve it. (Let it freeze solid, uncovered, then cover tightly with plastic wrap until you are ready to serve it.)

11. Cut with a hot knife and serve still frozen.

**Yield: 1 9-inch pie, or 10 servings**

# PEACH CRUNCH PIE

This pie, filled with luscious summer fruit in a rich sour cream custard and topped with a walnut streusel, is one of our most popular desserts.

**Preparation Time:** 45 minutes (including making crust)

**Baking Time:** 1 hour 10 minutes

1 unbaked single 9-inch pie crust (page 212)

■ **Filling**

1½ cups sour cream
1 egg
1 cup granulated sugar
2 teaspoons kirsch (substitute vanilla extract)
¼ cup unbleached white flour
½ teaspoon nutmeg
½ teaspoon salt
5 cups peeled and thinly sliced fresh peaches or nectarines (substitute drained unsweetened canned peaches, fresh apples, or reconstituted dried apricots)

■ **Streusel Topping**

½ cup coarsely chopped walnuts
2½ tablespoons granulated sugar
2½ tablespoons brown sugar
¼ cup unbleached white flour
1½ teaspoons ground cinnamon
Pinch of salt
4 tablespoons butter, cut into several pieces

1. Preheat oven to 450°F and place rack in center of oven.

2. **To prepare filling:** In a large mixing bowl, stir together sour cream, egg, 1 cup sugar, kirsch, ¼ cup flour, nutmeg, and ½ teaspoon salt. Stir in peaches. Pour into unbaked pie shell.

3. Bake for 10 minutes, then reduce heat to 350°F and bake for 10 minutes.

4. **While pie is baking, prepare streusel topping:** Place walnuts, granulated sugar, brown sugar, flour, cinnamon, and pinch of salt in a large bowl or food processor and cut together briefly. Add butter to bowl or processor, and cut in just until mixture resembles coarse crumbs. Do not cream mixture or allow butter to melt into crumbs. Refrigerate until ready to use.

NOTE:
To peel peaches easily, drop in boiling water for 10 seconds. Drain and slip off skin.

5. Remove pie from oven and sprinkle evenly with topping. Return to oven and continue to bake at 350°F for 45 to 50 minutes, until all but very center of pie seems a little puffed, juices are bubbling from middle of pie, and topping is lightly browned.

6. Remove from oven, cool on a rack, and serve at room temperature; or refrigerate and serve cold. Store tightly wrapped in refrigerator.

**Yield: 1 9-inch pie**

**NOTE:**
**It's normal for filling to appear curdled.**

### Picking Fruit

■ ■ ■

*Most of us pick our fruit from the produce department of a supermarket, not ripe from the vine. So how can you tell if it is ready?*

**1. Sniff it.** *Does it smell like a pear? Is that the glorious scent of late summer peaches? If it smells good and smells like the fruit it is, it likely will taste good and fruity too.*

*Scent-sensitive fruit:*

*Strawberries*
*Pears*
*Thick-skinned melons (cantaloupes)*
*Peaches*
*Nectarines*

**2. Gently run your hand over it (don't squeeze!).** *If it feels a little tacky or sticky, it should be sweet and delicious. (Ask your grocer not to wrap everything in plastic: It's not good for the environment and you can't check your fruit.)*

*Sticky sweet fruit:*

*Smooth-skinned melons*
*Papaya*
*Mango*

# WILD BLUEBERRY PIE

At the height of summer, take the kids, the dog, and some sandwiches and spend an afternoon in the sun listening to the hum of the day, languidly picking blueberries for pie. Pick them just as they begin to ripen so they aren't too sweet, and pick enough so you can enjoy the spicy sweetness all year. Wild blueberries freeze very well.

**Preparation Time:** 45 minutes (including making crust)

**Baking Time:** 45 minutes

1 unbaked double 9-inch pie crust (page 212)

■ **Filling**

4 cups fresh wild blueberries, soaked in salt water for ½ hour, cleaned, rinsed, and drained (substitute huckleberries or drained defrosted frozen wild berries or domesticated berries, but if you use domesticated berries, add 2 tablespoons lemon juice to filling)
1 cup granulated sugar
⅓ cup all-purpose flour
⅛ teaspoon ground cloves

1. Preheat oven to 425°F and place rack in center of oven. Place a rack immediately below the center and set a foil-lined cookie sheet on it to catch any drips from pie.

2. **To prepare filling:** In a large mixing bowl, combine blueberries, sugar, flour, and cloves. When they are evenly mixed, pour into unbaked pie shell.

3. Dampen edge of shell with a little water all the way around pie. Gently fold top crust in half and transfer it to pie. Unfold and center dough on pie. Trim edges to match bottom layer.

4. Folding two layers under, pinch together to create a tightly sealed, attractive edge to pie. Using a fork or tip of a small knife, make a pattern of small holes or slits in top of pie. Place in center of oven and bake at 425°F for 10 minutes. Reduce heat to 375°F and bake for 30 minutes, until juices are bubbling out of center.

5. Remove from oven and cool briefly on a rack. Serve warm or at room temperature, with ice cream or whipped cream if you like.

**Yield: 1 8- or 9-inch pie**

NOTE:
The pie is best eaten the same day, but can be stored overnight tightly wrapped at room temperature or in refrigerator.

NOTE:
A friend suggests a little crystallized ginger grated into whipped cream to top blueberry pies. It is delicious.

# FRESH FRUIT ICE

Here is the perfect fruit ice recipe; don't bother looking any further. This is ideal for those times when fresh fruit seems the best choice to follow a meal, but the occasion calls for a special dessert. The clear, sparkling colors look like jewels in a crystal glass, and the crisp, refreshing flavor finishes any meal wonderfully. Because it works well with almost every fruit available at any time of year and it can be made (and dished up) well ahead, this is an ideal dessert for a large dinner party.

Linda Youtzy contributed this recipe to the *Carnegie Treasures Cookbook* and, with the kind permission of the Women's Committee, we share the recipe with you.

**Preparation Time:**  20 minutes

**Freezing Time:**  1 hour (depends upon your ice cream maker)

> 1½ cups fresh fruit (nectarines, blueberries, pineapple, melon, kiwi, papaya, and pears all work well, or try your favorite)
> ¾ cup granulated sugar
> ½ cup fresh lemon juice (2 to 3 lemons)
> ½ cup fresh orange or grapefruit juice (2 oranges)

■ **Garnish**

> Fresh mint leaves, slices of fresh fruit, or edible flowers (see note, page 35)

1. In a food processor or blender, purée fruit with sugar and juices, or purée 1 cup fruit and reserve ½ cup to garnish the ice.

2. Pour purée into an ice cream maker and freeze according to manufacturer's instructions. (Strain mixture through a wire-mesh sieve if you want a very clear rather than creamy ice. We like ours creamy and full of texture, and so do not strain the purée.)

3. Scoop out into individual dishes (stemmed crystal glasses look very elegant) and serve garnished with fresh mint leaves, fruit, or edible sweet flowers such as forget-me-nots, violas, or rose petals.

**Yield: 3 cups ice**

# STRAWBERRY-RHUBARB PIE

Spring is officially here when the rhubarb is ready. The brightly tart flavor, mellowed just slightly by spring strawberries, will wake you from your long winter's nap.

**Preparation Time:** 45 minutes (including preparation of the shell)

**Baking Time:** 1 hour

**Cooling Time:** 30 minutes

1 unbaked double 9-inch pie crust (page 212)

■ **Filling**

4 cups sliced fresh rhubarb stems (1¼ pounds), or substitute defrosted frozen rhubarb, but pie will be drier
1 pint fresh strawberries, washed, patted dry, and stems removed (if they are large, cut into quarters)
⅓ cup minute tapioca (substitute all-purpose flour)
1⅓ to 1½ cups granulated sugar (homegrown rhubarb and wild strawberries tend to be slightly more tart than domesticated, and some people prefer sweeter flavors, so adjust sugar to suit your needs)
½ teaspoon ground cinnamon
2 tablespoons butter

1. **To prepare filling:** Place rhubarb, strawberries, tapioca, sugar, and cinnamon in a large glass or stainless steel bowl, mix well, and allow to sit for 15 minutes.

2. Preheat oven to 400°F and place rack in center of oven.

3. Pour rhubarb mixture into unbaked shell, mounding it toward center. Dot filling with butter, cut into teaspoons.

4. Use water to dampen lip of pie shell. Loosely fold top crust in half and transfer it to pie. Unfold and center on pie. Trim upper crust to match lower. Folding under, pinch two layers of crust together to create a secure and attractive edging to pie.

5. With a fork or small knife, make a pattern of small holes or slits in top of pie. Lightly dust with a pinch of sugar and place in oven. Put a cookie sheet lined with foil on shelf directly below pie to catch any drips.

6. Bake at 400°F for 10 minutes, then reduce heat to 375°F and bake for 40 to 45 minutes, until juices are bubbling out of slits in center of pie.

**7.** Remove from oven and allow to cool on a rack for 30 minutes or more before cutting. Serve warm or at room temperature (with vanilla ice cream!). Cover tightly and store at room temperature for 1 day, longer in the refrigerator. (It is best if served the same day.)

**Yield: 1 9-inch pie, or 8 pieces**

---

**Wild Berry Myth #1**

■ ■ ■

### Wild Berries Don't Need Pectin

*Imagine that you've just gathered a quart of luscious wild berries in spite of the bears and mosquitoes. You've retrieved the big kettle from the top shelf without falling off the chair, and located lids for all the jars. Think of the satisfaction you'll feel seeing the sparkling jelly jars lined up on the pantry shelf and the pleasure of your friends when they receive them as gifts. You begin the hot, tedious work, following the recipe to the letter, and after several hours you end up with—failure.*

*Chances are it's not your fault. Even though recipes state that certain berries don't need extra pectin to jell, our experience has been exactly the opposite. We have never found any Alaskan berry that will always jell, no matter what. Even the supposedly goof-proof ones like cranberries, highbush cranberries, nagoonberries, and red currants are variable in their natural pectin content, depending on their ripeness, and cooking and storage conditions.*

*You can save yourself a lot of time and frustration by using this simple pectin test. Extract the juice from the berries using your favorite method and cool the juice to room temperature. Mix 1 tablespoon juice with 1 tablespoon highproof grain alcohol (such as Everclear) in a jar. If it forms a gelatinous blob, there is enough natural pectin in the berry juice to jell by itself. Two or three separate lumps mean the juice is moderately high in pectin; flakes indicate low pectin content that will not jell by itself. With this knowledge, you can adjust the sugar and acid proportions and add extra pectin, if necessary, to produce gorgeous jelly every time.*

**NOTE:**
The custard can be made 1 day ahead, covered and refrigerated, and the desserts assembled early the day they will be eaten.

# STRAWBERRIES ROMANOFF

Strawberries and cream seem a perfect match. Lightly flavor the cream with sherry and you have an extraordinary dessert.

**Preparation Time:** 30 minutes

**Chilling Time:** 30 minutes

6 egg yolks
½ cup granulated sugar
½ cup Amontillado or cream sherry
5 cups fresh strawberries (substitute raspberries, huckleberries, or blueberries)
2 cups heavy cream
½ cup sour cream

1. Chill 10 stemmed glasses. Prepare a double boiler or set a large, round-bottomed, metal bowl over a pot of simmering water on medium heat.

2. Gently whisk together yolks, sugar, and ¼ cup sherry in bowl over simmering water. Continue stirring until mixture is foamy, about 1 minute. Gradually add remainder of sherry, stirring constantly until mixture is foamy throughout and thickened to a fluffy saucelike consistency, about 5 minutes. Remove from heat and chill mixture.

3. Wash, dry, and hull strawberries. If they are large, cut them into uniform, bite-size pieces. (Reserve 10 whole strawberries for garnish.)

4. In a large mixing bowl, whip cream until it is stiff.

5. In a separate large mixing bowl, stir together cooled custard and sour cream. Gently fold in whipped cream.

6. Carefully spoon ¼ cup custard into each chilled glass. Add a layer of ½ cup strawberries and top with additional custard. Decorate with a whole berry. Refrigerate until ready to serve. Serve chilled.

**Yield: 8 to 10 servings**

# CRÈME BRÛLÉE

A perfect example of simplicity as elegance, this classic dessert is suited to the grandest occasion, yet takes almost no time to make, can be made several days ahead, and doubles or triples easily. This delicate honey-flavored custard will become a standby for your fanciest dinners and a welcome treat for a quiet evening.

**Preparation Time:** 20 minutes

**Baking Time:** 40 minutes

**Chilling Time:** several hours or overnight

**Completion Time:** 5 minutes

  2 cups half-and-half
  1 cup heavy cream (no substitutions)
  ¼ cup honey
  7 egg yolks
  1 teaspoon vanilla extract
  ½ cup brown sugar

1. Preheat oven to 325°F and place rack in center of oven. Arrange 6 custard cups in a large baking pan.

2. In a large pot over medium high heat, or in the microwave, warm half-and-half and heavy cream with honey to about 115°F, or warm-bath temperature. Transfer to a large bowl with a spout.

3. Gently whisk in yolks and vanilla, just until combined, but not frothy.

4. Strain mixture through a wire-mesh sieve into a large pitcher, then pour into custard cups.

5. Set cups in baking pan and fill pan with 1 inch of hot water. Cover with an inverted cookie sheet and bake 35 to 40 minutes, until a knife inserted in center of a custard comes out clean. (Try not to overbake, which will toughen custard.) Remove from water bath and chill thoroughly. Cover tightly when completely cooled.

6. Preheat broiler. Sprinkle each custard with a thin coating (about 1½ teaspoons) of brown sugar and pat smooth. Set cups on a cookie sheet and place under broiler until sugar is melted and beginning to brown. Serve immediately.

**Yield: 6 servings**

NOTE:
The custards may be prepared through step 5 and kept tightly wrapped in refrigerator for up to 1 week.

NOTE:
The custard should still be cold, even though sugar is melted. This is best accomplished if you are sure your broiler is quite hot before you put custard under it, and if layer of brown sugar is not too thick.

# CHOCOLATE MOUSSE

This is the perfect mousse: The season is always open and there is no bag limit.

**Preparation Time:** 30 minutes

**Chilling Time:** 1 hour or overnight

- 2 ounces unsweetened chocolate, chopped into ½-inch chunks
- 2 ounces semisweet chocolate, chopped into ½-inch chunks
- 2 tablespoons butter
- 1 cup egg whites (about 8)
- ½ cup granulated sugar
- 1 cup heavy cream
- 1 tablespoon dark rum (substitute other flavorings if you prefer)

■ **Garnish**

Whipped cream, chocolate curls, or chopped walnuts

1. Chill 6 or 7 fancy glasses (champagne or parfaits look very nice).

2. In a small pot in a warm water bath over low heat, or in a small covered glass dish on high in the microwave for 2 to 3 minutes, melt both chocolates and butter together until smooth.

3. While chocolate is melting, place egg whites in a large mixing bowl and whip until frothy. Continue to whip, adding sugar gradually, until stiff but not dry.

4. In a separate bowl, whip heavy cream to firm peaks.

5. Working very quickly, pour chocolate into egg whites, stirring with a large balloon whip. Stir just to combine all chocolate with a little egg white, then add whipped cream and fold together. Just before completely combined, add rum and finish folding together.

6. Using a pastry bag fitted with a large fluted tip, pipe (or spoon) into chilled glasses and chill for at least 1 hour before serving.

7. Garnish with a dollop of whipped cream, chocolate curls or shavings, or chopped walnuts.

**Yield: 7 to 8 servings**

# PART 3

# FROM THE PANTRY

(INCLUDING BUTTERS, SPICES,
MARINADES, DRESSINGS,
SAUCES, STOCKS, AND OTHER
EMBELLISHMENTS)

# FLAVORED BUTTERS

Adding herbs and seasonings to plain butter allows you to add interest to a dish quickly, easily, and without complicated sauces. Let a bit of butter full of flavors melt over a grilling steak; add the seasoned butter to the pan after you've lightly fried meat, chicken, or fish, swirl to combine with the pan juices, and pour over the whole dish; or toss steamed vegetables or pasta with melted herbed butter. The combinations and possibilities are unlimited. Here are several of our favorite flavored butters. The preparation time for each is 15 minutes.

### ■ Garlic Butter

> 1 tablespoon minced fresh garlic
> 1 teaspoon medium-dry sherry (substitute fresh lemon juice)
> ¼ pound butter, softened
> ¼ teaspoon salt
> Freshly ground black pepper

1. In a small mixing bowl, beat minced garlic and sherry into softened butter. Add salt and pepper, taste, and adjust the seasoning.

2. Use at once, or place on a sheet of plastic wrap and roll into a tube, twist ends, and store in refrigerator for 1 week, or in freezer for up to 3 months.

3. Slice to use as needed for cooking vegetables, meat, chicken, or fish. Melt and use for garlic bread.

### ■ Anchovy Butter

> 2 to 4 anchovy fillets, mashed (or use 1 to 2 tablespoons anchovy paste)
> 1 tablespoon fresh lemon juice
> Several grindings of black pepper
> ¼ pound butter

1. Proceed as for garlic butter.

2. Slice and melt over steaks or grilled fish (especially good with swordfish).

### ■ Basil-Mustard Butter

> ¼ cup coarsely chopped fresh basil
> 2 tablespoons Dijon mustard
> ¼ pound butter
> ¼ teaspoon salt
> Freshly ground black pepper

1. Purée basil and mustard together in a blender until smooth.

2. Proceed as for garlic butter.

3. Slice and use in scrambled eggs, with steamed vegetables, or over poached or grilled seafood.

### ■ Bourbon Butter

1 cup good-quality bourbon or Scotch (no mild whiskeys, please)
1 tablespoon chopped fresh chives (or green onions)
1 teaspoon fresh lemon juice
½ teaspoon Dijon mustard
¼ pound butter
¼ teaspoon salt
⅛ teaspoon freshly ground black pepper

1. In a small pan over medium heat, cook bourbon and chives together until liquid is reduced to about ¼ cup. Remove from heat and cool.

2. Proceed as for garlic butter.

3. Slice and melt over grilled steaks.

### ■ Dill Butter

1 tablespoon minced fresh dill (1 teaspoon dried)
1 teaspoon fresh lemon juice
¼ pound butter
¼ teaspoon salt
Freshly ground black pepper

1. Proceed as for garlic butter.

2. Slice and melt over poached, grilled, or baked seafood, or toss with steamed vegetables.

### ■ Lemon-Caper Butter

4 teaspoons chopped capers
4 teaspoons fresh lemon juice
2 teaspoons freshly grated lemon zest
¼ cup butter
¼ teaspoon salt
Freshly ground black pepper

1. Proceed as for garlic butter.

2. Slice and melt over grilled chicken, grilled or baked seafood, or steamed vegetables.

### ■ Lemon-Garlic Butter

2 tablespoons fresh lemon juice (grate and squeeze 1 lemon)
2 teaspoons freshly grated lemon zest
2 teaspoons minced fresh garlic (2 large cloves)
¼ pound butter
¼ teaspoon salt
Freshly ground black pepper

1. Proceed as for garlic butter.

2. Slice and use wherever you might use garlic butter. Particularly good on baked or grilled seafood or chicken.

### ■ Tarragon Butter

2 teaspoons fresh lemon juice
1 teaspoon dried tarragon (1 tablespoon fresh)
1 teaspoon minced fresh chives (substitute green onions)
½ teaspoon Dijon mustard
¼ pound butter
¼ teaspoon salt
Freshly ground black pepper

1. Proceed as for garlic butter.

2. Slice as needed—it's good on almost everything except dessert. Melt over lightly fried fish, use to baste roast chicken, on steaks or chops, or mixed with steamed vegetables.

# HIGHBUSH CRANBERRY— APPLE BUTTER

This relish has been a favorite in southeast Alaska at least since the thirties, when this recipe appeared in a University of Alaska Cooperative Extension pamphlet. Longtime Alaskan Nicki Hopper introduced it to us when we were looking for a good accompaniment for smoked turkey and pasta salad (page 32). We also enjoy it with pork chops, deer, moose, ham, on pancakes, and hot honey-yogurt scones (page 156).

**Preparation Time:**   4 hours

    1 pound dried apples
    2 quarts warm water
    2 quarts washed highbush cranberries, picked early,
        before they are too ripe and before a frost*
    Sugar
    1 teaspoon ground cinnamon
    ½ teaspoon ground cloves
    ¼ teaspoon salt
    3 tablespoons fresh lemon juice (1 lemon)

1. Soak apples in a large stainless steel or enamel pot in warm water for 1 hour. Add highbush cranberries and cook over medium-high heat until soft.

2. Press mixture through a sieve to remove seeds and skin. Measure pulp and return it to pot. Add three quarters as much sugar as you have pulp, then stir in cinnamon, cloves, and salt. Cook until sugar is thoroughly dissolved and butter has a bright glasslike (rather than milky) appearance. Add freshly squeezed lemon juice and pack in sterilized canning jars. Seal in a hot-water bath according to instructions with jar lids (or freeze in 1-cup containers).

**Yield: 14 cups**

**\*Picked after a frost, highbush cranberries have a somewhat skunky aroma. Although we know people who prefer to pick them only after a frost, most prefer them picked before.**

# GARAM MASALA

Keep this freshly ground mixture of spices on hand to liven up a good curry. This recipe makes enough to last for a while and enough to share with a friend who enjoys curries. (In a tiny decorative spice jar, it makes a welcome holiday or hostess gift.)

**Preparation Time:**   20 minutes

⅓ cup whole cardamom seeds
2½ tablespoons whole cumin seeds
2½ tablespoons whole black peppercorns
1½ tablespoons whole cloves
2 whole nutmegs, crushed
2 tablespoons ground cinnamon

1. Preheat oven to 350°F. Spread cardamom, cumin, peppercorns, cloves, and nutmegs on a cookie sheet and toast until lightly browned (about 10 minutes), or cook at low heat on top of stove in a large pan, stirring frequently.

2. Grind to a powder in a blender, food processor, or coffee grinder. Add cinnamon and mix well.

3. Store in an airtight container in a cool dark place. Add as seasoning to curries or Indian dishes. This keeps well for up to a year.

**Yield: about ½ cup**

# GANACHE

This chocolate icing meets every criteria: It's quick, easy, deliciously chocolaty, and can be used for almost everything. In an emergency, just a spoonful right out of the container hits the spot.

**Preparation Time:**   15 minutes

8 ounces semisweet chocolate chips (1⅓ cups)
1 cup heavy cream

1. Place chips in a medium bowl.

2. Bring cream to a boil in a small pot over high heat, or in a 2-cup bowl in microwave. Pour boiling cream over chips and whisk until completely smooth.

3. Cool to room temperature but still pourable, then dip cookies, strawberries, or tiny tartlets in ganache, set on racks to drip and harden, and serve at once. Or pour over a cake, spreading until evenly coated; or pour over ice cream; or whip until stiffened and lighter in color, flavor as you like, and use to fill cakes or truffles.

4. Store ganache tightly covered and refrigerated for up to 2 weeks.

**Yield: 1¾ cups**

■        ■        ■

# BROWN RICE

Steamed brown rice is a classic dish that can be dressed up or down as the occasion demands, and is always in good taste.

**Preparation Time:** 5 minutes

**Cooking Time:** 45 minutes

    2 tablespoons oil
    2 cups brown rice
    4 cups water
    1 teaspoon salt
    1 teaspoon pepper
    1 bay leaf
    ½ teaspoon thyme

1. Heat oil in a large pot over medium-high heat. Add rice and stir until it begins to crackle, about 2 minutes.

2. Add water and seasonings. Cover pot, bring to a boil, and reduce heat to a low simmer. Cook for 45 minutes, until rice is fluffy and has absorbed all the water.

3. Remove from heat, transfer to a serving dish, and serve at once.

**Yield: 6 to 7 cups**

# MALLORQUINA MARINADE

This is a robust treatment for grilled seafood. Perla Meyers, in her book, *The Seasonal Kitchen*, recommends it with prawns or scallops; this version goes beautifully with salmon, halibut, and almost any other fish.

**Preparation Time:** 15 minutes

**Marinating Time:** 2 hours to overnight

⅔ cup olive oil
¼ cup freshly squeezed lemon juice (1 large)
1 tablespoon hot dried chili peppers, crumbled
1 teaspoon finely chopped fresh basil (substitute ½ teaspoon dried)
1 large sprig of fresh oregano (or 1 teaspoon dried)
1 teaspoon dry mustard
4 teaspoons minced fresh garlic (2 large cloves)
1 large pinch of chopped parsley, fresh or dried

**Yield: enough marinade for 2 pounds of seafood**

1. Combine all ingredients in a large flat-bottomed enamel or glass container.

2. Add seafood of your choice and marinate, refrigerated, for 2 hours, or up to overnight, before grilling or broiling.

# TERIYAKI MARINADE

Grill or stir-fry teriyaki-marinated chicken, fish, or meat.

**Preparation Time:** 5 minutes

**Marinating Time:** 1 hour to overnight

¼ cup tamari or soy sauce
¼ cup dry sherry
¼ cup honey
2 tablespoons safflower oil
1 teaspoon minced ginger
1 teaspoon minced garlic (1 large clove)
1½ teaspoons oriental sesame oil*

**Yield: 1 cup**

*****See mail-order sources, page 237.**

1. Combine all ingredients in a glass mixing bowl.

2. Marinate 2 pounds meat, chicken, or fish, refrigerated, for 1 hour, or up to overnight.

# KING JONATHAN MARINADE

Our friend Jonathan Douglas prepared a wonderful meal of grilled fresh king salmon for us one evening. He revealed his secret: this marvelous marinade from *The New York Times Cook Book*. It has been one of our favorites ever since. Although listed there as a marinade simply for grilled salmon, it is good and simple with every type of fresh fish. With kind permission, we pass the recipe on to you.

**Preparation Time:** 15 minutes

**Marinating Time:** 2 to 4 hours

> ½ cup olive oil
> ½ cup dry vermouth
> 1 tablespoon freshly squeezed lemon juice
> ½ teaspoon salt
> 2 teaspoons dried parsley
> Pinch of each: dried thyme, marjoram, and sage
> Dash of freshly ground pepper

1. Combine all ingredients in a flat-bottomed enamel or glass container.
2. Add up to 3 pounds fresh fish fillets or steaks and marinate, refrigerated, for 2 to 4 hours before grilling or broiling.

**Yield: enough marinade for 3 pounds of fish**

---

### Tamari or Soy Sauce?

■ ■ ■

*Most people quite satisfactorily use soy sauce, tamari, and shoyu interchangeably. For people who enjoy oriental food, the differences among them are significant, and using the right sauce in the right place gives a dish authenticity.*

*All are products of fermented soy beans. Soy sauce and shoyu are made from soy combined with wheat; tamari originated as the by-product in the production of miso and consequently is usually made of soy and rice or very little wheat. All are made in varying degrees of saltiness, thickness, and darkness, which allows the cook to choose a sauce that adds just the right touch to a dish without overpowering a delicate flavor.*

*We use tamari in our cooking because, unlike many domestic soy sauces that are artificially fermented, it is made according to the traditional fermentation process, and because its flavor seems to fit our needs.*

# PIE CRUST

The trick is not to cream, stir, knead, or beat but to "cut" pie dough. You want the butter in tiny little pieces barely bound together with the flour by a little water. Keep everything chilled so the butter does not melt into the flour, and remember that flour becomes tough and strong with handling. "As easy as pie" is not as easy as it seems, but it's not difficult if you keep the basic principles in mind.

**Preparation Time:** 30 minutes

■ **For a 9-inch single-crust pie**

1½ cups unbleached white flour
¼ pound butter, margarine, or shortening, chilled
3 tablespoons very cold water

■ **For a 9-inch double-crust or 10-inch single-crust pie**

2 cups unbleached white flour
¼ pound plus 2⅔ tablespoons butter, margarine, or shortening, chilled
¼ cup very cold water

■ **For a 10-inch double-crust pie**

2¼ cups unbleached white flour
¼ pound plus 4 tablespoons butter, margarine, or shortening, chilled
5 to 6 tablespoons cold water

1. **To prepare any size pie crust:** In a mixing bowl, cut flour and butter together using a pastry cutter, 2 knives, your fingers, or a food processor fitted with a steel blade until mixture resembles coarse meal. Sprinkle mixture with water, 1 tablespoon at a time, tossing gently with a fork, just until dough begins to come together. (Take care not to stir or knead dough, which will toughen it.)

2. Gently gather dough into a ball. If dough is warm or very soft, wrap and refrigerate for 30 minutes to prevent butter from melting into flour when you roll out dough.

3. **To prepare a single crust:** Roll out on a well-floured surface to a circle 3 to 4 inches larger in diameter than your pie pan and about ⅛ inch thick. Slip a long spatula or knife under dough to loosen it and carefully fold dough loosely in half and place in pie pan. Unfold, center it in pan, and trim edges so they overhang pan by ½ inch. Folding under itself, pinch overhanging dough

to make an attractive edge that stands up on lip of pie pan. Refrigerate until ready to fill.

4. Fill and bake as directed in recipe.

5. **To prepare a double crust:** Divide dough into 2 parts, one slightly larger than the other. Refrigerate the smaller piece. Generously sprinkle work surface with flour and roll out larger piece of dough into a circle 3 to 4 inches larger than your pie pan and ⅛ inch thick. Carefully slip a flat spatula or long knife under dough to be sure it is loose from work surface, then loosely fold dough in half. Lift dough and place it on half of pie pan. Unfold dough to cover other half of plate. Trim edges of dough so that they overhang pan by ½ inch. If there are tears or parts where dough does not cover plate, moisten with water and patch with a bit of dough.

6. After pie is filled, sprinkle more flour on work surface and roll out remaining bit of dough to a circle about 2 inches in diameter larger than pie pan and ⅛ inch thick.

7. Use water to dampen lip of pie shell. Loosely fold top crust in half and transfer it to half of filled pie pan. Unfold and center on pie. Trim upper crust to match lower. Folding under, pinch two layers of crust together to create a secure and attractive edging to pie.

8. With a fork or small knife, make an attractive pattern of small holes or slits in top of pie. Bake as directed in recipe.

**Yield: 1 pie shell**

NOTE:
**Unbaked pie shells may be wrapped and frozen to be baked later —convenient for last-minute quiches or pies.**

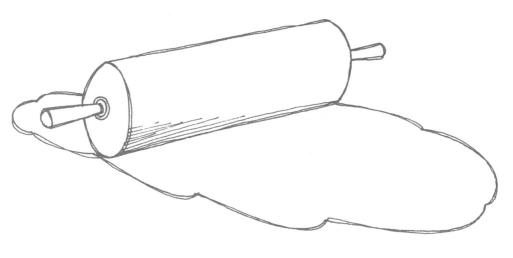

# ROASTED RED PEPPERS

Peppers become tender and sweet with just a hint of smokiness when they have been roasted. Sliced or chopped, they are good in salads, soups, and sandwiches. Marinated in olive oil with a bit of garlic and perhaps a fresh basil leaf, they become an appetizer or flavorful addition to pasta dishes. Puréed, they complement a grilled steak or fish fillet handsomely.

**Cooking Time:**  5 minutes

**Resting Time:**  3 minutes

 1 large red bell pepper

1. Place pepper directly on a burner on high heat or under broiler. (Turn on the overhead fan!) Cook and turn pepper until charred on all sides. Remove from heat and place in a paper bag if you have one handy. Allow to rest until cool.

2. Carefully remove blackened skin. Cut pepper in half, remove stem, seeds, and interior ribs. Cut into strips and marinate or purée, as needed.

**Yield: ½ cup sliced pepper**

■         ■         ■

# R & H CHEESE SPREAD

Deborah "R." Marshall and Scott "H." Miller, founders of the Fiddlehead, really like this herbed cream cheese.

**Preparation Time:**  15 minutes

 8 ounces cream cheese
 ⅓ cup mayonnaise
 ¼ cup thinly sliced green onions (3 to 4 medium)

1. Beat all ingredients together in a medium mixing bowl.

2. Cover and refrigerate up to 1 week. Use on sandwiches, as dip for vegetables, on baked potatoes, or as an omelet filling (see recipe, page 55).

**Yield: about 1 cup**

# SALAD CROUTONS

Croutons are the real reason people eat salad. Keep some on hand.

**Preparation Time:**  15 minutes

**Baking Time:**  20 minutes

> 3 tablespoons safflower oil
> 3 tablespoons butter
> ¼ teaspoon Worcestershire sauce
> ¼ teaspoon minced garlic or garlic salt
> ¼ teaspoon salt
> ⅛ teaspoon pepper
> 4 cups cubed stale bread (use sourdough, herb, honey-butter-oatmeal, bran, whole wheat, or pumpernickel, but not a sweet bread such as orange-mace-raisin)

1. Preheat oven to 325°F. Lightly oil a large cookie sheet.

2. In a small pot over medium heat, combine oil, butter, Worcestershire, garlic, salt, and pepper (or melt together in a small bowl in the microwave for 1 minute). Stir until butter is melted. Pour into a large mixing bowl.

3. Add cubes of bread and, using your hands or two large spoons, gently toss together until evenly mixed.

4. Spread seasoned bread evenly on cookie sheet. Bake for 10 minutes. Use a spatula to turn and redistribute croutons. Return to oven and bake for 10 minutes more, just until croutons are dried and crisp but not browned. (Cooking time varies with type and staleness of bread. Watch closely to be sure croutons don't burn.)

5. Remove from oven and cool on cookie sheet. Transfer to airtight containers to store for up to 1 week.

**Yield: 4 cups**

# SALAD SEEDS

Sprinkle these roasted seasoned seeds in salads, on soups, or over steamed vegetables.

> ½ cup raw sunflower seeds (available in health food stores*)
> ⅓ cup untoasted sesame seeds
> 1 to 1½ teaspoons tamari or soy sauce

1. Preheat oven to 325°F.

2. In a large mixing bowl, stir seeds together with tamari.

3. Spread on a large, lightly oiled cookie sheet and bake for 15 minutes. Using a metal spatula, stir and redistribute them. Return them to oven to bake for another 15 minutes. Bake until dried and very lightly browned.

4. Remove from oven and cool on pan, then transfer to an airtight container and store at room temperature for up to 2 weeks.

**Yield: 1 scant cup**

**\*See mail-order sources, page 237.**

■       ■       ■

# BLUE CHEESE SALAD DRESSING

Thick and chunky and creamy all at once, this dressing makes the most of a simple green salad.

**Preparation Time:**  15 minutes

> 1 cup mayonnaise
> 5 ounces blue cheese, crumbled
> ¼ cup orange or apple juice
> 2 tablespoons sour cream
> 1 tablespoon apple cider vinegar
> 1 tablespoon finely grated onion

1. In a large mixing bowl, with a wooden spoon or electric mixer set on low, beat together mayonnaise and blue cheese until it is as lumpy or as smooth as you like.

(You can use a food processor fitted with a steel blade if you like it smoother rather than lumpier.) Add remaining ingredients and mix well.

2. Transfer to a glass or plastic container and store tightly covered in refrigerator for up to 1 week.

**Yield: 2 cups**

■         ■         ■

# ORIENTAL VINAIGRETTE

This makes an intriguing change from the usual oil-and-vinegar dressing.

**Preparation Time:** 15 minutes

    1 cup safflower or corn oil
    ⅓ cup rice wine vinegar (available in oriental markets or health food stores*)
    1 tablespoon peeled and grated fresh ginger
    1 teaspoon minced fresh garlic (1 large clove)
    1 teaspoon soy sauce or tamari
    1 teaspoon oriental sesame oil*
    Salt and pepper to taste

1. Whisk all ingredients together in a small bowl. Allow to sit at room temperature for ½ hour.

2. Strain through a wire-mesh sieve and use to dress salads of cold oriental noodles, vegetables, or leftover meat or seafood. Store dressing, covered, at room temperature for up to 1 week.

**Yield: 1⅓ cups**

**\*See mail-order sources, page 237.**

# FIDDLEHEAD HOUSE DRESSING

We've been trying for years to describe this adequately, and there seems to be only one description that fits: indescribably good. Originally made by Joan Daniels at the Bread Factory, in Anchorage, this salad dressing has been Alaska's favorite for over 20 years.

**Preparation Time:** 15 minutes

> ½ cup good-quality mayonnaise
> ½ cup seeded and coarsely chopped tomatoes
> ⅓ cup coarsely chopped onion (1 small)
> 2 tablespoons apple cider vinegar
> 2 tablespoons safflower oil
> 3 to 4 fresh parsley sprigs, washed and squeezed
>    dry (about ½ tablespoon freshly chopped parsley)

1. Place all ingredients in a large blender or food processor. Purée until smooth.

2. Transfer to a 2-cup container, cover, and store refrigerated for up to 3 days. Serve with salad or as a vegetable dip.

**Yield: 1½ cups**

# FIDDLEHEAD VINAIGRETTE

This is a classic match for green salads, pasta salads, or chilled steamed vegetables.

**Preparation Time:** 10 minutes

> ¾ cup good-quality olive oil
> ¼ cup red wine vinegar
> 2 teaspoons Dijon mustard
> ½ teaspoon minced garlic (1 small clove)
> ½ teaspoon salt
> ½ teaspoon pepper
> ¼ teaspoon dried thyme

1. Whisk all ingredients together in a small bowl or pitcher.

2. Store covered at room temperature for up to 1 week, whisking thoroughly before each use.

**Yield: 1 cup**

# BÉCHAMEL SAUCE

This simple cream sauce gilds cannelloni (page 130) or magically turns little bits of seafood or chicken and fresh vegetables into a pleasant Sunday-morning dish or quick Monday-night supper.

**Preparation Time:** 15 minutes

2 tablespoons butter
2 tablespoons flour
1½ cups milk or half-and-half
1 bay leaf
¼ medium onion
1 whole clove
¼ teaspoon salt
¼ teaspoon grated nutmeg

1. Melt butter in a small saucepan over medium-high heat. Whisk in flour, reduce heat to medium low, and cook together while stirring for 3 to 5 minutes.

2. Slowly whisk in milk. Raise heat to high, bring to a boil, and reduce heat to low. Attach bay leaf to quartered onion with clove and add to sauce. Cook gently, stirring occasionally, until thickened, 5 to 10 minutes.

3. Remove onion, bay leaf, and clove. Stir in salt and nutmeg. Remove from heat but keep warm until ready to use.

**NOTE:**
The béchamel can be prepared 2 to 3 days ahead, cooled, and kept refrigerated. Reheat gently when ready to use.

**Yield: 1½ cups**

"What I love about cooking is that after a hard day, there is something comforting about the fact that if you melt butter and add flour and then hot stock, it will get thick! It's a sure thing! It's a sure thing in a world where nothing is sure."
    —*Nora Ephron*

# SALSA

Use this cooked spicy tomato sauce to give your meal a Mexican accent.

**Preparation Time:** 15 minutes

**Cooking Time:** 50 minutes

> 1 tablespoon olive oil
> 2 cups large-diced onion (1 large)
> 2 cups large-diced green pepper (1 medium)
> 1 teaspoon minced garlic (1 large clove)
> 2 14-ounce cans diced tomatoes (substitute crushed tomatoes or chop canned whole tomatoes)
> ½ teaspoon crushed red pepper (more or less depending on how hot you like things)
> 1 teaspoon salt
> ¼ teaspoon pepper

1. Heat oil in a 2-quart pot over medium-high heat.
2. Add onion and green peppers, stir, and cook for 5 minutes.
3. Stir in garlic and cook for 1 minute, but do not allow garlic to brown.
4. Add diced tomatoes and crushed pepper, reduce heat to low, and simmer, uncovered, for 45 minutes.
5. Add salt and pepper, taste, and correct seasoning.
6. Use at once over rice, eggs, or beans; or store covered and refrigerated for up to 1 week, or frozen for up to 1 month.

**Yield: 1 quart**

*Mexican Rice Grande:* One of the Fiddlehead's most popular meals is quickly made at home. You need cooked brown rice, salsa, Cheddar cheese, and if you want, sour cream and guacamole.

Fill a soup bowl with hot brown rice. Spoon salsa over top and top with cheese. Melt cheese under broiler. Top dish with sour cream and guacamole and serve at once.

# FRESH CILANTRO SALSA

The hot and spicy flavor of this salsa is particularly good with grilled meat or fish.

**Preparation Time:** 20 minutes (with a food processor, 10 minutes)

**Resting Time:** 2 hours

- 2 cups seeded, small-diced tomatoes (about 3 medium)
- 2 tablespoons finely diced red onion (substitute white or yellow)
- 2 tablespoons finely diced green onion, including tops (about 2)
- ½ teaspoon minced fresh garlic (1 medium clove)
- ¼ cup finely chopped fresh cilantro (there is no flavor substitute)
- 1 jalapeño pepper, minced
- 1 tablespoon finely chopped fresh oregano (or ½ tablespoon dried)
- 1 tablespoon red wine vinegar
- ½ teaspoon salt (or to taste)
- ½ teaspoon pepper

1. Combine all ingredients in a small nonreactive (non-aluminum) bowl. Cover and refrigerate for at least 2 hours before using. (If you have a food processor, just put all ingredients in it and process quickly to the consistency you like best.)

2. Serve with fajitas, tacos, grilled fish or chicken, chips, or wherever a spicy Mexican accent seems appropriate.

**Yield: 2 cups**

**NOTE:**
Best if used within 1 or 2 days.

**NOTE:**
Be extremely careful when working with fresh hot peppers: Wash your hands, knife, and work surface immediately after cutting peppers to avoid burning your skin. Avoid touching your face or eyes until you have thoroughly washed your hands.

# GUACAMOLE

Everyone loves this sauce/dip/sandwich spread/salad.

**Preparation Time:** 20 minutes

> 1 cup peeled, pitted, and mashed avocado (about 2 avocados)
> ½ cup seeded, small-diced tomato (1 small tomato)
> 1½ tablespoons fresh lime juice (substitute lemon if necessary)
> 1 tablespoon finely diced red onion (substitute green onions)
> 1 teaspoon chopped fresh cilantro (no substitute)
> ½ teaspoon minced fresh garlic (1 medium clove)
> ½ teaspoon salt
> ¼ teaspoon pepper
> ¼ teaspoon minced fresh jalapeño pepper (more or less, depending on how spicy you like things)
> 1 drop Tabasco sauce

1. Place all ingredients in a large mixing bowl and, using a fork or an electric mixer set on medium, stir together until combined but still a little lumpy.

2. Transfer to a medium container. To prevent guacamole from turning brown, put plastic wrap directly on surface of mixture so that no air can reach it. Refrigerate until needed. It is best used the same day.

**Yield: 1½ cups**

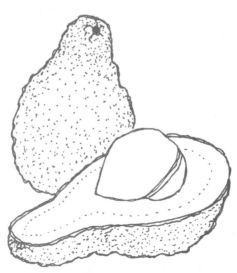

# HOT PEANUT SAUCE

Yes, it's hot!

**Preparation Time:** 15 minutes

½ cup peanut butter, chunky or creamy
¼ cup oriental sesame oil (available in oriental
   markets or health food stores*)
2 tablespoons soy or tamari sauce
2 tablespoons rice wine vinegar (available in oriental
   markets or health food stores*), or substitute cider
   vinegar
1 tablespoon minced fresh ginger
1 tablespoon minced fresh garlic (3 to 4 large cloves)
1 tablespoon finely chopped green onions
1 tablespoon oriental hot oil (available in Oriental
   markets or health food stores*)
1 tablespoon chopped fresh cilantro (parsley can be
   substituted in this recipe)

1. In a large mixing bowl, using an electric mixer set on
   high, whip together peanut butter, sesame oil, soy
   sauce, rice vinegar, ginger, garlic, green onions, hot oil,
   and cilantro until creamy in appearance.

2. Transfer to a small container, cover tightly, and store
   for up to 2 weeks in refrigerator.

3. Add to stir-fried vegetables, chicken, pork, or noodles.

**Yield: 1 scant cup**

**\*See mail-order sources, page 237.**

**NOTE:**
The peanut sauce
recipe doubles easily
so you can make extra
to have on hand when
you need it.

# MARINARA SAUCE

This all-purpose tomato sauce is good with pasta, over meats, in sandwiches, with vegetables, and in casseroles. Make lots and freeze some for later.

**Preparation Time:** 15 minutes

**Cooking Time:** 30 minutes to 1 hour

　　　　2 tablespoons olive oil
　　　　½ to ¾ cup chopped onion (1 medium onion)
　　　　1 teaspoon minced garlic (1 large clove)
　　　　1 bay leaf
　　　　2 teaspoons dried basil
　　　　2 teaspoons dried oregano
　　　　¾ teaspoon dried rosemary
　　　　1 28-ounce can crushed tomatoes in purée (substitute diced, or chop canned whole tomatoes)
　　　　1 cup dry red wine (burgundy or cabernet sauvignon)
　　　　1 6-ounce can tomato paste
　　　　1 teaspoon salt
　　　　1 tablespoon pepper

1. Heat oil in a large heavy-bottomed pot over medium heat. When oil is hot, add onion and cook gently until translucent and tender but not browned.

2. Add garlic, bay leaf, basil, oregano, and rosemary. Stir and add remaining ingredients. Bring slowly to the boil, stirring frequently (be careful not to scorch the bottom). Reduce heat to low and simmer uncovered for 30 minutes or more.

**NOTE:**
**This may be frozen for future use.**

3. Use immediately or store, covered, in refrigerator for up to 1 week.

**Yield: 1½ quarts**

# COURT BOUILLON

Salmon is particularly good simply poached. This court bouillon, a basic stock in which to poach fish, highlights its flavors well. If fish of any kind appears regularly at your table, keep this on hand: It is easy to prepare, perfect for low-fat, low-cholesterol needs, and brings out the best in fish.

**Preparation Time:** 15 minutes

**Simmering Time:** 30 minutes

    4 quarts water
    ½ cup white wine vinegar
    2 tablespoons salt
    4 cups thinly sliced onion (about 4 medium)
    3 cups thinly sliced carrots (about 4)
    3 cups coarsely chopped celery with tops and leaves
       (5 or 6 ribs)
    3 bay leaves
    6 parsley sprigs (or 2 tablespoons dried)
    2 teaspoons dried thyme
    1 tablespoon whole black peppercorns

1. Combine all ingredients in a 6-quart pot over high heat. Bring to a boil, reduce heat, partially cover, and simmer stock for 20 to 30 minutes.

2. Strain court bouillon through a colander or wire-mesh sieve into four 1-quart containers (or several smaller containers depending on your needs). Cover and keep refrigerated for 3 days, or freeze until ready to use.

3. To poach fish, place fillet, steak, or whole fish in a pan and add court bouillon halfway up side of fish. Bring just to a boil over medium-high heat, immediately reduce heat to a very slight simmer (boiling toughens and dries out fish), cover pan, and cook until fish flakes easily (figure 10 minutes for every inch of thickness).

4. Remove fish from pan, dress with a simple squeeze of lemon, toasted almonds, hollandaise sauce (page 40), a flavored butter (see recipes, pages 204–206) or as you like. Serve poached fish hot or chilled.

**Yield: 4 quarts**

# CHICKEN STOCK

If you're planning a chicken dish for dinner, buy bone-in breasts (ask the butcher to bone them for you if you don't feel adept at it) and put the bones on for stock while dinner is cooking. When dinner is over, you'll have stock for soup the next day. This technique is so easy, so good, and so economical that making chicken stock will become a habit.

**Preparation Time:**   10 minutes

**Cooking Time:**   1 to 2 hours

>    1 pound chicken bones, preferably uncooked, but
>       cooked will do
>    1 medium onion, peeled and quartered
>    1 medium carrot, peeled and cut into 2-inch pieces
>    1 celery rib, cut into 2-inch pieces
>    3 mushrooms
>    2 parsley sprigs (substitute 1 teaspoon dried)
>    1 bay leaf
>    ½ teaspoon dried thyme
>    ½ teaspoon whole peppercorns
>    1 or 2 whole cloves
>    A squeeze of lemon or a splash of white wine
>    1 quart cold water

1. If bones are fresh, rinse them in cold water. Place all ingredients in a large pot over high heat and bring to a boil. Reduce heat to a very low simmer and cook gently for at least 1 hour. Skim off froth as it appears on stock.

2. Strain through a colander (lined with cheesecloth if you have any) into a large bowl. Refrigerate, uncovered, until cooled.

3. Remove fat and pour stock into serving-size containers. Cover and refrigerate to use within a week, or freeze for later.

**Yield: 1 quart**

**NOTE:**
It is handy to freeze some stock in ice cube trays to use in sauces that call only for a small amount. Keep frozen cubes in bags in freezer to use when needed.

# VEGETABLE STOCK

This rich vegetable broth is the basis of many of our soups.

**Preparation Time:** 20 minutes

**Cooking Time:** 30 minutes

  3 quarts water
  3 to 4 onions, 1¼ to 1½ pounds, peeled and quartered
  3 medium carrots, about ¾ pound, peeled and cut
    into 2-inch pieces
  3 medium celery ribs, cut into 2-inch pieces
  6 mushrooms
  1 medium potato, about ½ pound, unpeeled, well
    scrubbed, and quartered
  3 fresh parsley stalks (substitute 1 tablespoon dried)
  1 fresh lemon wedge
  1 to 2 whole cloves
  1 to 3 peeled garlic cloves
  1 bay leaf
  1 teaspoon dried thyme
  ½ teaspoon black peppercorns

1. Place all ingredients in a large pot. Bring to a boil over high heat, then reduce heat to low and simmer gently for 30 minutes, until vegetables are completely cooked.

2. Strain stock through a colander and discard vegetables. Use stock immediately, or pour into containers, cool, cover, and freeze for later use.

**Yield: 2 quarts**

**NOTE:**
The stock will be enriched by the addition of almost any vegetable. Try tomatoes, zucchini, corn, beans, or parsnips, but add members of the cabbage (broccoli, cauliflower, radishes) and bell pepper families only for soups and stews that include them (their taste can be overwhelming). Always use vegetables that are fresh and unspoiled.

**NOTE:**
This recipe doubles easily.

# FISH STOCK

Homemade fish stock gives a good fresh flavor to fish soups or chowders. Keep some ready in the freezer and . . . soup's on!

**Preparation Time:**  15 minutes

**Cooking Time:**  30 minutes

> 3 pounds fresh fish heads and bones*, rinsed twice (blood and gills removed from head)
> 2 quarts water
> 2 cups dry white wine (substitute 1 lemon, halved)
> 2 cups coarsely chopped onion (1 medium)
> 1 cup coarsely chopped celery (2 or 3 ribs)
> 2 bay leaves
> 2 tablespoons dried parsley, or 4 or 5 parsley stems
> 1½ teaspoons black peppercorns

**NOTE:**
**The stock keeps for up to 1 week in the refrigerator, or may be frozen and defrosted when needed.**

1. Place rinsed bones in a large (2-gallon) pot with other ingredients. Bring to a boil over high heat, then reduce heat to a simmer. Skim foam from surface as it appears and simmer stock for 20 to 30 minutes.

2. Strain through a colander into two 1-quart containers and chill or freeze until needed.

**Yield: 2 quarts**

**\*Use red snapper or other white fish if possible. Use salmon only for stock to be used in salmon dishes. Shrimp or crab shells make good stock also.**

■                              ■                              ■

# TOMATO CHUTNEY

Long-time Fiddlehead chef and manager Susan Kirkness contributed this tangy chutney to the kitchen pantry. Its flavor goes well with saag panir (page 124), lamb curry (page 86), and other spicy dishes. Try it as an omelet filling or spread on ham sandwiches.

**Preparation Time:**  20 minutes

**Cooking Time:**  3 hours 15 minutes

> ½ cup minced fresh garlic (1½ whole heads; see note, page 115)

4 ounces fresh ginger
2 tablespoons cider vinegar
1 14-ounce can diced tomatoes (substitute crushed
    tomatoes)
1 cup honey
2 teaspoons salt
½ teaspoon cayenne
⅓ cup raisins

1. Peel garlic and ginger. Purée in a food processor with
   vinegar.

2. Place purée, tomatoes, honey, salt, and cayenne in a
   medium-size heavy-bottomed pot over medium heat.
   Bring to a boil, reduce heat to low, and simmer, stirring
   frequently, until it has thickened and become darker
   and more "glassy" in appearance (3 hours cooking time).

3. Stir in raisins and cook for 10 minutes.

4. Pack into sterilized 1-cup jars and store in refrigerator,
   tightly wrapped, for up to 1 month.

**Yield: 2 cups**

# HOT SPICED CIDER

Fragrant with winter spices, hot cider warms cold hands
and damp spirits.

**Preparation Time:**   20 minutes

"Dress for the weather
and not the vehicle."
    —Harold Hopper

    2 quarts apple juice or cider
    1 orange, cut into ½-inch slices
    1 small lemon, cut into ½-inch slices
    12 whole cloves
    4 whole allspice seeds
    1 cardamom seed

1. Combine all ingredients in a large nonreactive (nonaluminum) pot over medium-high heat. Bring just to boiling point and lower heat to a simmer.

2. Simmer for 10 minutes. Ladle into mugs and serve at
   once.

**Yield: 2 quarts**

# SOURDOUGH STARTER

**Sourdough** is a colony of active yeast, a "mother dough" used to leaven new doughs. Before dried and compressed yeasts or baking powders became available to bakers, all raised breads and pastries started with a bit of sourdough.

Sourdoughs taste different in different parts of the country because they tend to become dominated by the local airborne microflora. For reasons that are not clearly understood, the older the sour, the more resistant it is to contamination by outside yeasts. Analysis of old sours indicates that the sourdough yeast is a different organism from the yeast used in bakers' yeasts, and in fact, bakers' yeast may inhibit the growth of a true sourdough yeast colony.

## ■ Starting a Starter

The easiest and most reliable way to start your own sourdough is to begin with a bit (¼ cup will do) of sour from an older active one:

1. Put starter in a sterile glass or crockery jar, add equal parts water and flour (for ¼ cup starter add ½ cup flour and ½ cup water), stir well, cover, and allow to sit overnight at room temperature, until mixture is actively bubbling.

2. Refrigerate starter, loosely covered, until you need it. (Sourdough starter can be frozen for long-term storage.)

If you don't know anyone who can give you a bit of starter, start your own from scratch:

> ½ cup plain active-culture yogurt
> ½ cup warm (110°F) water
> ½ cup white flour
> 1 teaspoon granulated sugar or honey
> (Optional: Some people add ¼ teaspoon dry yeast to guarantee the sour will become active. This does change the flavor somewhat.)

1. Stir all ingredients together with a wooden spoon in a large, sterile glass or crockery jar.

2. Cover jar and set in a warm spot for 24 to 48 hours, until dough is permeated with bubbles.

3. Feed sour with ½ cup each flour and water and let it sit, covered, overnight again.

NOTE:
If you have a yogurt maker, use it to ferment the sour. Otherwise, the top of your refrigerator is a good warm and undisturbed spot.

**4.** Use at once or store, covered loosely, in refrigerator. Sourdough can be frozen for up to 6 months.

## ◼ Caring for Your Sourdough

The yeasts need to be fed regularly, once every other week at least. If you do not use your sourdough frequently, remember to stir in a bit of flour and water every so often so there is fresh food for them. They do seem to enjoy rye flour, so add some as a treat occasionally. Frozen sours should be thawed and used or fed every 6 months.

If blackish water begins to collect on the surface of the dough, stir it back in or pour it off and add fresh flour and water. (It is a reminder that you need to make pancakes or bread soon.)

If the water collecting on the dough is pink, discard the whole thing, sterilize the pot, and start over: The sour has been contaminated with a foreign substance and is breaking down.

Keep one wooden bowl and spoon to use only for your sourdough bread. Then, should you ever lose your sour, you can start a fresh one just by adding flour and water to the bowl, stirring with the spoon, and leaving the mix overnight. The sourdough yeast spores in the wood should be sufficient to activate your dough and give you a new starter.

Use your sour frequently, particularly if it is a young one. This keeps it fresh and active and prevents contamination by molds or outside yeasts.

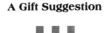

**A Gift Suggestion**

◼ ◼ ◼

*Every new home needs a pot of sourdough. Give newlyweds or the family moving into the house next door a pot of active sour, a sourdough bread recipe, and your best wishes for a long and bubbly life.*

# MULLED WINE

Not too sweet and slightly spicy, this warm drink is welcome whenever the temperature drops and clouds begin to gather.

**Preparation Time:**  15 minutes

**Cooking Time:**  20 minutes

   1¼ cups granulated sugar
   ⅔ cups water
   1½ lemons, sliced or coarsely chopped
   1 orange, sliced or coarsely chopped
   1½ tablespoons whole cloves
   ½ teaspoon ground cinnamon
   ½ teaspoon ground nutmeg
   3 tablespoons freshly squeezed lemon juice
   1½ liters red wine (burgundy)
   2 cups sherry (medium dry)

■ **Garnish**

   1 orange, cut into ½-inch slices with short sticks of
      cinnamon stuck in centers
   1 apple, cored and cut into ½-inch slices

1. In a large pot over medium heat, combine sugar, water, lemons, orange, and spices. Boil for 5 minutes.

2. Strain through a wire-mesh sieve into a large glass or plastic container, pressing out all juice from fruit, and stir in lemon juice.

**NOTE:**
Make ahead through step 2. Store refrigerated until ready to use.

3. Combine spice mixture, wine, and sherry in a large enamel or stainless steel pot over medium-high heat. When simmering, pour into heat-resistant punch bowl, float orange and apple rings on top, and serve at once.

**Yield: about 2 quarts**

"Her hopes were a good deal like Alaskan weather, so far below zero that she could scarcely read the thermometer."
   —*Anna Fulcomer*

PART 4

# RESOURCES

# THE COOKBOOK SHELF

As much as we love to cook and eat, we enjoy reading about cooking and eating. Here is a brief list of those books we refer to time and time again for inspiration and satisfaction.

**Alice, Let's Eat,** by Calvin Trillin. New York: Random House, 1978.

Amid all the serious and pretentious food books, Calvin Trillin's good humor and clear prose remind us that food is fun.

**The Asian Cookbook,** by Charmain Soloman. New York: McGraw-Hill Book Co., 1979.

This comprehensive book includes recipes from India to Korea and all points in between. All are clearly written and well adapted to the American kitchen. It includes thorough explanations of unfamiliar products and offers substitutions wherever possible.

**The Bakers' Manual,** by Joseph Amendola. Rochelle Park, NJ: Hayden Book Co. Inc., 1972.

This book has very useful, easy-to-understand charts that show baking faults and possible causes for all types of baked goods, and excellent explanations of the role of each ingredient in baking.

**Beard on Bread,** by James Beard. New York: Alfred A. Knopf, 1974.

We've found some good, unusual breads in this book. The directions are clear and the book includes good basic bread-baking instructions.

**The Best of Sunset, Recipes from the Magazine of Western Living,** by the Editors of Sunset Books and *Sunset Magazine*. Menlo Park, CA: Lane Publishing Co., 1987.

These are the best of the recipes published in *Sunset* over the years collected into one convenient volume. They reflect the abundance of fresh vegetables, fruit, and fish found on the West Coast, and are extremely reliable. In addition, each recipe includes a dietary analysis.

**The Blue Strawberry Cookbook,** by James Haller. Harvard, MA: Harvard Common Press, 1976.

For those who want to extend their creative boundaries and can function with a minimum of supervision, the wildly creative *Blue Strawberry* is ideal. Be forewarned: This is not a book for the timid, the indecisive, or the rigidly structured cook. Essentially, it is a license to do whatever you want in the kitchen, with lots of ideas you may not have thought of yet.

**The Breakfast Book,** by Marion Cunningham. New York: Alfred A. Knopf, 1988.

**Carnegie Treasures Cookbook,** by the Women's Committee, Museum of Art, Carnegie Institute, Pittsburgh. New York: Atheneum, 1984.

This book is full of good recipes, the suggested menus are inventive, the table settings are dazzling and inspiring, and the art reproductions are wonderful. (Unfortunately the book is now out of print. If you locate a copy, latch on to it.)

**Chef Paul Prudhomme's Louisiana Kitchen,** by Paul Prudhomme. New York: William Morrow & Co., Inc., 1984.

Louisiana's most famous chef gives terrific recipes for blackened redfish, jambalaya, and gumbo. Don't ignore the cookie recipes either.

**Classic Italian Cooking** and **More Classic Italian Cooking,** by Marcella Hazan. New York: Alfred A. Knopf, 1978 and 1980.

Food writers and critics seem to agree that these two volumes are the definitive cookbooks for Italian cuisine.

**The Cuisine of the Sun,** by Mirelle Johnson. New York: Vintage Books, 1979.

The flavors of Provence and Nice provide a sharp contrast to classical French cuisine. This small but informative book offers recipes and insights on the indigenous ingredients.

**The Encyclopedia of Fish Cookery,** by A. J. McClane. New York: Holt, Rinehart and Winston, 1977.

The key word here is "encyclopedia:" Everything you need to know about almost every fish in the world is in this book. The acompanying recipes are good, though fairly traditional. The book is a must for serious seafood cooks.

**Entertaining,** by Martha Stewart. New York: Clarkson N. Potter, Inc., 1982.

Martha Stewart is everywhere. Her books are full of good recipes that work and beautiful illustrations that make you dream. She'll inspire you.

**Food**, by Waverly Root. New York: Simon and Schuster, Inc., 1980.

If you wonder about the origins and history of everyday, or not so everyday, ingredients, read this book. Attractively illustrated with artwork from the centuries and full of remarkable bits of lore, this book is fascinating for the student of history as well as the cook by avocation.

**Foods of the World**, by the Editors of Time-Life Books. Alexandria, VA: Time-Life Books, 1970.

This series gives authentic and usable recipes from all over the world accompanied by insights into the culture of each country. Fascinating and enlightening reading with well-tested, easy, and delicious recipes.

**The Four Seasons Cookbook**, by Tom Margittai and Paul Kovi. New York: Simon and Schuster, 1980.

The Four Seasons restaurant in New York pioneered innovative cooking with an emphasis on using the freshest available seasonal ingredients. The recipes reflect a mostly classical French tradition and exhibit obvious care and thought. The food is elegant and delicious.

**The Frog Commissary Cookbook**, by Steven Poses, Anne Clark, and Becky Roller. Garden City, NY: Doubleday and Co., Inc., 1985.

This book is from a restaurant, unfortunately now closed, in Philadelphia. We like its cross-cultural style of cooking. The salads, baked goods, desserts, entrées, in fact all the recipes, are truly exceptional. The authors have included anecdotes and bits of useful information throughout the book, making it good reading as well as a good cookbook.

**The Good Cook/Techniques & Recipes**, by the Editors of Time/Life Books. Alexandria, VA: Time-Life Books, 1981.

This series clearly illustrates and explains all manner of cooking methods, followed by recipes gathered from sources all over the world. The recipes work and invariably taste great, and the introductory information tells you why and how.

**The Greens Cookbook**, by Deborah Madison. New York: Bantam Books, 1987.

Greens Restaurant in San Francisco is noted for its brilliant vegetarian cuisine. The recipes in the book come from its successful and seasonal menus, and some reflect the same serious Zen philosophy that went into the development of the restaurant.

**James Beard's American Cookery**, by James Beard. Boston: Little, Brown and Company, 1972.

This book is valuable not only tor the hundreds of recipes, but also for the historical insights and opinions James Beard, the dean of American cuisine, shares with us.

**James McNair's Salmon Cookbook**. San Francisco: Chronicle Books, 1987.

**Joy of Cooking**, by Irma S. Rombauer and Marion Rombauer Becker. Indianapolis: Bobbs-Merrill Co., Inc., 1973.

This book is like having everyone's grandmother's recipes at your fingertips. It is a large and comprehensive book, often the ultimate source for fundamental information and recipes.

**La Technique**, by Jacques Pepin. New York: Pocket Books, 1976.

As Pepin says in the introduction, "is not a picture worth a thousand words?" His text is profusely illustrated with photographs demonstrating basic methods and classical French recipes.

**Madhur Jaffrey's Indian Cooking**, by Madhur Jaffrey. Woodbury, NY: Barron's Educational Series, 1983.

**Madhur Jaffrey's World-of-the-East Vegetarian Cooking**, by Madhur Jaffrey. New York: Alfred A. Knopf, 1981.

These are excellent books, easy to follow, with reliably delicious recipes, backed up by good information about Eastern foods.

**Mastering the Art of French Cooking**, by Julia Child and Simone Beck. New York: Alfred A. Knopf, 1970.

**Mexican Regional Cooking**, by Diana Kennedy. Cambridge, MA: Harper Colophon Books, 1984.

For years Mexican tood meant tacos and chili to most Americans. Diana Kennedy demonstrates the diversity and flavor of Mexican cooking in all of her highly readable books on the subject.

**M.F.K. Fisher's Translation of Brillat-Savarin's The Physiology of Taste**, by Jean Anthelme Brillat-Savarin, translated and annotated by M.F.K. Fisher. New York: Harcourt Brace Jovanovich, Publishers, 1949.

Reading this book is sort of like reading Shakespeare: It seems to be filled with nothing but overused, hackneyed clichés. And then you realize you've been unwittingly quoting him for years, that this is *the* source. The book is charming and delightful to read, and quite up-to-date.

**Any book written by M.F.K. Fisher:**

She writes gracefully witty and wise books on food, cooking, life, and aging. Reading her books is like sitting in front of the fire with good friends after a good meal: You enter into a warm, meditative, contented state of pleasant dreams and general goodwill toward all, where life is livable and even noble.

**The Moosewood Cookbook**, by Mollie Katzen. Berkeley: Ten Speed Press, 1977.

All the Moosewood cookbooks are excellent sources of vegetarian recipes that satisfy everyone. This, the first one, guided us through the formative years of the Fiddlehead. The index can be hard to use, so just read through the book until you come across an inspiration.

**The New York Times Cook Book**, by Craig Claiborne. New York: Harper and Row, 1961; and *The New New York Times Cookbook*, by Craig Claiborne with Pierre Franey, New York: Times Books, 1979.

Craig Claiborne and Pierre Franey bring a wide range of experience to these two volumes. The recipes are drawn from a multitude of different cuisines, carefully adapted to the American kitchen. Look in these books for great recipes for everything from appetizers to desserts.

**On Food and Cooking**, by Harold McGee. New York: Charles Scribner's Sons, 1984.

This is an in-depth, but accessible, look at the chemistry, physics, and mechanics of cooking. When neither the *Joy of Cooking* nor your mother can explain why your angel food cake is flat and gummy, this author will (and somehow still be appetizing about it all).

**The Original Thai Cookbook**, by Jennifer Brennan. New York: Coward-McCann Inc., 1981.

This is a wonderful book with a multitude of great curries, soups, and noodle dishes.

**Paul Bocuse's French Cooking**, by Paul Bocuse. New York: Pantheon Books, 1977.

**The Seasonal Kitchen**, by Perla Meyers. New York: Vintage Books, 1975.

**The Silver Palate Cookbook**, by Julee Rosso and Sheila Lukins with Michael McLaughlin. New York: Workman Publishing, 1982.

This may be the book that defined American cuisine in the eighties. The recipes, clearly written and sensibly imaginative, emphasize fresh foods prepared with a minimum of fuss. The little tidbits of wisdom and anecdotes served up with the recipes make the book a pleasure to read as well as use.

**Square Meals**, by Jane and Michael Stern. New York: Alfred A. Knopf, 1984.

This is a hilarious look at the cuisine and culture of the U.S. since the turn of the century. The chapter on the cuisine of suburbia was required reading at the Fiddlehead staff table. The recipes work, too, in case you've forgotten some of the basics you grew up on, like Rice Krispie cookies or California dip.

**The Tassajara Bread Book**, by Edward Espe Brown. Berkeley: Shambala, 1970.

We owe our bread to this book.

Airmail Over Auke Lake—Small planes are almost as common as cars in Alaska, especially since most communities are not linked by road. Airplanes bring the world to even the most remote spots in Alaska.

AIRMAIL over AUKE LAKE
JUNEAU - ALASKA

# MAIL-ORDER SOURCES

If you have difficulty locating some ingredients at your local grocery (or if you don't have a local grocery), contact these or other mail-order suppliers.

| COMPANY | WHAT IT CARRIES |
|---|---|
| **For Alaskan Seafood** | |
| **DEJON DELIGHTS**<br>P.O. Box 712<br>Haines, AK 99827<br>(907) 766-2505<br>*Call or write for brochure.*<br>*Accepts major credit cards.* | Alaskan-style smoked salmon, lox, salmon caviar (seasonally), and salmon jerky |
| **FREDERICK & NELSON'S**<br>Food Department<br>Fifth & Pine<br>Seattle, WA 98118<br>(206) 682-5500<br>*Call or write for details.*<br>*Accepts major credit cards.* | Alaskan-style smoked fish (and a wide range of other delicacies) |
| **JERRY'S MEATS**<br>9141 Glacier Highway<br>Juneau, AK 99801<br>P.O. Box 33379<br>Juneau, AK 99803<br>(907) 789-5142<br>*Call or write for details.*<br>*Accepts major credit cards.* | Alaskan-style smoked salmon, crab, and other seafood, including Kodiak scallops |
| **SALMON RIVER SMOKEHOUSE**<br>P.O. Box 40<br>Gustavus, AK 99826<br>(907) 697-2330<br>*Call or write for brochure.*<br>*Accepts M.C. and Visa.*<br>*Ships via Federal Express.* | Alaskan-style smoked halibut, smoked salmon, smoked trout, and smoked salmon spread |
| **SALMON SHOPPE**<br>201 South Franklin<br>Juneau, AK 99801<br>(907) 586-2522<br>*Call or write for brochure.*<br>*Accepts major credit cards.* | Alaskan-style smoked salmon, canned salmon, fireweed honey, Alaskan jams and jellies, and black seaweed |

| COMPANY | WHAT IT CARRIES |
|---|---|

**TAKU SMOKERIES**
230 South Franklin Street
Juneau, AK 99801
(907) 463-3474
*Call or write for brochure.*
*Accepts major credit cards.*

Alaskan-style smoked salmon, lox, and (in season and available via Federal Express) fresh halibut and fresh salmon

*For Fiddleheads and Other Unusual Things*

**AUX DÉLICES DES BOIS**
4 Leonard Street
New York, NY 10013
(212) 334-1230
*Call or write for brochure.*
*Accepts major credit cards.*

Fiddlehead ferns, beach asparagus, and lots more very unusual treats

**DEAN AND DELUCA**
560 Broadway
New York, NY 10012
(800) 221-7714
*Call or write for details (no catalogue).*
*Accepts major credit cards.*

beach asparagus, fiddlehead ferns (in season), as well as an excellent variety of other food products

**LARRY'S MARKETS**
14227 Pacific Highway South
Seattle, WA 98168
(206) 242-5200
*Call or write for details.*

beach asparagus, edible flowers (occasionally), fiddlehead ferns (in season), and many other things

**NEW PENNY FARM**
(207) 768-7551
*Call for details.*

Fiddlehead ferns (in season), gourmet potatoes

**NICHOLS GARDEN NURSERY**
1190 North Pacific Highway
Albany, OR 97321
(503) 928-9280
*Call or write for catalogue.*
*Accepts major credit cards.*

unusual seeds and herbs to grow your own

**ORLANDO SPECIALTY**
1213 East Pine Avenue
Orlando, FL 32824
(407) 856-1611
*Call or write for catalogue.*
*Accepts major credit cards.*

beach asparagus, fiddlehead ferns (in season), and other treats

*Jams, Jellies, Honey, and other Preserves*

**AMERICAN SPOON FOODS**
1668 Clarion Avenue
P.O. Box 566
Petoskey, MI 49770-0566
800 222-5886
*Call or write for catalogue.*

dried cherries, chutney and relishes, jams and jellies, and many other treats (some of the preserves are made without the addition of sugars)

**ALASKA HONEY FARM**
1812 Central Avenue
Fairbanks, AK 99709
(907) 456-7202
*Call or write for details.*

fireweed honey

**ALASKA HONEY AND POLLEN**
15524 Old Glenn Highway
Eagle River, AK 99577
(907) 696-2526
*Call or write for details.*

bee pollen and fireweed honey

| COMPANY | WHAT IT CARRIES |
|---|---|

**SUSAN BROOK**
P.O. Box 93
Gustavus, AK 99826
(907) 697-2348
*Call or write for catalogue.*

Alaskan wild berry jams and jellies, wild berry syrups, chutneys, highbush cranberry catsup, kelp pickles, and spruce tip syrup

**TOKLAT APIARIES**
1153 Donna Drive
Fairbanks, AK 99712
(907) 457-2440
*Call or write for details.*

fireweed honey

*Oriental Foods*

**UWAJIMAYA**
P.O. Box 3003
Seattle, WA 98114
(206) 624-6248
*Call or write, or visit the stores in the Seattle International district or Bellevue. Accepts major credit cards.*

an amazing array of oriental products including: lemongrass, miso, dried mushrooms, rice wine vinegar, rice, rice flour, sesame oil, soy sauce, tamari, Thai curries, tofu, as well as cooking utensils, silks, fans, kites, tablewares, and cookbooks

*Whole Grains and Natural Foods*

**ARROWHEAD MILLS**
Box 866
Hereford, TX 79045
(806) 364-0730
*Call or write for catalogue.*

dried beans, dried unsweetened coconut, organically grown grains and flours

**WALNUT ACRES**
Penns Creek, PA 17862
(717) 837-0601
*Call or write for catalogue.*
*Accepts M.C. and Visa.*

wide selection of whole foods, including flours, grains, rice, and prepared products

*Good General Selection*

**DE LAURENTI'S FOOD MARKET**
1435 First Avenue
Seattle, WA 98101
(206) 622-0141
*Call, or write, and ask for Curt Chambers, who handles all mail orders.*
*Or visit the store in the Pike Place Market.*
*Accepts major credit cards.*

an excellent selection of Italian foods, including black beans (canned and dried), capers, dried unsweetened coconut, Dutch dark cocoa and many varieties of chocolate for eating or cooking, olive oil, fresh truffles, dried mushrooms, semolina flour, sourdough starter, tomato products, balsamic, raspberry, and other vinegars, plus cheeses, prosciutto, salami, and other perishables available by 1-day air service.

**GB RATTO'S**
821 Washington Street
Oakland, CA 94501
(415) 832-6503
*Call or write for catalogue.*
*Accepts major credit cards.*

a wide selection of Italian foods, including capers, herbs, mushrooms, olives, California olive oil, pastas, semolina flour, tomato products, balsamic and other vinegars, and cooking utensils

*Mail-Order Grocers (for people living in rural or bush Alaska)*

**FOODLAND**
Willoughby Avenue
Juneau, AK 99801
(907) 586-3101
fax (907) 586-6775
*Serves northern southeast Alaska by air.*
*Call, fax, or write for details.*
*Set up charge account or receive goods C.O.D.*

excellent grocery selection, including capers, chèvre cheese, oriental products including a miso-making kit, rice flour, semolina flour, tofu, tomato products, and fresh produce, including cilantro, fresh herbs, jalapeño and other products, and lemongrass (occasionally)

**PRAIRIE BUSH SHIPPERS**
4000 West Dimond
Anchorage, AK 99515
(907) 243 3225
fax (907) 243-3241
*Serves all of Alaska.*
*Call or write for catalogue.*
*Ships freight collect.*

wide range of groceries, plus specialty items available upon request

**RAINBOW FOODS**
200 Seward Street
Juneau, AK 99801
(907) 586-6476
*Serves all of Alaska.*
*Call or write for details.*
*Accepts major credit cards.*

organically grown grains, herbs, spices, teas, beans of all colors, carob chips, dried unsweetened coconut, honey, maple syrup, millet, molasses, nuts, semolina flour, vinegars including balsamic and raspberry, whole wheat pastry flour, as well as vitamins and cosmetics

**SUPERBEAR**
PO Box 33379
Juneau, AK 99803
(907) 789-0173
*Serves all of southeast Alaska.*
*Call or write for details.*
*Set up payment arrangements in advance.*

excellent selection of groceries, including Alaskan-style smoked fish, black beans, capers, chèvre cheese, oriental products, semolina flour, tomato products, vinegars including balsamic and raspberry, fresh produce including cilantro, fresh herbs, jalapeño and other peppers

# INDEX